EASY MONEY

ROGER M. OLIEN

AND DIANA DAVIDS OLIEN

EASY MONEY

OIL PROMOTERS

AND INVESTORS IN

THE JAZZ AGE

The University of North Carolina Press

Chapel Hill and London

HD
9565
O 647
1990

© 1990 The University of North Carolina Press
All rights reserved

Library of Congress Cataloging-in-Publication Data

Olien, Roger M., 1938–
Easy money : oil promoters and investors in the jazz age / by
Roger M. Olien and Diana Davids Olien.
p.   cm.
Includes bibliographical references.
ISBN 0-8078-1928-X (alk. paper)—ISBN 0-8078-4291-5 (pbk. :
alk. paper)
1. Petroleum industry and trade—United States—Finance—Corrupt
practices—History—20th century.   2. Speculation—United States—
History—20th century.   3. Fraud—United States—History—20th
century.   4. United States—Economic conditions—1918–1945.
I. Olien, Diana Davids, 1943–   .   II. Title.
HD9565.O647   1990
364.1′68—dc20
90-50017   CIP

Manufactured in the United States of America
94 93 92 91 90   5 4 3 2 1

In memory of
John J. Redfern, Jr.,
W. D. Noel,
and E. E. Reigle

CONTENTS

Contents

A section of photographs follows page 72.

PREFACE

The Lawyers, Doctors, Hatters, Clerks
Industrious and lazy,
Have put their money all in stocks:
In fact, have gone oil crazy.[1]

THIS DITTY, "as sung in New York, Philadelphia, and all the principal cities of the Union where ile fever abounds," describes one of the great speculative manias of nineteenth-century America. Others, in land and in canal and railroad shares, preceded it, and many more would follow it.

Charles P. Kindleberger is one of the few scholars to examine speculative manias. In a pioneering work he explains what happens in booms in terms of investor "irrationality." Kindleberger describes "mob psychology" and "the irrationality of the gullible and greedy" over a vast expanse of European and American history. He concludes that, though they need a little help from government occasionally, capital markets work well: "Modern excesses burn themselves out without damage."[2] Manias, thus, are aberrations, unrelated to the regular conduct of business or to the general health of the economy.

We believe that this view is open to question when speculative booms and manias are viewed with greater attention to detail than Kindleberger's broad overview permitted. A number of significant topics deserve further study, including the social and economic basis of speculative booms, the expectations and mentalities they reflect, the apparent difficulty of increasing assets during booms, the relation of fraudulent business activity to manias, and the effect of law enforcement on fraudulent boom-time activity.

The literature on mining and securities speculation has addressed these subjects in piecemeal fashion. We believe that these topics can be delineated more sharply through examination of a single industry during a limited period of time. The best candidate for such scrutiny is the domestic petroleum industry during the era of World War I. The remarkable boom of this period exceeded even that of the 1860s, when the industry was young. The latter period, moreover, saw the scope of activity spread over the entire country, far beyond the financial communities of major eastern cities. The oil industry, given to volatile boom-to-bust cycles and to speculative high-risk activity, was the popular favorite of small investors during much of the postwar period. One can trace their motivations and fates most clearly in oil.

The postwar period serves a scholar interested in speculation well because it was one of the most expansive and optimistic in our history. Jazz-age Americans from all income brackets believed they could make quick riches. Widespread prosperity, accentuated by striking booms in some sectors of the economy, encouraged investors and promoters alike to assume that there was never a better time to build fortunes. They did not expect to use special resources or expertise to do so; they agreed with industrial titan John J. Raskob that "anyone can be rich." Investors looked to become wealthy by buying into glamorous new ventures in such areas as real estate, oil, and communications, while promoters expected to prosper either by using investor capital or by stealing it.

The role of promoters in launching ventures in high-risk enterprises also deserves additional attention, especially with regard to their relations with investors. Again, oil is ideal as the focus of this investigation because capital formation in the independent sector of the industry has traditionally relied on promotion to fund exploratory activity. In oil, as in real estate and other businesses, promoters have raised capital for activities that are economically and socially useful. As we have shown in *Wildcatters*, promoters have long been a creative, vital, and constructive part of the American oil industry. During the twenties in particular, the vast expansion of domestic oil reserves was largely the accomplishment of promoters who risked their careers—and other people's money. The antics of dishonest promoters notwithstanding, promotion of high-risk ventures is legitimate and important in an open economy.[3]

It is particularly challenging to go beyond the general outline of promotional strategies and assess how well they functioned. The main problem for scholars is the relative absence of a paper trail for small businessmen. Small independent oilmen did not normally keep voluminous records on the day-to-day details of business, and when businesses ended in ruin, there was even less incentive to preserve their records. Similarly, Americans of all income brackets received huge quantities of mail promoting investments during the teens and twenties, but remarkably little of this material has found its way to archives. Many people simply discarded such "junk mail" when they received it; those who responded and lost money had little reason to keep the promotional literature as souvenirs of financial misjudgment. The fullest collections of materials come from ventures that landed promoters in trouble—with investors and often with the law. Thus the surviving record may produce a skewed view of promoters as a group.

Fortunately, much evidence relating to promoters is now in the care of the National Archives and its branches. We are especially indebted to Barbara Rust of the Southwest Branch (Fort Worth) and to Aloha P. South of the Civil Division in Washington for highly efficient management of our requests for materials. Our work was also aided by Anita Voorhies at the University of Texas–Permian Basin, Richard Mason and Janet Neugebauer of the Southwest Collection at Texas Tech University, Dr. Bobby Weaver of the Panhandle-Plains Museum, and the staffs of the Barker Texas History Center at the University of Texas at Austin and of the Permian Basin Petroleum Museum, Library, and Hall of Fame, Midland, Texas. Mr. Clyde Barton provided valuable help in picking up the trails of promoters in local land records, while Rose Mary Malone and Arthur G. Randall secured important material for us in Wyoming.

We have also benefited greatly from critiques and suggestions at various stages of work, notably from Forrest McDonald, J. Conrad Dunagan, Betty and Leo Byerley, and Nicholas C. Taylor. Clyde Barton, Ford Chapman, J. Conrad Dunagan, John Hendrix, Robert Leibrock, Joe B. McShane, W. D. Noel, John J. Redfern, Jr., Ed Reigle, William Thams, and Oliver Wood provided valuable encouragement for our research. Drs. Duane M. Leach and H. Warren Gardner of the University of Texas–Permian Basin also gave us welcome support for its completion. Major funding was provided by the Communities Foundation of Texas. We have had complete control of the research and writing of this book, and thus we are solely responsible for its content.

EASY MONEY

ONE

Getting Rich Quick

KLONDIKE on the Hudson River? A bonanza gold and platinum mine within a few miles of Manhattan? The hundreds of Russian immigrants who invested in the Iridium Gold and Platinum Company in 1921 believed so, and that their $1 investments would bring fast returns of $600! If investors hesitated, Iridium's promoters, who included a former United States consul general to St. Petersburg and the editor of a Russian-language newspaper, even offered guided tours of their fantastic mining operations, complete with commentary and sales literature in Russian. A skeptic could see concrete evidence of the company's vast mineral riches. All it took was a short train ride to Yonkers.

The field trip was cleverly devised to erode peasant cunning with hope and greed. It began in a corner of an ordinary-looking potato farm, where the promoters threw several shovelfuls of topsoil into a rock-crushing machine. After churning and grinding the earth for a few seconds, the machine spat out a handful of bright gold nuggets at the feet of the astonished visitors. Seizing on the excitement of the moment, salesmen delivered a rousing forecast of vast wealth that would be drawn from mother earth. Then they hauled the noisy crusher to another corner of the field and repeated the demonstration, producing pea-sized nuggets of glistening platinum. If potential investors were still reluctant to part with their cash, the salesmen offered "evidence" of lucrative stray silver veins, directly under their feet. Few investors needed that reassurance: here was the chance of a lifetime! Caught up in the potato lot bonanza, neighboring farmers also took to their fields with shovels and buckets in feverish searches for Yonkers gold and platinum. Belief in the geological miracle thus spread beyond the community targeted by Iridium's promoters.

There were skeptics, especially in the office of the United States attorney, who caught on to the scheme when the gold rush in Yonkers potato fields became a matter for wider notice and humorous comment. The investigators did some digging of their own and discovered that the total assets of the company were a rock crusher, several gold nuggets, and $30 worth of platinum. Iridium did not even own the Yonkers farm. In due course the officers of the company were indicted in 1922 for the fraudulent sale of over 500,000 shares in their enterprise. To the end, however, Iridium's president swore the company had a bonanza; he had prospected in Alaska, Montana, and California, and he knew pay dirt like that in Yonkers when he saw it.[1]

The Iridium Gold and Platinum Company was not one of the grander scams of its time, nor were its investors uniquely naive. In 1921 imaginative Chicago promoters did a lively trade in shares of the League of Nations; they claimed that they would be able to pay mammoth dividends, because of "the great value of the League to humanity."

Nova Adolphus Brown, who peddled shares in many enterprises, promoted the Lexington Chocolate Company. He foresaw great profits to be made by selling cod liver oil chocolate bars to people who wanted the nutritional benefits of cod liver oil without its rank taste.

The directors of the Birmingham Motors Corporation of Jamestown, New York, offered their investors the unparalleled opportunity to own the manufacturer of the world's first no-axle automobile.

H. Kent Holmes promoted the American Aircraft Arms Company, a venture which would produce an antiaircraft gun with twenty-four barrels that could all be fired at once. He explained that the concentrated firepower would bring down enemy airplanes without the need to aim the gun.

The George Alot Land Company peddled farmland that was located in the bed of the Mississippi River, admitting that the property was "unimproved except for running water."[2]

Compared to these colorful lures to the hapless investor, the scheme of Boston's Carlo Ponzi, the most notorious swindler of the 1920s, was a model of sober rationality. Ponzi merely promised his investors a 50 percent dividend in ninety days, through his purchases of international postal exchange coupons and exploitation of differing exchange rates. When the ninety days were up, Ponzi offered to pay both the original investment and the handsome dividend, and during the early months of his promotion, he actually did so. In most instances, however, he persuaded his clients to reinvest both the capital and the proceeds, thus leaving him with

Getting Rich Quick

the funds for the time being and postponing a final reckoning of accounts.

In the meantime, Ponzi paid "dividends" out of capital paid in, because the whole postal coupon scheme was bogus. His get-rich-quick clientele grew with dizzying speed, and long lines of investors crowded the doors of his office. In one month alone he took in about $2.5 million. The scale of his operations made him a byword for fraudulent promotion and gave Ponzi, who went to jail, immortality in the annals of easy money.[3]

Many promotions enjoyed the initial success of Ponzi and Iridium because faith in getting rich quick was more pervasive in America following World War I than jazz, flappers, and bathtub gin. Wartime prosperity created an expansive, optimistic mentality in much of the nation and helped launch genuine booms in real estate, the stock market, and oil. Some luck, some hustle, or a combination of both would seemingly yield windfall wealth, both for investors and for those with whom they trusted their money. So wonderful were opportunities that neither capital nor experience was necessary. The humblest investor would turn a few dollars into a fortune. The rawest promoter would build a business empire on a shoestring. Everyone would "get in on the ground floor," everyone would see dollars multiply, and every proposition was "can't lose." In short, anybody who really wanted to would land on Easy Street. Only the great stock market crash marked Easy Street as a dead-end road.

It is far easier to identify the end of the great jazz-age speculative mania than to account for either its mentality or its duration. What brought so many Americans to try their luck as investors that sales of securities doubled between 1912 and 1922? What encouraged so many persons to look for easy money? Why, as one observer wryly noted, did it seem that "the man who said that a sucker is born every minute underestimated the supply?" Most of all, out of all the speculation, why did so few speculators get rich? Why was it so hard to succeed when it looked as though success had never been so certain?[4]

Any explanation of frenzied speculation must start with money in speculators' hands. Simply put, as the result of wartime conditions, Americans had more money to invest. Between 1914 and 1918 the number of persons reporting incomes in the $50,000 to $100,000 range rose from approximately 5,000 to 13,000, and the number whose incomes were in the $30,000 to $40,000 range rose from about 6,000 to over 15,000. Despite a brief postwar recession, the number of persons who made more than $5,000 a year trebled from 1910 to 1929. For an increasing number of affluent Americans, after the bare costs of living were met there was money to spare for vacations, commercial amusements, luxuries, and investment.[5]

Farther down the income pyramid, many people who were not affluent enjoyed wartime prosperity. Excepting a few areas such as home building and construction, most industries had more jobs. Seven hundred thousand persons joined the work force in 1916–17, and 600,000 the following year. These war workers included women and blacks, entering jobs previously closed to them. Generally sympathetic to workers' demands, wartime wage boards permitted wage hikes in most industries. Coal miners, for example, won large increases in May and December 1917, with a further raise in 1918. Not all workers did so well, but by 1918 the average wage earner's income was nonetheless estimated at 63 percent higher than in 1914. Inflation eroded some of the benefit from the increase: the cost of a quart of milk or a dozen eggs, for example, doubled during the war. But with more family members able to find work and with pay envelopes fatter than ever, the working household was still likely to have gained economically as a result of the war.[6]

Farmers fared even better than workers. War brought soaring prices for farm products. Between August 1915 and August 1918, for example, prices of corn and oats doubled. In May 1917 wheat futures hit $3.25 per bushel, a record high at the Chicago Board of Trade. Cotton brought thirteen cents a pound in 1913; at the end of August 1918 its price leaped to thirty-seven cents, the highest in fifty-two years. Even if what they bought rose in price, as farmers complained, their net income rose from $4 billion to $10 billion during the war years. Many a farmer took profits and bought an automobile; the appearance of the automobile as a regular feature of American rural life was a result of wartime prosperity. Some farmers cannily reasoned that they would never see farm prices equal wartime levels, sold out at war's end, and moved to town or California. Others less farsighted and more prone to speculate plowed their capital into more farmland and equipment, bought at highly inflated prices. Making a losing bet on continued high prices, they would be sorely pressed after 1920 to make payments on mortgages and notes. If hopes for a farm bonanza in the twenties proved illusory, however, wartime gains down on the farm were real. In 1919 farmers had an ample supply of spare cash.[7]

Not everyone made out as well. Amid all this prosperity, there were groups of Americans who fell behind economically as they watched their

Getting Rich Quick

neighbors get ahead. Persons living on limited capital and fixed incomes found that wartime inflation destroyed their economic security. The minor bureaucrat, the retired schoolteacher, and the military pensioner alike had to prune their budgets. They could see prosperity all around them, but it was beyond their reach. Desperate to halt the alarming erosion of their financial positions, these people were easily tempted to stake their dwindling capital on long-shot gambles for riches. Failing lucky windfalls, their economic prospects were grim: if they missed Easy Street, they were on the road to the poor farm.[8]

The atmosphere of patriotic frugality generated by government policymakers during the war, however, tended to obscure the difference between voluntary and involuntary thrift. No matter how much money Americans made, from 1917 to the end of the war economic mobilization and government anxiety over scarcity of wartime supplies made it increasingly hard to spend. Those who might have bought a bungalow in the suburbs or built a larger barn had to postpone plans when Priority Circular No. 21 put a lid on nonwar construction. Homeowners who wanted to redecorate found they could not buy dining room armchairs or sideboards with mirrors, while brass bedsteads had fewer rods and smaller head and foot pieces. There were half as many electric heating appliances, oil stoves, and sewing machines available, and government authorities ordered production of waffle irons, peanut roasters, and soup kettles stopped. Genteel shabbiness was enforced at Uncle Sam's direction.[9]

Consumers who liked to put much of what they earned on their backs faced frustrations in the form of policy directives amounting to sumptuary laws. The War Industries Board decided that Americans could survive with shoes in a color range limited to white, black, and two shades of tan. Bedroom slippers were a forbidden luxury. Feminine modesty notwithstanding, manufacturers had to shorten the tops of ladies' shoes. Men could no long buy double-breasted coats, and the styles, heights, trim, and brim-widths of their straw hats came under government regulation. Beginning with limitation of consumer choices, policymakers moved by autumn 1918 to deciding that there would be no new styles whatever in shoes, ladies' hats, and fountain pens for at least six months. Even time was brought under control; after October 1, 1918, manufacturers were forced to cut watch production by 70 percent.[10]

The appeal to the patriot's heart also reached his stomach. America's tireless food administrator, Herbert Hoover, told the public it must accept

Easy Money

wheatless Mondays, meatless Tuesdays, porkless Tuesdays and Saturdays, and one meatless meal a day—but that was only the beginning. Americans were urged to use Victory bread, made with 20 percent nonwheat flours. To conserve sugar, bakers had to cut back making cookies, cakes, pies, and pastries by 30 percent, while ice cream manufacturers had to cut their production by a quarter. Nor could a hungry diner evade the rules by eating out. Not only were restaurants held to the same guidelines as homemakers, but they could not serve bread unless requested, bacon or bread as a garnish to food, butter in greater than one-ounce servings, roast beef or steak more than once a week, or sugar in sugar bowls. In compensation, Hoover urged Americans to grow vegetable gardens, and he allowed the price of prunes to rise to 8½ cents a pound to head off shortages in 1918.[11]

In this wartime environment of forced frugality, Americans saved an unprecedented proportion of their incomes. The rate of saving reached 9.1 percent by 1917–19, a rate not again attained until 1944. As pockets filled with dollars unspent on consumer goods, the federal government urged patriotic Americans to put their money into war bonds. Newspaper and magazine advertisements, posters, and George Creel's ubiquitous "Four-Minute Men" all admonished citizens to "Win the War—Buy a Bond!" Over 22 million persons did so. That number included experienced investors, but there were many other bond buyers, prodded by peer pressure and stimulated by patriotism, who would not ordinarily have saved money at all. Nearly one-third of all Liberty Bonds were bought by persons with annual incomes of $2,000 or less, people more likely to put their money into groceries and clothing in normal times.[12]

The war bond campaign succeeded in all income brackets and reached citizens in the largest cities and smallest hamlets alike. Its message swayed Americans who had never before had easy access to investments outside their immediate neighborhoods, persons who had never seen a securities broker, let alone done business with one. No securities sales effort of the past could compare with the massive sales campaign for war bonds. It was a brilliantly successful promotion, and in the end more than 18 million Americans became securities owners for the first time. Thanks to Uncle Sam, they flooded the pool of potential small investors.

Once the war ended, therefore, many Americans found themselves not only with some savings but also with a start on investment, the fruit of

Getting Rich Quick

prosperity and frugality. But as they rejoiced in peace, they celebrated the end of wartime austerity; they were tired of thrift and ready for hedonistic extravagance. As one proponent of the simple life lamented, "Reckless spending takes the place of saving, waste replaces conservation." The National Prosperity Bureau, organized by businessmen, told Americans in 1919, "Buy what you need now!"[13] After months of having their shoe colors, furniture designs, and daily diets dictated to them, Americans were entirely willing to do so. They found, moreover, that higher paychecks and the device of installment payments opened a cornucopia of consumer options to them, ranging from automobiles and radios to color-coordinated bed linens and mouthwash. The average person not only could aspire to own more things but was also inclined to admire those who had the means to do so. Thus a journalist told the readers of *Nation's Business* that his ideal American was "rich, fat, arrogant, and superior."[14]

Getting rich, being rich, and enjoying riches became dominant themes in American culture during the jazz age. Advertisers were quick to exploit the public's preoccupation with riches. They presented their products as the ones the rich lived with; by using advertised products, they implied, the ordinary consumer could share the experiences of the wealthy.[15] Politicians knew voters wanted to be rich; Calvin Coolidge solemnly proclaimed, "Brains are wealth, and wealth is the chief end of man."[16] Clergymen and evangelists recast their message in terms of material gain. The dean of the University of Chicago Divinity School, for one, told the press a man could make more money if he prayed about his business, while Bruce Barton portrayed Jesus as an ace businessman whose parables were the best advertising of all time. As William Leuchtenburg has noted, "Religion was valued not as a path to personal salvation or a key to the riddle of the universe but because it paid off in dollars and cents."[17]

But so were many other aspects of life. When Robert and Helen Lynd asked the inhabitants of "Middletown" why they worked so hard, they were told that money was the main goal. Money, in Middletown as elsewhere, was the basis of social status. As one Middletowner remarked on how old-timers "placed" newcomers in terms of where and how they lived, "You see, they know money, and they don't know you." Money and material possessions defined one's place in that community; money was the antidote to social insecurity. Most Americans knew, however, that they would have to do more than work hard to reach beyond simple comfort to

Easy Money

riches. Their money would also have to work for them: they would need to invest it.[18]

Though they began investing in war bonds, the 3½ to 4½ percent interest these instruments offered would not make small investors wealthy. Bondholders quickly learned that bonds could be put to creative uses, with a view to a better return than from holding them to maturity. Banks, for example, accepted war bonds as collateral for loans. Securities peddlers accepted bonds at full value, rather than the lower redemption value of bonds that were not held to maturity. Many novice investors learned that from Liberty Bonds they could move into more exciting and speculative activities and make more money than Uncle Sam offered: all they needed was opportunity.

When aspiring investors studied local opportunities for placing their money, they found few appealing prospects. Farmland and farm loans ceased to be attractive when farm product prices plunged in the early 1920s; nor was slow-moving stock in a local savings and loan association alluring. Another traditional conservative investment, local real estate, was unattractive because outside major cities or booming areas like Florida and California most prices were flat. None of the local opportunities was likely to make anyone rich quick.

Depositing money in the bank was equally unattractive. Even those who did not seek instant riches were under pressure to invest their money rather than save it, because the rate of inflation exceeded prevailing interest rates. Money placed in the bank shrank a little every year. This was common knowledge, but anyone who lacked it could read it in the form of expert advice printed in mass circulation magazines. John J. Raskob, financier and one-time president of General Motors, told readers of the *Ladies' Home Journal* as much: "No one can be rich merely by saving. Putting aside a sum each week or month in a sock at no interest, or in a savings bank at ordinary interest, will not provide enough for old age unless life in the meantime be rigorously skimped down to the level of mere existence. And if everyone skimped in any such fashion, then the country would be so poor that living at all would hardly be worthwhile."[19] Pinning one's hopes on 3 percent interest was foolish and vaguely un-American. Saving did not lead to the good life; a penny saved was no longer a penny earned. More adventurous investment was the only avenue to future security and comfort; it was the road to prosperity.

Getting Rich Quick

Investors received strong encouragement to plunge into risky ventures from advertising men and journalists. Popular magazines regularly carried tales of instant millionaires, created overnight by profitable real estate or oil investments. In 1917, for example, readers of the *Scientific American* learned that the southwestern oil fields were "making millionaires at . . . a dizzy rate; men who three or four years ago were in the down-and-out class are millionaires many times over today." The following year the *Saturday Evening Post* told its readers that oil fields were "where fairy tales come true," where "new kings of oil appear upon the stage, and fortunes by the hundreds—yes, even by the thousands . . . all spring up like magic overnight." Similarly, in 1926 *Harper's* published a Florida land boom feature describing the "poor woman who bought a lot in Miami in 1896 for $25 and sold it this year for $150,000." The author of the article reflected, as must have many a reader, "Remembering the painful slowness of saving, I was struck hard by the quick ease with which these fortunate people gained assurance against dependence."[20] Feature writers stressed that the overnight millionaires did not become rich as the result of work, intelligence, or any other special advantage: what happened to them could have happened to anyone. Anyone could get rich.

Speaking as an expert on the subject, John J. Raskob argued that the petty capitalist who invested intelligently could become a rentier, living comfortably on the proceeds of a small invested capital by setting aside as little as $15 a month. Thus, he assured readers of the *Ladies' Home Journal*, prosperity was "attainable by anyone."[21] The obvious problem for the would-be rentier was inadequate access to investment opportunities. Raskob admitted this difficulty: "If he thinks of investing in some stock, he has nowhere to turn for advice. He is not big enough to get much attention from his banker, and he has not enough money to go to a broker."[22] Instead, he found other people selling what he could afford, people delighted to give him personal attention.

Swarms of itinerant stock salesmen rode the trains and drove the dusty rural roads of America to gather in the dollars of the new investors. They accepted any purchase, however small; they soothed nervous novices with promises of wonderful gains. What they sold sounded respectable, as did the firms they represented. In fact, most of them worked for bucket shops and fly-by-night brokerage firms. The frequently indicted C. W. Cannon styled his operation in Manhattan as "Cannon, Stamm, & Company, members of the Consolidated Stock Exchange of New York." Harold Boericke, another securities illusionist, found one Edwin Baruch and made him an associate in "Baruch & Company," thus trading on the celebrity of Bernard Baruch and Baruch Brothers. Boericke's investors received letters mentioning "our Mr. Baruch" as a renowned investment authority; for Boericke's purposes, one Baruch was as good as another. These stock peddlers were always ready to cultivate small investors.[23]

More reputable brokerage houses also dealt directly with the new crop of investors, sending them newsletters, tip sheets, telegrams, and promotional letters and following up with phone calls. Brokerage firms as well as individual promoters often selected certain groups for ventures that informed investors would turn down. Farmers, factory workers, clergymen, and unmarried women were favorite targets. One group of promoters, for example, directed a sales campaign at farmers in Henry County, Missouri, in 1921. The slick out-of-town visitors invited most of the county to a festive barbecue, and their hospitality paid off in the form of over $100,000 in sales of shares in a tire and rubber company of dubious worth. The event became newsworthy because it took place just at the time the Missouri College of Agriculture sent a trainload of agricultural experts and exhibition cattle to Henry County to offer farmers current instruction in scientific stock breeding. The farmers, more interested in a free meal and easy money, left the experts and their prize cows ignored and stranded on a siding at the railroad depot.[24]

While shares in all sorts of speculative ventures sold well, some enjoyed special popularity. During and after the war, oil stocks led all others in investor appeal, challenging the longer dominance of hard-rock mining shares as speculations. The popularity of oil was obvious in the portfolio of one small investor, a seventy-year-old Massachusetts hairdresser; it included 10 shares of Anglo-American Oil, 110 shares of Elk Basin Consolidated Oil, 6 shares of Producers and Refiners Oil, 51 shares of Federal Oil, 300 shares of Hudson Oil, 20 shares of Merritt Oil, 250 shares of Northwest Oil, 20 shares of Cosden & Company (also oil), and 5 shares of American Telephone and Telegraph. An Atlanta housewife, a somewhat more conservative speculator, held 85 shares of Hecla Mining, 4 shares of American International Corporation, 500 shares of Hudson Oil, and 100 shares of Mason Valley Mines. Both investors were thus clearly trying highly speculative issues. Nonetheless, a genuine boom in the petroleum

Getting Rich Quick

industry made it easy to sell oil stock to small and large investors alike, and reputable Wall Street firms were as ready to do so as the bucket shops.[25]

In addition to oil and mining stocks, shares in ventures relating to modern technology sold briskly throughout the twenties. Promoters hurried to cater to the investors' preference for stocks in motion pictures, radio communications, aviation, and automobile manufacturing. The increasing popularity of motion pictures in particular made it easy to attract investors for even poorly managed and fraudulent film productions. In 1921 the Vigilance Committee of the National Association of the Motion Picture Industry estimated that investors had put about $50 million into fraudulent motion picture ventures during the previous year. Though investors often lost their stakes in these schemes, losses did not discourage further speculation. Indeed, when oil and real estate eventually paled, the stock market became even more attractive to investors. By 1928 investor commitment to stocks reached a level one disgruntled savings bank president compared to a siege of malarial fever; he lamented that "savings banks are deluding themselves if they hope there will be an immediate or considerable return of savings from Wall Street." At the same time, stock swindles were so notorious that Chicago crime boss Al Capone complained, "It's a racket. Those stock market guys are crooked."[26]

For investors large and small, one of the most enticing alternatives to the stock market was land in the southern parts of Florida and California, where sunshine was an asset and land values had nowhere to go but up. Observers explained the Florida phenomenon in a variety of ways. The climate was perfect for winter vacations—warm, sunny, suitable for outdoor sports all year. Places like Palm Beach became popular resorts for wealthy celebrities who had given up Riviera playgrounds during the war. There was the relative proximity of Florida to northern population centers, and its accessibility by automobile via the Dixie Highway or by train on the Florida East Coast Railroad. Above all, there were the thrilling tales of spectacular fortunes made in Florida by developers such as George Merrick, Carl B. Fisher, J. W. Young, and D. P. Davis: their careers proved that Florida investments brought quick riches.[27]

The catalyst binding all these ingredients was modern advertising. As one journalist put it, it made the Florida speculation into "Eldorado, the Klondike, and the South Sea Bubble rolled into one." Promoters not only filled Florida newspapers like the *Miami Herald* with advertising, but branched out across the United States. George Merrick, for one, ran full-page advertisements in the *New York Times*; his publicity department sent out a flood of promotional literature to newspapers, magazines, and individual investors. In order to mount this campaign, double crews of workers filled eight-hour shifts around the clock, using electric duplicating machines that could whip out a single-page release or letter in a split second. With this publicity barrage, Merrick, like many other Florida land promoters, opened sales offices in northern cities.[28] Other Florida promoters targeted rural America for investors and sent out corps of lecturers to declaim on Florida's wonders to small-town clubs and civic groups. Rural newspapers, often hard-pressed for copy, received a steady supply of Florida features and "news" releases. So, for that matter, did major dailies like the *New York Times*.

Nationally circulated newspapers and periodicals routinely carried the promise that investments were magic in Florida. They told and retold the same stories: of the Coast Guardsman who picked up ocean frontage for twenty-five cents and sold it for a million; of a soldier who traded an overcoat for ten worthless beach acres that came to be valued at $25,000; of the two schoolteachers from Boston who ignored their banker's advice and invested $1,000 in Florida lots, selling them for $3,000 in only three weeks. It was believable when the *New York Times* told its readers that in Florida even laborers owned limousines and "fine houses." What these tales emphasized was that just plain folks—tourists in Model T's, elderly retirees, vacationing wage earners—people with neither money nor expertise—were cleaning up in Florida; Florida offered the little guy a chance to strike it rich.[29]

The promise of quick riches was much more likely to capture the reader's attention than the occasional cautionary observation that the Florida boom would not last forever. Some journalists, moreover, went out of their way to assure readers that Florida real estate was a low-risk investment. Felix Isman, for example, told *Saturday Evening Post* readers that the state of Florida was doing "everything possible" to protect investors from swindlers; that there was less danger in Florida speculation than in investments anywhere else; and that the wealthy who had invested in Florida "know what they are doing." One of the knowledgeable wealthy people who invested in Florida development was Isman's publisher.[30]

By the height of the boom in 1925, the radio offered an effective new way to reach prospects in urban and rural America alike. The ever-creative Merrick sponsored a Coral Gables orchestra and prompted Irving Berlin to write "When the Moon Shines in Coral Gables" in order to broadcast the wonders of his Florida town lots. Had one tried, it would have been difficult not to hear about the marvels of real estate investments in Florida.[31]

The Florida promoters also capitalized on the popular taste for exotic locales stimulated by the movies. They gave their new developments names worthy of cinematic fantasy—Olympia, Eldorado Heights, Comfort Gardens, Utopia, and Hollywood-by-the-Sea—and they recreated Spanish mansions, Venetian palazzi, Moorish arcades, and medieval cloisters in their subdivisions. Working with the swampy Florida terrain, many developers dug canals to aid drainage; turning necessity to advantage, George Merrick imported Venetian gondolas and gondoliers to ply his canals. Like the world of cinema, Florida blended the real and the fantastic. For that matter, there was a strong element of storybook wonder in the way in which land was created from swamps, lagoons, and sand dunes. Carl Fisher, for example, used landfill to create much of Miami Beach from mangrove swamp, while D. P. "Doc" Davis built his Davis Islands development from the shoals and marshes of Tampa Bay. No wonder one writer asked, "Where, outside of a fairy book, does one find islands rising from the sea and crowned with Aladdin palaces almost overnight?" Florida seemed like the place where something came from nothing, where the too-good-to-be-true regularly came true. It readily sustained hopes of easy money.[32]

Once Florida captured public imagination, curious tourists flocked to the state. Real estate promoters encouraged this migration, for they saw a likely investor in every visitor. Promoter Merrick ran three weekly excursions to Coral Gables from points as distant as Montgomery, Alabama, some 800 miles away; on a less regular basis, he ran "inspection tours" from New York, Chicago, and San Francisco. When Merrick's potential investors signed up for his trips, they received a package that included transportation, two or three days' room and board, and entertainment free of charge. Another developer put on dances in towns throughout the Middle West; admission was free, as was the trip pressed on the prospects who attended them.

Many people paid their own way to the Sunshine State, crowding onto

Easy Money

trains, booking passages to Jacksonville or Miami on steamers, or bouncing along in the family flivver. At the height of the boom in the summer of 1925, the resultant traffic on the eighteen-foot-wide Dixie Highway near Miami resembled "a dense, struggling stream," and Miami itself was "a seething cauldron of humanity." The city looked like a frontier town, as its temporary citizens engaged in a mad scramble for overnight fortune. It was a promoter's paradise.[33]

Once the casual visitors arrived in Miami, they were besieged by regiments of land salesmen. Eager young men wearing straw hats and white golfing clothes buttonholed pedestrians, offering them free lunches, dinners, barbecues, clambakes, bus tours, boat trips, and lectures. Other salesmen drove up and down streets in flashy open cars, alternating their raucous sales pitches with honking saxophone solos. When either feet or ears became fatigued, the weary visitors relaxed in overstuffed easy chairs in the numerous real estate offices on Miami's main streets while sales agents entertained them with glossy pictures and colored maps of new subdivisions.[34]

Sooner or later most people left downtown Miami to take the free bus or boat tours to development sites. The excursions varied in length from one afternoon to several days, but they all included extravagant oratory from hired lecturers on the wonders of Florida. Never outshone in promotional artistry, George Merrick hired the "peerless prince of platform English," William Jennings Bryan, to sell for him. Bryan, who shared a raft in one of Merrick's Venetian pools with Gilda Gray, the Original Shimmy Girl, expounded on Florida's charms with some sincerity; he himself had made handsome profits in Florida land speculation, and Merrick paid him over $100 a day to deliver what one journalist described as "sort of a sermon" on Florida. Promoters less intent on uplifting and educating their prospects treated them to baby contests, vaudeville acts, and alligator wrestling. It was all free, until the visitor signed on the dotted line—but even then, promoters made life easy for their customers.[35]

Units in what most developers sold went for relatively small prices, and signing purchase contracts for lots did not require buyers to part with large sums of money immediately. Widespread installment sales made it easy for thrifty small-town visitors to buy lots on speculation, thinking to sell them for quick profits. Developers commonly required only small down payments, $50 or $100; they readily agreed to monthly payments of

Getting Rich Quick

only a few dollars. After days of hearing of the wonders of Florida, the newcomers began to believe they too could be real estate tycoons, selling to buyers eager to take the lots off their hands. Before they had to make any payments, they would reap spectacular profits. Snowbirds easily became plungers.[36]

Those who chased even shorter-term gains could enter the game by paying binders, as little as 5 percent of the asked prices of the properties. Once they paid the binders, the speculators were not obliged to pay the first installments—usually 25 percent of the purchase price—until the titles to the properties cleared. This process often took at least four to six weeks, and it could drag on for months because title offices were swamped with business. In the meantime, the purchasers could sell their purchase contracts at a profit. As salesmen pointed out, taking advantage of the situation would permit investors to purchase multiple lots with the same amount of "up-front" money that single-lot purchases required. The scheme also contained the assurance for small speculators that if they continued to leverage through binders, they could expect their financial juggling to yield quick profits from which they would pay installment obligations as they came due. The booming trade in binders sent them spiraling upward—and the supply of eager investors and buyers seemed unlimited. In short, speculators expected to make a profit by selling property before they had to pay for it.[37]

Spiraling prices obscured risk, as one land salesman recalled: "One of these wild plungers whom I happened to meet . . . himself pointed out to me that, in order to justify the price which he had just paid for a certain city property, he would have to build on it an office building 200 stories high with all the rooms let in perpetuity at the prevailing enormous rents. He knew, of course, that such a thing was utterly impossible, but he didn't care in the least. He also knew that he could hand on this gem of an investment to somebody else at a vastly increased price, and by the time I met him again a few days later he had actually done so."[38] Still, the narrator was surprised that his friend sold his property so quickly. The inflation of prices in boom times made it hard to foresee real profits from operations, and it was ever more likely that the prices of investments would outstrip all plausible return.

Caught up in the speculative whirl, it was very difficult for participants to have realistic calculations of assets and liabilities. It was easy to generate

Easy Money

paper profits, harder to assess the real costs and risks of making them. A promoter who resorted to advertising, promotional tours, and hired celebrities had bills to pay at the end of each month, and they were no illusion. Many promoters had no idea of how much money they owed or how much was owed them. In the words of one journalist, "The nice balance of outgo against income was not understood."[39]

There were other serious problems with boom-time land trading, especially in doing business with obliging strangers. Few people invested with brokers they knew well. It was easy, under such circumstances, for salesmen to misrepresent the locations of properties and to sell lots they did not own. Underwater lots, swampland tracts, and bogus titles proliferated as trading soared.

Florida speculation reached its highest pitch late in the summer of 1925. Thereafter, a variety of mishaps cooled boom fever. The first sign of a break came when the transportation bottlenecks on the highways and Florida East Coast Railroad proved chronic. In August the railroad declared an embargo on freight, except for food and mail. Building materials could no longer move by rail, causing immediate setbacks for developers who were rushing to complete hotels to cash in on the winter tourist trade. Some of the freight was carried by a makeshift flotilla of coastal steamers until January 1926, when a ship capsized and sank in the Miami ship canal, blocking the marine entrance to the city. This mishap further curtailed tourism because it made the transfer of passengers to shore time-consuming and inconvenient. In the face of mounting transportation bottlenecks, the flow of tourists and speculators diminished during what should have been the high season for Florida promotion.[40]

It was clear by the end of January 1926 that the bonanza winter Florida developers counted on was not going to appear. Optimistic projections were lowered every day, and in the end winter tourism amounted to only one-tenth of what had been expected. Land buyers were scarce, and trading came to a standstill. The stall signaled the critical phase in speculation. Without fresh investment, values would plummet and prices would decline. Day by day, boom turned to bust. Obligations assumed in the hectic days of the preceding summer began to come due, and many traders were pressed for cash.

The end of the Florida boom was hastened by increasingly negative press coverage outside the state. Bankers in the Northeast and Middle

Getting Rich Quick

West were responsible for some of it; they were alarmed by the drain of capital from their institutions to Florida during 1925. The Massachusetts Savings Bank League, for example, estimated that in the summer of that year over 100,000 depositors in the state transferred money to Florida. Ohio bankers felt so threatened by the flow of capital to the South that they took out newspaper ads advising against travel to Florida. Stories of land swindles, like that carried out by a young woman calling herself Florence Nightingale, made even the pro-Floridian pages of the *New York Times*, and the Better Business Bureau announced that it was investigating some Florida land promotions. In an attempt at a counteroffensive, the governor of Florida and some prominent Florida investors told the press that the state was cracking down on "fly-by-night speculators," but Florida's attraction for new investors nonetheless diminished.[41]

By the summer of 1926 the Florida boom had run its course. With a few exceptions, development halted. Binders went unpaid, contracts were breached, venture after venture went into receivership, real estate offices closed, and some banks failed. Nature provided a grim climax to the downturn: on September 19, 1926, a giant hurricane smashed into the Miami area, leaving nearly 400 people dead, 6,300 injured, and 50,000 homeless. In effect, economics and the elements combined to end the fantasies that were the stock-in-trade of Florida promoters, putting a period to many small investors' dreams of getting rich quick.[42]

What was left when the boom was over? Paper profits and fraud aside, the Florida boom did stimulate permanent development. The area of most intense activity lay along Florida's southeastern coast, particularly in the stretch between Miami and Palm Beach. The boom, however, also reached the Gulf Coast, notably in the Tampa Bay area, and the central citrus orchard regions. Using bond issues, the new cities created by Florida developers took on large-scale construction of roads, parks, street railways, city buildings, and water and sewage systems. Though some plans were fanciful—like Thomas Edison's suggestion to establish rubber plantations in the Everglades or the scheme of motion picture promoters who thought the Florida swamps could come to rival Hollywood in the production of jungle adventures—a great amount of swamp and marsh was cleared, drained, and put under cultivation in the southern part of the state.[43]

Once these places grew, economic growth picked up further north,

Easy Money

especially at Jacksonville, a major port and transportation terminus for the eastern part of the state. Developers seeing potential in the "sunny South" extended land promotion into other states: there were local real estate booms in Mississippi, Alabama, and Georgia, and even Asheville, North Carolina, attracted developers. None of this, of course, could compete with the explosive growth in Florida, where population more than doubled.

If growth was real, why did so many promoters and investors lose money in Florida? The most general answer is that, in the excitement of the boom, they embraced the intuitive notion that risk diminishes during a boom. Having done that, they then assumed that their ventures were risk free. Small fry in particular failed to realize that they were at the end of the speculative food chain. Though developers like Merrick put big capital into projects, early success stories played up giant profits made on small investments. Once Florida land prices rose, land that was attractive for development—large tracts near centers of growth—became more expensive. On a small investment, all a promoter or speculator could afford was small, distant, or both. Less desirable properties cost more to sell; it was harder to pass them and the risk attached to buying them along to someone else. Promoters who specialized in small sales were also progressively disadvantaged. As the boom progressed, competition for small sales grew fiercer and, hence, more costly. In short, those who bought little and late had virtually no chance of increasing their assets, but the can't-lose mentality of boom times made it seem like Florida speculation was guaranteed to yield easy money.

With the benefit of hindsight, some analysts who looked at the Florida debacle noted that what happened in Florida resembled land booms at other times and in other places. In many respects, earlier real estate promotions in California, starting with those of the 1880s, were the models for what was done in Florida. Nineteenth-century land promoters in southern California, for example, perfected the techniques of earlier western developers, such as selling lots from impressively drawn maps and pictures, and cultivating investors with free excursions and food. Like Florida, southern California's climate and bustling speculation acted as a potent lure for tourists, retirees, and small-town folk in search of excitement and a chance to enter the real estate game. With the newcomers' arrival, the ranks of California realtors swelled. During the first quarter of

Getting Rich Quick

1923, for example, over 27,000 real estate sales licenses were issued by the state of California. The novices entered a trade that was both complex and promising, because California promoters found that the techniques they used to promote real estate development transferred to that new and potent magnet to investors' dollars, oil. In short, what would sell town lots would sell oil wells.[44]

Whether by geological or historical accident, most of North America's major oil fields have been discovered in underpopulated and desolate regions; the Permian Basin of Texas and New Mexico and the Rocky Mountain Overthrust are familiar examples. California offers an exception to this general rule. Indeed, some of the important California oil discoveries of the early twentieth century took place in areas where real estate developers had already been selling town lots and small farms. Thus as early as 1892 Edward L. Doheny, once a mining prospector, discovered the City field in Los Angeles, around what is now the site of Dodger Stadium. Before World War I, a promoter of Huntington Beach town lots joined forces with an encyclopedia printer to boost sales of their respective commodities, neither of which had attracted many buyers; they gave a free town lot to anyone who bought a set of encyclopedias. After the war, oil was discovered under those twenty-five-foot lots, which came to be worth $2,000 each. Real estate promotion also preceded the discovery of oil in both Long Beach and Santa Fe Springs, but in other parts of Los Angeles and Orange counties industrial suburbs grew up around oil fields. In either instance, real estate and oil development were linked in regional growth.[45]

By the early twenties, especially in the Los Angeles area, the techniques of real estate promotion merged with those of oil promotion with spectacular results. As one journalist described it, "Nothing had been easier than for the real-estate salesman and operator to turn to oil. Many a real-estate man is now drilling for oil, and thousands of real-estate salesmen . . . are selling oil units. The paraphernalia, the equipment, the officers, the personnel, the sales technic [*sic*]—all were there. Why not make killings in two directions instead of one." Or, as another observer reflected in August 1923, "Oranges may be out of season in Los Angeles just now, but oil is very ripe."[46]

Observers also noted that the real estate booms sometimes preceding oil promotions contributed to investor willingness to buy into oil; real estate booms "created an extremely favorable attitude and atmosphere for buying and selling." In other words, it seemed easy to get rich quick: realtors had done so. As one Californian summed it up, "Money has come so easy, especially in real estate, that they are willing to take a little gamble."[47]

Many southern Californians, keenly aware of oil activity around them, itched to try for boom-time fortunes. People who commuted to work had daily visual evidence of oil's importance. They drove through neighborhoods peppered with derricks and producing wells; they saw, or at least heard of, gushers and wild wells. They could see streets clogged with traffic, and they could watch developers transform vacant lots into tidy subdivisions. They had read or heard stories of quick riches, of people like the illiterate German day laborer who came into an income of $3,000 a day, or of the newly rich barber who decorated his shop door with a sign: "Cadillac Salesmen Call At My House." Such tales made it easy to believe that a fortune could grow from small beginnings, that "oil money is the easiest money on earth." As a Los Angeles banker commented, "People here are especially gullible. That is because speculation is in the air, because people think of it [southern California] as the land of easy money, and because for so many it has proved to be." As in Florida, early success made fantasies all the more believable.[48]

Those who watched the southern California oil boom unfold in the early 1920s were impressed with the number of investors of obviously modest means who took seriously the promises of quick fortune. Workers down on their luck were tempted to grab for quick riches. Nellie Scanlan of the *New York Times* reported that the people who took a Los Angeles oil promotion tour with her in August 1923 included farmers from Iowa and Missouri "who dropped money raising wheat," a New York realtor, a middle-aged woman who taught voice, a mechanic "who had lost nearly everything, including his wife," a boardinghouse mistress, and an elderly man who boasted of having invested in fourteen oil wells. Scanlan particularly noticed working women among investors, "drab, wrinkled women, with work-knotted hands and shabby clothes." The *Saturday Evening Post*'s Albert Atwood, on a similar tour a month earlier, had seen "oil-begrimed workmen and sad-looking women with smelly babies; many bore upon their faces and persons unmistakable signs of both ignorance and poverty, although they were of no one class or group." Atwood found women and the elderly especially numerous; as he went on a weekday tour, perhaps this was not remarkable. But he also saw younger married couples: "A pathetic-looking, poorly dressed young woman, with a face half-gone, evidently burned off in a cookstove explosion, was handing a Liberty Bond over to a salesman. The husband, dressed in the roughest working clothes, sat by with an expression as intelligent as that of a faithful ox."[49]

The promoters recruited these small investors with "The Four B's Method—Busses, Barkers, Ballyhoo, and Boobs." As early as November 1909, oil promoters had used a variant of it to attract investors to oil wells at Coalinga; then a twelve-car train brought in 200 well-heeled visitors who were treated to oysters, crab, asparagus, roast duck, and sparkling burgundy as part of their tour. Promoters of the early twenties had no need to go to such lengths: their potential investors were willing to settle for a bus ride and a ham sandwich. Promoters hired men and women to round them up by canvassing neighborhoods, giving away free tickets for the tours. Ticket pushers became so numerous and aggressive in Long Beach that the city barred them from blocking sidewalks with their handouts. If a prospect took a ticket, he or she could board one of the many busses lining streets in downtown Los Angeles and Long Beach, chartered for a day of oil field inspection. For that matter, even without a ticket one would be welcomed aboard the busses—which not infrequently contained people hired to fill the seats and thus make the excursion look popular.[50]

Once these tours were under way, their routes varied. Often busses took prospective investors for some sightseeing before heading to the promoters' well sites. Sales personnel explained these diversions as innocent recreation, but the sightseeing was carefully planned to build sales. One tour took visitors down to the ocean to view tankers full of oil, emphasizing the worldwide importance of the local bonanza. Another tour wound through Beverly Hills as the guide pointed out homes of movie stars. Buster Keaton was given special mention as an investor in oil. The tour thus demonstrated that great wealth was real, visible, and enjoyable. Sometimes busses cruised through areas where fortunes had been made from small investments in real estate. By the time the tourists arrived at the oil fields, they were already "thinking rich" and dreaming about hobnobbing with the wealthy and famous.[51]

The busses unloaded their human cargo at the red and white "sucker tents" erected artfully amid derricks and wells; as the *Times* reporter reflected, "There is no more convincing argument for buying oil units than to look out at those four-hundred-odd peaks of scaffolding and to know that 20,000 people are drawing monthly dividends from them." But prospects were not given much time to reflect on this scene before they were herded into the tents. They sat down at long tables, and smartly dressed salesmen handed out sandwiches and coffee, urging the tourists to eat all they wanted. Before the last cup of coffee was poured, sales people raised the tent flaps to provide a backdrop of the surrounding derricks. They then invited the audiences to guess at the production of the closest well and write their guesses on slips of paper, along with their names and mailing addresses. When the guesses were read aloud, the highest one usually won and the lucky person received a token prize. Naturally his name and those of the other contest entrants went on the promoters' "transient sucker" lists.[52]

After the contest was over the barkers stepped up to their blackboards and began their sales harangues, using rehearsed themes to prod the "mullets," as they were often called by the bigger "fish," into abandoning caution and common sense. The pitch usually began by expanding grandly on the satisfactions of wealth, making it clear that only "bondage to fear and doubt" separated their audiences from it. Most pitchmen emphasized the slim return on money in a bank account and went on to fill their blackboards with irrefutable evidence of the fabulous gain that would follow from buying into their ventures. Not uncommonly, they predicted quick 500 percent returns and described these projections as "conservative." Passing on to the potentially discouraging subject of risk, they often minimized it by distorting the meager legal restrictions on promotional activity. They described the very fact that the promoters had Corporation Commission permits to sell securities as endorsement of their schemes by the state of California. If the state approved, how could the investors go wrong? And if pursuing riches seemed like a gamble, what fun was life without the occasional risk?[53]

After the warm-up, sales personnel circulated through the audience, urging people to sign up for shares, certificates, units, or whatever parts of the deal they had to peddle. Sale prices varied. Often promoters pushed $100 units, but when this was beyond the reach of investors, promoters allowed them to buy smaller units or to pay on the installment plan. When even this adjustment failed to make the tourists reach for their billfolds, a salesman would ask them how much money they had with them; the amounts turned out to be what the promoter would settle for. In the absence of cash, clients offered jewelry and fur coats. Liberty Bonds were always accepted. In any event, after hours of sitting, eating, and listening to high-pressure salesmen it was difficult for prospects to leave without buying something, especially after the promoters' shills made enthusiastic purchases to build a bandwagon effect. For this reason promoters found the tours profitable, though many of the mullets had little money. The return to the promoters ranged from $3,000 to $5,000 or more for a day's work. Once they paid for their sales personnel, performers, busses, tents, and the food, they still had capital for legitimate business, if they wished to pursue it.[54]

A high rate of investor recruitment was not the only feature of bus tour oil promotions that appealed to promoters. There were also important legal advantages because the sales pitches were largely oral, and little evidence remained for postal inspectors or investigators from the Federal Trade Commission to scrutinize. In the unlikely event that the California Corporation Commission's two Los Angeles field men took an interest in possible violations of the law, there was scant material to support complaints. Indeed, the ineffectiveness of the commission was in itself an inducement for promoters; only the barest and crudest kinds of fraud were detected and punished.[55]

But what were the bus tour investors' chances of making the fortunes they sought? Though many promoters acted in good faith and drilled wells in the hope of producing oil, the small investors were unlikely to prosper for a variety of reasons. No oil well was a sure thing; a dry hole was always a possibility. Moreover, most of them bought such small parts of the ventures, often less than 1/1,000 of the whole, that even a good well would take decades to pay back the amounts they invested, let alone yield profits. Investors in one Long Beach promotion, for example, bought interests in ten-foot-square leases for $500. Purchasers were to receive seven-sixteenths of the one-eighth royalty on any oil found under their tracts. The *Oil Weekly* estimated that, had the promoter brought in a 10,000-barrel well, the yearly return to the investor in one unit would have been $36. Hypnotized by visions of oil bonanzas, purchasers of such small interests did not realize how little they received or how massively overcapitalized the ventures were that they bought into. Nor were they likely to understand that even strong initial production would decline over time. Whatever happened in such promotions, the investors assumed most of the financial risk; promoters rarely staked many of their assets on such speculations, though they usually reserved between one-third and one-half of any production that might be found. Thus the odds were great that the bus tour investor would get little or nothing for his investment, except a cold sandwich and a hot bus ride. There was no chance of moving to a Beverly Hills mansion by way of an oil field bus tour.[56]

Though few investors made any money, so potent was the combination of illusion and ignorance, so powerful the speculative urge generated by regional boom-time growth, that promoters continued to do a thriving business during much of the twenties. When federal authorities began to take an unwelcome interest in Texas promoters, some of them merely transferred operations to southern California. Thus speculation remained intense in California over a longer period than in Florida.[57]

Whether on the stock market or in Florida and California, when jazz-age Americans found themselves with some, though not enough, money, they were tempted to try for quick profits. Day by day, in many different contexts, the media assured them this was possible: it was the American dream. General prosperity and some spectacular examples of boom-time growth made it easy to believe in unparalleled opportunity. But the view of real growth encouraged visions of fantastic fortune, the kind of return on investments only successful speculations on the longest odds could yield. Indeed, for a sensational return on a small investment, the odds had to be exceptionally long. What both promoters and investors in search of quick riches usually forgot was that it was much harder to get rich quick than it seemed, even when opportunities were real. The chance to get rich quick on a small investment was usually illusory. As in California, nowhere was this more readily demonstrable than in the booming American petroleum industry.

The Black Gold Rush

OOBS LURED BY ballyhoo were not the only people eager to invest in oil. During the teens and twenties the petroleum industry offered genuine investment opportunities. Sophisticated investors with few delusions about getting rich quick found them highly attractive, for industry growth during the first three decades of the twentieth century was both undeniable and spectacular. As strong demand and high prices encouraged exploration, wildcatters made exciting discoveries in state after state. There were oil booms in California, Texas, Oklahoma, Louisiana, Arkansas, Kansas, Kentucky, and Wyoming. Every new discovery produced new "oil kings" like Josh Cosden, Harry Sinclair, E. W. Marland, and Thomas B. "Mad Tom" Slick, and newspapers and magazines publicized their success and boosted the oil industry. No wonder investors and operators large and small, veteran and novice, honest and otherwise, rushed to get in on the action. The opportunities were real, but so were the unavoidable risks which actually increased during the oil booms. It was both tempting and easy to get into oil, but it was much harder to succeed in it.

The basis of the remarkable growth of the petroleum industry in the early twentieth century was the rapid rise in national demand for refined products. Between 1900 and 1920 energy consumption grew by 250 percent in the United States; in the same period the petroleum industry's share of the energy market rose sevenfold. Much of the increased demand was for fuel oil—in industry, home heating, and railroad and marine transportation. As gas stoves became popular in home cooking, more natural gas found urban markets. But it was the skyrocketing demand for gasoline which gave the greatest push to industry growth. Modern transportation depended upon gasoline, and, more than anything else, the automobile created the mass market for petroleum products. At the close of the nine-

Easy Money

teenth century there were roughly 8,000 registered motor vehicles in the United States. By 1916 Americans owned 3.5 million autos, a remarkable increase, which was surpassed by 1921 when there were 10.5 million cars on the road. Many people purchased automobiles well before their homes had indoor plumbing or central heat. With the automobile appeared that twentieth-century phenomenon, the gas station. Precisely where the first one opened has been a matter for argument, but by 1915 there were 30 of them in Detroit, and a year later Los Angeles boasted 200. America raced into the automobile age, and by 1921 it was clear that petroleum would play a major role in the American economy for the foreseeable future.[1]

Petroleum would also have a major role in the military strategy of all major powers in the twentieth century, as World War I demonstrated. The world's navies switched from burning coal to fuel oil before the war; during the war, military tacticians made increasing use of automobiles, trucks, tanks, and aircraft, all of which used gasoline. Much of the petroleum used in the Allied war effort came from the United States; an estimated 133 million barrels of petroleum and petroleum products reached Europe between 1914 and 1918, some 70 million barrels of this total during 1917–18. There was some substance, then, to Lord Curzon's oft-quoted remark that "The allies floated to victory on a wave of oil," and the wave came from America.[2]

Mounting demand, both domestic and foreign, triggered an oil boom of massive proportions in the United States. Prices and activity alike turned upward in 1916. In response to both civilian and military consumption, the average price of crude rose to $1.10 per barrel from $.64; the number of wells drilled jumped from 14,157 to 24,619. Prices continued to climb to $1.56 in 1917. The following year wartime consumption of petroleum outstripped domestic production and imports combined. The domestic oil industry drew heavily upon stored oil and spot shortages occurred; fears mounted, particularly among scientific experts and government officials, that the United States was running out of oil. Responding to tight supplies, crude oil prices soared, reaching $2.00 per barrel in 1919 and an all-time high of $3.07 in 1920. As prices rose, so did exploratory activity. In 1920 nearly 34,000 wells were drilled, more than double the number of 1915. The following year oil production reached 472,183,000 barrels, more than double the production of the previous decade. The accelerated growth of refinery capacity spurred by wartime demand con-

The Black Gold Rush

tinued during the 1920s. Beyond question, the industry was in an all-out boom: to judge from oil field activity, there never was a better time to make a killing in oil.[3]

With that thought uppermost in mind, operators and investors stampeded into the oil business. The wave of new company formations lasted for nearly four years. Between March 1 and June 1, 1918, for example, the *New York Times* reported that 270 oil companies capitalized at over $100,000 received charters. That figure made no allowance for numerous small firms and ventures organized as proprietorships, partnerships, and common law trusts; these forms of organization did not require state charters. The pace of company formation accelerated in 1919; in the month of November alone, 141 oil companies with total capitalization of nearly a half billion dollars were organized. So rapid was the proliferation of oil firms that by 1919 the *World's Work*, a reformist periodical, admitted that it could no longer evaluate every oil enterprise it heard about: "Thousands of oil promotions have sprung up, and it has been impossible to investigate them all." The oil rush was on.[4]

Appetite for oil speculation was insatiable, and investors bought into promotions as fast as promoters could contrive them. Observant journalists likened petroleum's attraction for investor dollars to magnetism, "the psychological magnet for that portion of the investing public that likes to gamble." In the year following armistice, investment in oil securities rose from $1.8 billion to $3.2 billion. So strong was the appeal of oil during the boom that it eclipsed hard-rock mining promotions, even in traditional mining centers like Denver and Salt Lake City. Veteran promoters of hard-rock mining issues hastily joined the oil bandwagon and peddled oil stocks.[5]

Many new oilmen had experience in other types of promotions. Dr. Frederick A. Cook, for example, raised money for Arctic exploration, and S. E. J. Cox promoted patent medicines and automobile parts. So great was the press of the black gold rush, however, that many a would-be tycoon with neither promotional experience nor adequate capital jumped into oil; printers H. H. Hoffman, Roy Westbrook, and Chester Bunker, attorneys P. M. Faver and Oscar Houston, insurance salesman Paul Vitek, and the Glasscock Brothers, theatrical tightrope walkers, were of that group, as were the ranchers and small-town bankers who organized the Lubbock-Bridgeport Oil Company.

The voracious public appetite for oil stocks also gave rise to trading operations of dubious honesty in cities across the nation. "Oil Exchanges," offices where lively trade in promotional issues took place, had long been common in oil field boomtowns and nearby urban centers. Wichita Falls had three exchanges in 1918; in 1919 Shreveport, Dallas, Fort Worth, and Tulsa all had such operations, run from storefront locations. As oil fever gripped the nation, exchanges appeared in Spokane, Salt Lake City, Chicago, and other towns far from the heart of the oil fields. The Chicago exchange consisted of five or six downtown storefront operations, whose front windows contained miniature derricks and bottles of crude oil set off by posters and flashily illustrated literature; inside, men and women worked at rows of desks and blackboards, listing and taking orders for stock offerings. The listings always included well-known companies, notably Standard Oil of New Jersey, along with many dubious companies. Such exchanges made the bulk of their sales to local residents who had caught oil fever; as one would-be oil investor from the Texas oil field town of Breckenridge reflected, "They felt, well, if they's buying stock and everybody gettin' oil wells, why they just couldn't go wrong with this stock."[6]

Oil fever spread through the New York financial district. Even more staid Wall Street houses proved susceptible to oil mania; the *New York Times* noted with surprise that petroleum ventures were being sold "by houses which some few years ago would never have thought it feasible or proper to promote petroleum companies . . . the glamour of the word oil having aroused their speculative interest." The *Times*, too, saw that Wall Street's new infatuation with oil was part of a speculative wave sweeping the country. With good reason, one analyst branded oil stocks as "the form of get-rich security now most popular with the public." The arena of hottest trading was the Curb Exchange, a stretch of Broad Street where, for a century and a quarter, stocks were traded on the street curb. By July 1919 millions of dollars were traded daily for shares, many of them in oil ventures. When the New York district attorney branded much of the Curb Exchange stock as worthless, the 300 exchange members moved indoors in an attempt to exclude outsiders. They went on to salvage the exchange's reputation by cutting down on the flourishing trade in bogus oil securities.[7]

Many of the oil ventures had the legitimate objective of making money by finding and producing petroleum, and it had never seemed easier to do so. Newspaper and magazine tales of mammoth gushers made finding oil seem like a simple task. As one journalist described north Texas in 1917, "So many gushers have been brought in of late that all that seems necessary to tap some rich pool of oil is to sink a hole in the ground and let nature do the rest. Discoveries of this sort have poured millions into the laps of lucky producers."[8]

But was it that easy to make a fortune? Journalistic hyperbole so attractive to potential petroleum investors never touched upon the many hazards to success that were unavoidable in the industry, the geological and financial risks faced by those who explored for oil. And in boom times, just when it was most appealing to go into exploration, those risks increased.

The most obvious geological risk in exploration was, and always had been, the failure to find petroleum. Dry holes yield no production income. Any well could be dry, even on the most promising lease or in the most prolific oil field. A geological fluke could turn what looked like a sure thing into a dead loss. Moreover, for a test well to be successful, it was not enough to find a mere trace of oil or gas; success required the eventual production of enough petroleum to cover exploration and production costs and still turn a profit. It was impossible to guarantee success at the time of spudding in or beginning a well, as oil field veterans knew.

Despite this problem, prospectors naturally had the best chance of success if they looked for oil as near to strong production as possible, trying their luck on acreage whose potential was "proven" by adjacent producing leases. Such acreage, of course, fetched high prices compared with land some distance from production and hence riskier to drill. Small operators with limited capital thus seldom bought into the safest areas for exploration; what they could afford entailed higher geological risks. That led them to rank wildcatting, looking for oil outside established productive regions where they faced a high probability of finding nothing.

There was one situation, however, in which small operators were sometimes able to prospect on acreage close to strong production, and that occurred when a producing oil field developed on land carved up among many owners. In places like Los Angeles, Santa Fe Springs, and Burkburnett Townsite where town-lot drilling was the rule, oilmen could often afford to buy very small tracts. Here there was a good chance of finding

Easy Money

oil, even if the tract's size might preclude drilling enough wells to produce a fortune.

With the commonsense technique of limiting geological risk by drilling as close to attractive production as possible, oilmen also began to consider the application of geological science, and by the late teens some large companies began to assemble geological staffs to find oil. The most favored scientific technique was the surface mapping of geological structures to locate oil-bearing subsurface formations. In many instances surface mapping led to important oil discoveries. But there were many places—like much of the Texas Gulf Coast or west Texas's Permian Basin—where flat plains lacking distinctive surface dips and elevations left geologists with nothing to map. Expensive geological help was thus of little value without additional information provided by drilling, and that involved taking the risks science was intended to sidestep or at least diminish.[9]

The application of geology to oil finding nonetheless made steady progress in the twenties. The application of geophysics to exploration marked a particularly useful, if expensive, step toward diminishing geological risk. But it took time for oilmen outside the major companies to understand and use either geology or engineering to limit risks. Many had doubts about putting scientists on their payrolls even when they could afford them. The president of one Oklahoma company, for example, decided to hire a geologist in 1918 but he gave him a bogus job title because he did not want to be teased about hiring a scientist. Yet another executive found geologists more exasperating than useful. He complained to a friend, "Rocks, rocks! Sam, all they talk about is rocks. Do they think we're running a stone quarry?"[10]

As for smaller companies and operators, while some may have taken to hiring an occasional geological consultant, most still worked with guesswork and know-how rather than science. The competitive advantages of scientific exploration were far from as great as they would one day be, and only major companies and large independents could afford to be on the cutting edge of the technologies, which had yet to prove their merit in the field. Many successful oilmen did without science.

Geology was of limited use in finding oil, but pseudogeology, an artful mixture of quasi-scientific terminology and pure fantasy, was of great practical value to promoters looking for money. The literate American

The Black Gold Rush

public had learned from popular journals that geology could be helpful in exploration. This aspect of the widespread popular faith in science gave promoters an advantage if they included some "geology" in their literature; a bit of pseudogeology could even lend the appearance of legitimacy and respectability to a promotion notably short on both characteristics.

When they were of an inventive turn of mind, promoters simply created their own "geologists" and attributed wondrous speculation about underground riches to them. The promoters of General Lee Development Interests, for example, touted their company figurehead, "General" Robert A. Lee, as "The Miracle Man of Geology, known far and wide as a geological engineer," to whom "the great Mid-Continental oil fields . . . are as an open book." What the General saw in the open book was "the mother pool of the Texas oil fields" and "the main continental oil axis which . . . marks the trend of all productive oil fields in continental North America."

The General's brand of pseudogeology drew on hard-rock mining's notions of a "mother lode," presumably a reflection of his vaunted ability in finding gold as well as oil. The General also borrowed from the old notion of oil belts or oil lines, speculation that developed in the Pennsylvania fields of the 1860s when oilmen discovered fields along a rough northeast to southwest line. This pattern gave rise to a grand theory of great underground oil rivers, stretching from Canada to Mexico, running northeast to southwest; if one drilled above one of these rivers, an unending bonanza of oil would be tapped. Some extended this theory to claim that the underground rivers eventually flowed into huge oil lakes, capable of yielding an unimaginable wealth of oil. All of this palaver was a great deal more exciting than the surface maps and stratigraphic analyses of scientific geologists. It was also easier for the naive investor to understand.[11]

The promoters of General Lee supplied their own pseudogeology, but it was not hard to find professional poseurs at earth science who could be hired to write about the "vast oil structures" the companies would tap and occasionally to come forward to reassure nervous investors. One of the grand masters of the art of pseudogeology was A. D. "Doc" Lloyd, who began life as Joseph Idelbert Durham and, because of his lively business and sexual escapades, had as many aliases as a Chicago bucket shop operator. A man of enormous energy and equally enormous appetites—he was said to have had six wives and weighed over 300 pounds—Lloyd dabbled

Easy Money

at many careers. Starting out as a drugstore clerk, he picked up fragments of both medicine and chemistry, which he put to use selling bottled remedies in a traveling medicine show. He taught himself the rudiments of mining engineering and may have prospected for gold in the Yukon and Mexico. In the course of his adventures, he also picked up a smattering of geological jargon. Very much a self-made man, Lloyd turned himself into a geologist: "Dr. A. D. Lloyd, M.D., Ph.G., C.E."[12]

Highly intelligent as well as eccentric, Lloyd embarrassed conventional geologists by actually identifying a number of areas that eventually produced enormous quantities of oil. When associated with Columbus Marion Joiner, for example, Lloyd not only located the East Texas field, the largest in the nation for decades, but also directed Joiner to the sites of what became prolific fields at Seminole and Cement, Oklahoma. How Lloyd came to point Joiner toward oil obviously owed nothing to orthodox geological science; orthodox thinking usually swore at Lloyd's theories, as in east Texas, an area generally dismissed by petroleum geologists in the twenties.[13]

Anyone familiar with conventional geology, moreover, certainly would not have recognized it in what Lloyd wrote. His "Report of Mineralogical, Geological, and Topographical Survey for the Signal Hill Oil and Gas Company of Blanchard, Oklahoma," written to sell stock in 1916, is a good specimen of Lloyd's science. He argued that the variety of colors observable in rocks and topsoil on the earth's surface could indicate underground petroleum. He reasoned that a film of oil on water exhibited an iridescent range of colors, and thus, when a great variety of colors existed in surface rock and soil, the variegation was caused by leaking petroleum gases: "The change of local color in these deposits is due to epogene action of inorganic gases and circulating waters." Lloyd waxed eloquent about water: "Water, being the greatest of solvent agents, is continually taking the widely distributed elements into solution. The water thus charged with minerals upon reaching the surface at a spring, the elements are participated [*sic*] in the earth by evaporation, oxidation, and recrystallization."[14]

But for Lloyd's annoying way of locating large oil fields from time to time, scientific geologists had no reason to notice him. Lloyd's fellow promoters, however, respected him as a master of his particular craft. The operators of the Big Diamond Oil and Refining Company, for example, found his Signal Hill report useful when they came to sell stock in 1917; they had leased land in the area Lloyd described. When the Federal Trade Commission investigated their operations in 1921, they referred to Lloyd as their "chemist and geologist," though there is no evidence they had ever met him; they told federal interrogators that Lloyd was "considered the best geologist in the state" (Oklahoma), "the best there was in the United States," and that he was Mexico's "engineer and geologist." The grand old man of pseudogeology had a name to conjure with.[15]

When pseudogeology lacked sufficient sales appeal, some promoters turned to magic. Clairvoyants, seers, oil smellers, oil dowsers, doodlebuggers, men with "little black boxes"—all claimed special abilities in finding oil. One Texas preacher, for example, said he could see oil under the earth at Petrolia with X-ray eyes: "He would hold his hands high over his head as though he was pointing to the heavenly bodies, and with closed eyes would majestically prance around—suddenly stop, shudder as though he had palsy, and, in a centaurian [sic] voice would declare that he was on the edge of an oil creek that was narrow, about fifty feet wide, and the main oil river would be found in the immediate vicinity."[16]

On occasion, promoters would tell prospective investors they had the assistance of a person with special powers or devices. S. E. J. Cox, for example, claimed to have the advice of a mysterious hermit. The promoters of General Lee Development Interests told prospective investors that the General had invented a "battery process" with which he located a gold mine in California in 1912, "the same instrument that had been proven adaptable to the petroleum industry, in the location of pools of mineral oil." As it happened, the General had tried this type of oil finding, but with a divining rod, rather than any mechanical device.[17]

General Lee's "battery process" was pure fantasy, but some prospectors really experimented with oil finding devices. O. W. Killam, who found the Mirando City field in south Texas, believed that "oil gives off a ray of some kind." A friend of Killam's recalled:

> He had a tin bucket that he carried around with something in it, and he'd swear that it would find oil. Of course, I was always kidding him about that. So he came out that morning, and we were making hole, drilling on the rig. . . . I saw him walking around through the brush about a hundred yards from the derrick. I could just see his

head toddling along, he was limping along. Finally, he came up to the rig and said, "Joe, you are not going to get it here; it's right over yonder about a half mile."

I said, "Mr. Killam, . . . you're too intelligent a man to believe in that darn tin bucket you've got there. I don't understand you."

It made him mad. He said, "I'll tell you what, I'll bet you a brand new Stetson hat every well I'll drill will be an oil well or a gas well."

I said, "I'll take that bet."

Of course he was making a lot of dry holes. So if I hadn't caught him in an angry mood, he would have never done a thing like he did. But, anyway, he'd make a dry hole, and he would come to me and say, "Well, go get your hat."

In 1956, after nearly forty years in oil, Killam still believed "that if you knew what to look for you could see an oil field on top of the ground." Geology and geophysics did not interest him.[18]

Wildcatters who did not resort to science, fraud, or necromancy usually relied on what was known as "trendology" or "yardstick geology." The wildcatters simply plotted locations within a region where oil had been discovered and searched for geographical patterns in discoveries. The simplest pattern was a straight line: placing a ruler on a map to connect two oil fields, they speculated that additional oil might be found between them on "trends." To scientists this was nothing more than random drilling, but there was a rational, if nonscientific, logic behind the approach. Oil did accumulate along shorelines and rock faults and in the sandbars of ancient rivers that might coincide with lines on a map.[19]

Having located a plausible trend, the wildcatters next entered the complex area of land transactions and financial risk. Under American law the ownership of minerals that lie under land ordinarily belongs to the owner of the land surface, but these subsoil or mineral rights may be separated from surface rights. When wildcatters dealt with landowners, they usually purchased only mineral rights, and the landowners ordinarily reserved part of these rights in the form of "royalty" interests. They were thus entitled to negotiable portions—ordinarily one-sixth or one-eighth—of the gross income from the oil and gas from the leases. The royalty owners' interests carried no obligation to pay any of the costs of exploration and production. Those costs were born by the holders of "working" interests.

The Black Gold Rush

All of these interests, mineral, royalty, and working, have always been widely traded. Oilmen have acquired and held them in order to spread their own investments, and they have divided and sold them to investors in fractional or percentage quantities, following a sequence determined by the extent of development in prospective areas. Leases and mineral and working interests were often traded even before oil was discovered, while trade in royalty interests picked up after oil's discovery in commercial quantities. Initially the wildcatters sought to acquire large blocks of leases at reasonable prices. With a great amount of acreage, if they found oil they had a reasonable chance of exploiting their discoveries to great profit by having sites for additional wells. With sizable spreads, moreover, they could try to raise capital for drilling by selling some of it to investors or other oilmen. When they did so, they effectively shared their risk with others, a wise tactic given the strong probability that rank wildcat ventures would be total losses. Selling off acreage gave them money for operations; if the wildcatters bought their acreage cheaply and sold it for far more than they paid, they had the necessary stake for their ventures. They could also keep enough acreage for themselves to make real money if they found oil.[20]

Among the small independent oilmen of the first four decades of the twentieth century, this form of lease trading, putting together a "spread" of leases and selling off parts of it, was the most common way of raising capital for exploration. Obviously the wildcatters had to have at least small cash stakes before they could buy leases, but when they bought in places that were geological frontiers or when the petroleum industry was in recession, it did not take much money to get started. The essential element was cheap acreage. Stock issues, certificates, salesmen, literature, promotional letters—all the costly devices of the stock promoters—could be avoided if the wildcatters could sell leases at a good profit.

Finding buyers, however, was usually a challenge. The best time to find them was when oil prices were high. But in such times there was strong competition for investor dollars in the petroleum industry, and there was stronger competition in the purchase and sale of leases. During slow times, when acreage was cheapest, investors were harder to find; knowledgeable people avoided wildcat leases if they could buy into less risky areas. Raising money by selling leases thus was not easy, and rank wildcat leases were especially hard to sell, though major companies sometimes

Easy Money

acquired "safety leases" when they were not expensive and thereby supported wildcat wells to obtain scientific data. Most other buyers were either completely unsophisticated investors or industry gamblers. At that, few of them staked much money on long shots and they rarely bought more than small interests. Their caution forced the promoters of wildcat wells to sell many small units—fractions of fractions of leases and royalties, or small interests in their venture in the form of stock or certificates or units—in order to raise capital. Sale of leases and other interests proved to be a costly and uncertain way to raise money, and it usually failed to cover skyrocketing costs of boom times.

To the unavoidable geological and financial risks of wildcatting, a boom added the additional financial hazard of high operating costs, and that was faced by everyone in exploration whether they wildcatted or not. Leases, services, and supplies were all more expensive during a boom. Thus in 1918, at the beginning of the Burkburnett Townsite boom in north Texas, it cost $10,000 to $12,000 to drill a well to shallow production at 1,600–1,900 feet. As the boom progressed, the shortage of drilling contractors and supplies pushed costs to $25,000 a well within a year. By 1920 it had risen to as much as $30,000. Even those prices were approximately half what it cost to drill some seventy-five miles farther south in booming Eastland and Comanche counties. Wells there were often at least 1,000 feet deeper than those at Burkburnett and cost $35,000 to $50,000 more. These prices stunned industry veterans; thirty years earlier they drilled wells of comparable depth in West Virginia for $6,000 and considered that expensive. And though drilling costs were highly variable from region to region, $3 a foot, or $6,000 for a 2,000-foot well, was probably a national average in the early twentieth century.[21]

Competent workers were scarce during boom times and consequently their wages were high. Supplies and equipment were also hard to come by, and the wildcatters who found them at premium prices still faced high freight costs. As many promoters learned only after the fact, outgo commonly exceeded income. Wildcatters, however, were rarely preoccupied with debits and accounts payable; no one took accountants along on treasure hunts. To novices at oil, moreover, the promise of future riches made high current costs seem unimportant.

Undeterred by the geological challenges and largely ignorant of financial risks, those who joined the black gold rush during the late teens and early twenties looked to a number of regions where activity was especially intense. They included the Los Angeles area in California; the Hot Springs area in Wyoming; northeastern Oklahoma's Osage County; Eldorado, Kansas; southwestern Arkansas; northern Louisiana; eastern Kentucky; and Goose Creek and Damon Mound on the Texas Gulf Coast.

The first discovery of oil in commercial quantities in Texas took place near the small town of Corsicana in 1895, but the state did not become a major oil producer until the 1901 discovery of the prolific Spindletop field near Beaumont. Within the next few years discoveries followed at Sour Lake, Saratoga, Batson, and Humble, and it was clear that the Texas Gulf Coast would excite prospectors' interest for decades to come. Though geological understanding of the region developed slowly in the absence of solid science, there were seepages, tar springs, outcroppings showing traces of oil, and springs permeated with hydrogen sulfide to pique oil finders' interest. Such evidence of petroleum was, of course, not limited to the Gulf Coast, and by 1910 wildcatting was scattered throughout Texas. The discovery of oil at Electra in 1911, for example, prompted an all-out boom in the Wichita Falls area, on the Texas-Oklahoma border. By this time Texas was the nation's sixth largest oil producing state. From north Texas, exploration moved south and west to Eastland, Comanche, Stephens, and Brown counties. In 1917 a discovery near the small town of Ranger in Eastland County touched off a boom in west central Texas that captured national attention. It came just as the war effort enhanced demand for petroleum and emphasized its strategic importance; initial production from the area led informed observers to think it would become one of the greatest oil producing regions ever known. Such beliefs helped create one of the most intense oil booms ever to occur in Texas.[22]

There were many attractions for small independents in north and west central Texas. These were regions of modest-sized farms and ranches. Landowners had been hurt by the severe drought of 1917; there were thus many people who were willing to sell all or part of their mineral rights for very low sums, pennies per acre in some instances. The classic tactic of buying a spread and selling leases to pay for a test well was often relatively easy to execute because the profit margins on lease sales were high and the wells sometimes spectacularly prolific, producing more than 10,000 barrels per day. The oil, moreover, was high-gravity, bringing producers premium prices and making even marginal wells profitable. Selling the oil was also easy because refiners rushed to lay pipelines into the region, which they thought capable of meeting national demand for decades.

Cheap leases, high grade oil, and a ready market attracted hundreds of small independents to north and west central Texas. By 1920 exploration progressed at a feverish pitch throughout an area some 200 miles long and 125 miles wide.[23] The speculative boom reached beyond the oil fields to touch off runaway growth in the nearby cities of Fort Worth and Wichita Falls. As one journalist described the result, "Oil fever . . . attacked almost every man, woman, and child in northern Texas. . . . Real estate agents, insurance brokers, lawyers, cattlemen, and many business houses dropped their customary vocations to sell oil stocks, which the Texas public absorbed as rapidly as the printing presses could grind them out."[24]

Though they lived at some distance from this activity, in the dusty small west Texas town of Lubbock, the trustees of the Lubbock-Bridgeport Oil Company were among those whom oil fever led to abandon their customary occupations and join the black gold rush.

The three men who organized the Lubbock-Bridgeport Oil Company were by all appearances a sober set of businessmen. R. H. Lowrey, a Lubbock businessman who had assets of about $250,000 and was a director of the Lubbock State Bank, fit the description of "solid citizen." L. I. Rouse was a retired Lubbock merchant with assets of about $50,000, principally in the form of town lots and farms. W. D. Crump, a local rancher and stock breeder, had assets of $187,000. The largest single investor, J. H. Jennings, held substantial farm and ranch property, worth nearly a quarter of a million dollars. In all, on the company's organization its trustees claimed assets of nearly $2 million, surely adequate to their purpose: the drilling of one wildcat well in Wise County, Texas.[25]

From a geographical point of view, Wise County was ideal for a wildcat test. The area was due northeast of Ranger and southeast of Burkburnett, on the edge of the corridor in which the hottest activity in Texas was going on. Bridgeport, on the west central border of the county, was tantalizingly close to proven production, at least on a small map. But on closer examination, prospects were less encouraging. Though wildcatters tried numerous tests in Wise County, none had been commercially productive—a record that would stand until 1947. If the area was on or near a large geological trend, as Lubbock-Bridgeport's directors could hope, earlier wildcatters failed to find it. From the beginning, the Lubbock-Bridgeport venture was highly speculative.

The Black Gold Rush

Like so many other promoters of wildcat ventures, Lubbock-Bridgeport's trustees' first strategy lay in minimizing their own risk through leasing acreage cheaply and selling off smaller leases. In the early months of 1919 they assembled a block of slightly more than twelve sections; for the lease, Lubbock-Bridgeport paid token rentals of $1 or less per acre, but it also agreed to drill a well to 3,500 feet or to oil, whichever came first. The landowners demanded that Lubbock-Bridgeport post performance bonds amounting to $12,500. The leases contained standard time stipulations: a beginning date for drilling (April 1, 1919) and an expiration date (February 10, 1922). Neither condition was bothersome. With three months' lead time, Lubbock-Bridgeport's trustees were sure they could spud in by April Fools' Day. In any event, the venture would succeed or fail within the three-year term of the lease.[26]

Novices at the oil game, Lubbock-Bridgeport's trustees hired equally inexperienced men to manage day-to-day operations. The manager they chose, J. E. Chase, was the young pastor of the First Christian Church of Lubbock. From a locally prominent cattle family, Chase was a thirty-third degree Mason—possibly the basis of his relationship with the other trustees. W. C. Jennings got the job of assistant to Chase and served as treasurer; in effect, he represented his father, J. H. Jennings. But young Jennings knew no more about oil than Chase; he was assistant cashier of the Security State Bank and Trust Company of Lubbock. Whatever the intentions of Lubbock-Bridgeport's directors in hiring such green help, it was not a wise move.[27]

Even so, the inexperience of the trustees and managers might not have mattered greatly if they had hired seasoned workers at the well site. A veteran driller did not need much supervision. By the midst of the boom, however, when the company looked for help, experienced hands were in short supply; the most capable drillers and helpers already had jobs, and even "boll weevils," green hands, commanded high wages. Once again Lubbock-Bridgeport's trustees substituted personal connections for experience, by hiring H. S. Cook, Chase's brother-in-law, as drilling superintendent. He lacked the barest conventional qualifications for the job, but at a time when it seemed as if anyone could make money in the oil business, it was easy to think that industry know-how was not necessary.[28]

Though prepared to dispense with practical experience, the trustees of Lubbock-Bridgeport knew that they had urgent need of cash. The modest capital paid in by the trustees was quickly exhausted by lease and set-up costs. Completion of the projected 3,500-foot well would cost about $35,000 according to initial estimates. The organizers of the venture might have contributed this sum, but they were already concerned about the unexpectedly high costs of leasing and bonding. As costs mounted so did directors' apprehensions about the venture, and they grew concerned to limit their personal exposure to risk. They therefore agreed to raise operating capital from the sale of leases.

Even before they had their leases in hand, R. H. Lowrey, the company president, tried to recruit salesmen to peddle Lubbock-Bridgeport acreage. Eager for funds, Lowrey was not fussy about whom he hired. He met one gentleman from Vancouver, Washington, for example, on a train in 1918 and sent him maps, data, and an order book; Lowrey pressed him to sell for the company, assuring him, "You can make some good money for yourself by pushing this just a little." Similarly, once the leases were in their possession, the trustees recruited J. E. Chase's brother Frank, who lived in St. Louis, to sell acreage. The asking price for these tracts varied from $12.50 to $100 an acre, depending on proximity to the test site. The initial sales goal was one-quarter of Lubbock-Bridgeport's acreage, surely enough to finance drilling and completion of one well. Any additional sales would provide capital for development or, in the event of a dry hole, a onetime profit for the venture. The trustees, conservative businessmen for the most part, were convinced that their investments in Lubbock-Bridgeport were secure and that they would prove more profitable than ranching and banking. In the long run, they would all be much richer.[29]

In the short run, however, until it actually sold leases, Lubbock-Bridgeport was hard-pressed for operating cash. On February 1, 1919, its first day of official business, the trust had only $10,000 on hand because the remaining initial subscription, $25,000, had not yet been paid in by the founders. This balance was far short of the money needed to commence operations. A new rig and related drilling equipment cost $25,000 at the beginning of the boom, but by early 1919 prices were not only higher, but equipment was hard to find. Wages and fuel for the projected 3,500-foot well would cost at least $5,000 more. Worse yet, if cash shortages caused operational delays, costs would increase further because if Lubbock-Bridgeport missed its deadline for spudding in, it would be required to forfeit its performance bond and pay one year's rent to hold the lease.[30]

As the clock ran, Chase, the young manager, found it hard to get operations under way. The drilling deadline came and went, and Lubbock-

The Black Gold Rush

Bridgeport forfeited the $7,500 bond and had to pay $7,747 in rental charges. Roused to action, Chase left Lubbock in April, traveled to Decatur, the Wise County seat, and bought a rig by postdating a check. Two weeks later the check bounced, and the bank refused to honor it until the Lubbock-Bridgeport's president signed over a $1,000 Liberty Bond of his own as security. This was not a promising beginning. When the rig was finally in company hands, Chase returned to the Lubbock office and assured the trustees that he would soon be ready to spud in.[31]

This proved overoptimistic. On delivery the rig lacked several basic parts, hard to find during the boom. When parts finally arrived in mid-May, they were the wrong ones, and Chase began a week-long, long-distance wrangle with his supplier, who did not want to accept them back.[32]

By this time Chase had learned that it was difficult to drill an oil well in Wise County from Lubbock, so he moved to Bridgeport. Even this adjustment produced problems because he forgot to file complete mail forwarding instructions and did not receive delivery on various bills until mid-July. The delay stalled some creditors, but most of them knew where Chase was and they pressed for payment. When bills came in more quickly than cash, the individual trustees of Lubbock-Bridgeport borrowed slightly more than $10,000 to pay workers and creditors who could not be stalled. It was painfully clear that the venture needed working capital, and soon.[33]

Fund-raising efforts finally got under way in May, when the promoters divided their collection of leases into forty-acre blocks and then into ten-acre blocks. They then priced tracts within one mile of the test well at $50 to $100 per acre, while they hoped to sell more distant leases for $12.50 per acre. The trustees next looked for buyers who would purchase at least forty acres and sell off parts of their leases to other investors thereafter. An initial flurry of sales encouraged J. E. Chase, who told his brother Frank that "calls for acreage come everyday." His enthusiasm was largely based on ignorance: sales of oil promotions usually ran strongly for an initial brief period and then dropped off quickly, as soon became apparent. By the end of May the only large sales had been made in St. Louis, where Frank Chase found eight investors who put up $4,000 for one tract. J. E. Chase was still optimistic that "this is the beginning of some nice business," as he told the company's attorney. As it turned out, there were few additional sales during the month.[34]

At the beginning of June, Lubbock-Bridgeport's management considered other sales strategies. The company's attorney suggested contracting with the New York bucket shops of L. H. Cook and Company to sell properties. When Chase contacted them, they were not interested. Chase then approached Harry Hines, a Dallas promoter, to unload Lubbock-Bridgeport's acreage; Hines accepted Chase's offer and signed a thirty-day exclusive contract to sell acreage at $10 to $100 on a 15 percent commission. Unfortunately, young Chase jumped at this opportunity too quickly, and in his haste to send Hines the leases he did not take the time to enter legal descriptions of the property on the blank lease forms. He assumed that Hines would sell as much as he could, complete the forms, and later notify the company of the specifics of the sales. Without intending to do so, Chase thus placed all of the major assets of the company in the hands of Harry Hines. Lubbock-Bridgeport's attorney described this as "a risky piece of business." Matters became further complicated when Hines inadvertently sold leases on land on which there were liens, and Lubbock-Bridgeport's creditors threatened litigation. Young Chase learned once again that there was more to the oil business than he or any of the trustees realized when they went into it.[35]

Despite Harry Hines's sales campaign, he produced little additional capital, and Lubbock-Bridgeport reverted to direct sales of leases. Their lack of experience and of connections once again frustrated the efforts of the promoters. Even salesmen were hard to find; the company tried recruiting but no one accepted its offer of employment. Without substantial lease sales, however, there was no money for company operations. As work in Wise County continued, cash ran out and creditors pressed for immediate payment. Oil Well Supply, for example, forwarded Lubbock-Bridgeport's note to the First National Bank of Fort Worth for collection, but the bank returned it after three attempts were rebuffed. When Oil Well Supply finally mailed the note directly to the company for payment, Lubbock-Bridgeport sent back a check on which it had already filed a stop payment order. While blame for "this nasty tangle," as young Chase described it, was freely passed among the directors, the company attorney was once more left to resolve company affairs by arranging payment.[36]

At this stage, the bankers in the Lubbock-Bridgeport group sought to solve the acute cash flow problem by applying for a loan at a Lubbock bank. Their individual credit ratings were sound, several of them had done business with the bank on other occasions, and the bank president approved the $5,201 note promptly, though he expressed strong reservations about letting the money go into an oil venture. He told rancher Crump that "this is the only time he has loaned any for that purpose." The bank president made an exception for Lubbock-Bridgeport, but he soon thought the better of it; when the directors came to draw on their credit the banker voided the note, and another Lubbock-Bridgeport draft bounced.[37]

During the fall of 1919, Chase himself ventured out on a sales trip in the hope of selling enough leases to pay off the mounting debt—probably about $50,000 by September. Ever hopeful, Chase traveled to Omaha, where he expected sales to be so brisk that the company might consider opening a sales office. Checking into the Hotel Conant ("Rates $2.50 and down"), he began to work the contacts he developed through earlier correspondence, only to find some of his contacts had cooled because recent oil swindles in the Middle West had received considerable publicity. Chase discovered that it was necessary to distinguish Lubbock-Bridgeport from the notorious bogus oil companies. Thus he reassured a rural doctor that "this is no fake stock-selling scheme nor a get-rich-quick proposition, but a real bona fide business investment."[38] When potential investors wanted further assurances on paper, Chase was ready to supply them. He wrote "At the present time we are approximately 1650 feet down. Geologists tell us we should reach the sand at about 1700 feet." The well would be completed to a producing horizon within a month and thus time was running out for investors who hoped to get in on the ground floor. According to Chase, opportunity was limited to a few select investors: "We have no agents or salesmen in the field nor are we at this time making any active campaign to sell our own leases. We have had offers to part with a division of our stock, but this we refused to do."[39]

What Chase told potential investors was literally true, but it was also highly misleading and designed to obscure Lubbock-Bridgeport's urgent need for cash. Failure to peddle a significant number of leases was, after all, the reason for the absence of an active sales campaign, just as the absence of salesmen was the result of failed recruitment efforts. Lubbock-Bridgeport urgently sought outlets for its leases, and if it was not sending out agents, it was certainly trying to get others to do so. Thus, before he set out on his sales tour, Chase attempted to persuade Harry Hines and Company to resume sales. He provided them with two pages of advertising copy that mentioned the location of the company leases on a "great plunging incline," and claimed that expert opinion held Lubbock-Bridgeport "should reach the sand at approximately 2700 feet." He expanded: "The unanimous judgment is that between 2500 and 3000 feet our best production will be found." Chase thus tried his hand at pseudogeology, coupling it with the standard injunction that time was running out: the company expected to reach pay formation "within the next fifty or sixty days." The result would be "quick action on the investment if we get a well." His final phrase was revealingly honest, so Chase's amateur advertising effort had little chance of competing with the inflated promises of more facile promoters. Worse yet, as investors bought what other promoters offered without getting rich quick, enthusiasm for oil investments flagged. Chase wrote to his friends from Omaha, "They [his potential customers] have been bitten so often they hesitate."[40]

By the end of 1919 Lubbock-Bridgeport had sold about $18,000 worth of leases, and it had spent about $87,000. The difference was made up by creditors, to whom they owed about $33,000, by lease purchasers, and by trustees. The company had cash in accounts totaling $7,378.36. As a financial proposition Lubbock-Bridgeport fell far short of fulfilling the hopes of the trustees, because they had failed to spread their risk and raise sufficient operating capital by selling leases. Instead, as the costs of operations mounted, the trustees assumed ever greater liabilities, secured by their farm, ranch, and urban real estate holdings in Texas. A venture that was supposed to have produced tidy profits yielded only personal losses.[41]

If finances were bleak, field operations were no more encouraging. As Lubbock-Bridgeport tried to drill its test, a steady sequence of boom-time operating problems stretched a six-week project over many months. In July 1919 drilling superintendent Cook shut down the rig for several days while he waited for replacement equipment, elevators, and a casing shoe.[42] Then he let the supply of fuel oil run out and the boiler, the rig's source of power, went out of service. The crew was idle until a tank car of fuel oil arrived several days later. Delay turned to misfortune; while the crew was unloading the car it caught fire, burned for several days, and consumed three weeks' supply of fuel. Two weeks passed before another tank car arrived at the site. When work resumed, the driller encountered salt water and had major water incursion and erosion problems. These met, several weeks of intermittent work followed before pipe stuck in the hole and drilling stopped again. The inexperienced drilling superintendent took control of operations and gave one great pull on the pipe with the powerful engine. As rig timbers creaked ominously, the crew fled from the floor; seconds later the rig collapsed.

The rig was a wreck, and expensive and scarce equipment was damaged beyond repair. Still, when management surveyed the damage, it decided to continue the operation. One month later the partially reconstructed rig still lay idle as J. E. Chase scoured north Texas for a crown block and an elevator, hard to find at any price during a drilling boom. With the optimism of youth and inexperience, Chase reassured a trustee, "Everything is going alright with the exception of the above."[43]

The rig was finally operative again two months after the accident, and drilling resumed until the crew botched a fishing job; that stopped work for another month. Two days after work resumed, the driller encountered cave-in problems requiring additional casing, which the company did not have. Drilling stopped for another week while Chase backtracked a past-due shipment of casing, only to learn that the factory had canceled the order because it was too far behind to fill it in the near future. No casing was on the way. The rig was idle again.[44]

Finally, at the beginning of December, Chase found more casing and fuel oil. The crew might have made up for the long series of delays if the weather had permitted, but as luck would have it, a "blue norther" arrived along with the pipe and fuel oil. It was too cold for the workers to unload the pipe, and the fuel oil was so cold that it would not flow. The rig was idle for another week. Then the cold front moved on and the crew was at last able to drill for several days, until they lost more tools down the hole and the rig shut down for another fishing job. A week later they fired the boiler once more and drilled for several days, until the weather changed and their fuel oil froze once again. With all these mishaps, the crew had drilled only 130 feet during the month of December.[45]

Nor did the new year see an improvement. The crew lost tools down the hole during the first week of 1920, requiring a fishing job that took several more days. When it was finished the crew ran out of casing, shut down the rig, and waited. New pipe arrived two weeks later but it was defective and the driller refused to use it. Thus, at the beginning of February, the operation was at a standstill.[46]

While drilling lagged, financial problems mounted. In order to meet them, in December 1919 Lubbock-Bridgeport tried to sell first mortgage bonds but found no buyers. Nor were leases selling any better. One of the few salesmen Lubbock-Bridgeport had by this time described discouraging conditions in Mount Vernon, Texas: "They [the potential investors] would not buy a twenty-dollar gold piece for $15.00." But unless investors bought Lubbock-Bridgeport's acreage, the company would continue without cash. A note for $10,000 to the Fort Worth National Bank came due and the company did not have funds to cover it, so trustees Crump, Lowrey, and Rouse once again assumed responsibility for the obligation. By the end of 1919 Lubbock-Bridgeport had only a shallow hole in the ground, but it was deeply out of pocket.[47]

Though only the most determined optimist could see a favorable outcome in the Wise County venture by the beginning of 1920, Lubbock-Bridgeport's trustees refused to give up. And there were a few encouraging signs that their labor and investments might yet pay off: other wildcatters were drilling in Wise County, twelve to fifteen miles from the Lubbock-Bridgeport lease, prompting talk of a "trend" in Decatur and Bridgeport. Another group of promoters planned to build a refinery nearby to process all of the as yet undiscovered Wise County oil. From this activity the Lubbock-Bridgeport crowd took heart, so much so that they bought shares in the refinery.[48]

It was necessary, however, to find additional financial expedients to keep Lubbock-Bridgeport alive long enough to benefit from the prospective Wise County boom. In December 1919, therefore, the company's attorney mapped out a conversion from trust to public corporation, a change that would permit the sale of securities. Since this was the only alternative to liquidation, the trustees accepted it. Thus the Lubbock Oil Corporation, capitalized at $100,000, began operations legally on January 24, 1920. The name was new but little else changed; the same officers and directors stayed on, though T. B. Saunders and N. F. Boone, Fort Worth cattle dealers, joined Lubbock Oil's board. The new corporation assumed all of the debts of its predecessor.[49]

Lubbock Oil looked strong on paper; its assets totaled $165,455.30, and its capital stock had a par value of $100,000, leaving a surplus of $65,455.30. These figures, however, were at best highly optimistic. Lubbock Oil had 2,825 acres under lease, a well short of half its planned depth, drilling machinery, and supplies, but the directors grossly inflated the market value of these assets. The leases, for example, were listed at $27.50 per acre, substantially more than the average current sales price—when leases sold. The investment in machinery, $44,708.71, was twice its resale value, while the unfinished well was valued at nearly $20 per foot, more than double the regional average, though the mistakes the crew made may have driven costs to that figure. More important for the immediate future, the company had only $7,651.56 on hand in the form of cash, a reflection of one of the venture's most serious problems, continued shortage of operating capital.[50]

Desperate to see stock sales bring in some quick money, Lubbock Oil's directors lost no time in exercising their newly won franchise. Through N. F. Boone they contacted advertising specialists and securities sales organizations, among them the Trade Circular Addressing Company and the Western Advertising Company of Fort Worth. Specializing in sucker lists and mailing services, the Trade Circular Addressing Company said it had the names and addresses of 4,735 millionaires, 148,000 doctors, 35,000 dentists, and 216,000 "Well-to-do Farmers, all worth $10,000 & over," and it boasted the trade of some of the leading oil promoters like Seymour E. J. Cox. Western Advertising of Fort Worth bid for Lubbock Oil's business on the strength of their campaigns for Dr. Frederick A. Cook's Texas Eagle promotion, among others. Lubbock Oil's directors learned, however, that these service companies unfortunately demanded cash up front, and the Lubbock Oil Corporation would have none until stock was sold. Before it could hire expert help it had to proceed with its own sales campaign.[51]

In short, reorganization as a corporation provided no solution for the company's ills. In February 1920, after a year of using their own resources to keep their venture going and seeing only discouraging results, Lubbock Oil's directors finally took the proverbial long hard look at their company. Field operations were "enough to run a fellow crazy," as J. E. Chase told his brother Frank. His employers, seeking some reassurance, made a belated attempt to secure scientific information on the geological potential of their leases and asked Chase to obtain some geological reports on Wise County. After some delay he did so, though once he had the information he broke his reading glasses on the train ride to his directors' meeting and was unable to report on them. But what Chase found was no help, and the directors could not wait for more expert opinions. They knew that Lub-

Easy Money

bock Oil would be overdrawn by the end of the month. It was time for action.

The directors' first step was to fire the inept drilling supervisor; even J. E. Chase agreed his brother-in-law had to go. Next, in view of the deterioration of the directors' own finances, the personal notes they had signed for Lubbock-Bridgeport were transferred to Lubbock Oil, making the new corporation owe an additional $24,500 to banks in Lubbock and Bridgeport. In a last-ditch effort, the directors urged heroic measures to sell the corporation's stock.[52]

Lubbock Oil's bleak financial situation did not keep its management from issuing optimistic financial statements. Thus it reported to Bradstreet's that, as of February 18, its assets were $244,600 while its liabilities were only $42,500. New drilling efforts by other Wise County wildcatters prompted the sudden and additional inflation of assets; indeed, in response to their activity Lubbock Oil boosted the paper value of its leases to $40 per acre. At the same time, however, it claimed real estate in Lubbock worth $72,000. J. E. Chase, unimpressed by this slight-of-hand, wrote Frank: "Mae [Mrs. Chase] has a lot of garden planted. She thinks she is going to make more from it than I do off the oil well. Maybe she will."[53] Meanwhile, to pump money into the company, its directors bought stock. They also succeeded in refinancing $40,000 of the corporation's debt at 6 percent, plus a 2 percent commission. Other initiatives to improve company finances, however, came to nothing. Efforts to interest the Atlantic Refining Company and other large companies in their leases fell through. At the same time, back on the rig, the underreamer broke and the driller ran out of casing.[54]

For Lubbock Oil, this was business as usual. Still not willing to give up, N. F. Boone devised a scheme for peddling leases through six sequential 640-acre lease syndicates, a device then popular among Fort Worth promoters. Believing that he could do better than Chase at sales, which was no doubt true, Boone took to the campaign trail. He contacted brokers in Cincinnati and other towns, offering a one-third commission on sales. Though this was an expensive way to raise money, Boone calculated that the return to Lubbock Oil would be $160,000, enough to complete the well to 3,600 feet and pay off the company's debts. By late April, however, it was clear that this scheme would fare no better than the others. Boone's one-third commission was less than many brokers of speculative stocks

The Black Gold Rush

ordinarily charged, so they were not eager to sell for Lubbock Oil. The lease-syndicate scheme ran afoul of blue sky laws in Kansas, where regulators refused to license it. Boone, moreover, had no feeling for potential markets. By the time he reached Kentucky, for example, a regional oil boom had been under way for two years and the market for oil securities was oversold. Boone complained to Chase, "They are simply gorged on oil stuff."[55]

Eastern money markets were just as unreceptive. New Yorkers, Boone told Chase, were distracted by the "Wanamaker Panic" in May, so his efforts at lease syndication fell through. Boone did not know that the New York district attorney had been pursuing bogus oil firms, and oil ventures had received considerable adverse publicity in the New York newspapers. Once again, his timing was poor. To cheer up the discouraged director, young Chase offered what little good news he could find: "Mr. Rominger's Brother went to see a Fortune teller the other day, or rather his wife did, and she told [her] that we had been having lots of trouble with the well, but that we were sure to get a well at 2800 feet." If finances offered no ground for optimism, clairvoyance would have to do.[56]

But the well did not come in, and by July the company was still desperate for operating capital. Wages cost $900 per month, and suppliers pressed for payment on goods delivered in May. Lowrey and Crump personally took over expiring bank loans, though not without some grumbling from the old rancher. Young Chase told his brother, "We are going to make it somehow, I know, but just how and where, I don't know." No one could have said how Lubbock Oil would succeed; even when the company lowered its lease price to $10 an acre, nothing sold. No matter what new tactics they tried, these inexperienced oilmen could not compete successfully for investor dollars. Nor did they know when to call their venture a failure: they were too deeply committed to it.[57]

And so they went on. During July the driller reached 3,500 feet, the contract depth, and stopped. The directors considered their alternatives: plugging the well or raising fresh capital to drill deeper. As they pondered, optimism won out over prudence because shows of oil had appeared that week—in a well only five miles away. They decided to drill deeper. Three of the directors bought $500 worth of lease syndicate units each, to provide about one-third of the estimated cost of drilling for a month or so. The rest of the money was nowhere in sight. Certainly it could not be raised in Bridgeport because hard times had nipped oil fever. J. E. Chase advised a friend: "The town is dead, very dead. Cotton crop a failure and miners on strike, and the oil business about blown up." If this were not enough, diphtheria struck down Chase and his children.⁵⁸

Struggling to keep going, Lubbock Oil then made a deal with its driller who, in exchange for $8,000 ($2,000 up front) and 750 acres of leases, agreed to deepen the well to 4,250 feet and to continue below that level at the rate of $4.50 per foot. Chase and Jennings burned up the telephone lines calling contacts in Fort Worth and rural west Texas trying to raise the necessary capital, with the usual result. Once more, shortages of cash delayed operations, for unpaid suppliers held up fuel oil shipments and took the company to court; that shut down the rig until the end of December. The only good news for Lubbock Oil at the beginning of 1921 was of a new well, thirty miles away; its own was still uncompleted. Jennings, the young company treasurer, wrote his mother that he still hoped for a 1,000-barrel well, "but that is too good to be true."⁵⁹

For that matter, no doubt young Jennings and Chase were also hoping that Lubbock Oil would catch up on their salaries, then six months in arrears. Both were flat broke, and Jennings was thrown out of the local Elks Club because he had not paid his dues. In response to urgent appeals, the directors personally paid out a few dollars to Chase, but they saved the company's meager operating capital to pay toward lease rentals, also past due.⁶⁰

Finally, on March 17, 1921, there was a small show of oil in the bailer. Here was a ray of hope at last! But hope vanished as quickly as it appeared, for as the driller reentered the hole to drill deeper, he lost his tools. The well sat idle for the next four months. In the absence of a genuine gusher, there was little incentive for Lubbock Oil to pay the costs of testing and completing the well. When the driller finally reentered the hole in July, the company learned that there was not enough oil to make commercial production viable. Faced with irrefutable proof of failure, the directors finally gave up the venture. They decided to plug the hole and salvage their casing and equipment.⁶¹

Even liquidating Lubbock Oil proved to be frustrating and time-consuming because the Wise County sheriff listed the equipment for forced sale to cover unpaid taxes. After some negotiation, Lubbock Oil sold its casing and equipment and paid some of its debts to suppliers, but it left its

The Black Gold Rush

two young employees high and dry. At age twenty-nine, J. E. Chase had lost $12,000–$15,000 on the venture, by his own calculation. By September 1921, he was reduced to begging rancher Crump for $100: "I am without clothes and money to live on." He was willing to take on blue-collar work in the Kansas City stockyards if a friend could help him land a job. Not as badly off, Jennings sought bank jobs outside of Wise County.[62]

Its business liquidated, all that remained of Lubbock Oil were mutual recriminations among its participants. Though he had helped hire Chase, rancher Crump complained to Lowrey that the young manager "had laid down on the job." For his part, poorer and wiser, Chase blamed the trustees and directors for misjudgments: they should have ended operations when drilling reached 3,500 feet and there was no oil, or, alternatively, once they got a show of oil, they should have put the well to a more conclusive test. He was willing to admit, "I may have made mistakes, business judgments having been at fault." Certainly that was so, but it was a fault he fully shared with Lubbock Oil's organizers. They had all looked for easy money in a business they knew nothing about. They never realized that costs—and hence financial risks—rise during speculative booms like the one that lured them into oil, and they all failed at sharing the high risks of their venture with others. Like so many other oilmen and investors, Lubbock Oil's directors were felled by oil fever.

For all these mishaps the directors of Lubbock Oil were squarely to blame. But developments over which they had no control also ran against them. If, in the spring of 1921, Lubbock Oil had gotten a 1,000-barrel well of the sort Jennings wished for, its problems would by no means have been solved. Nine months earlier, in June 1920, demand for petroleum turned down. The effect of this decline in demand was not evident immediately, for, as oil purchasers continued to replenish stores of oil which they had drawn down in recent years, oil prices in the field stayed high. Prices, however, could not hold up indefinitely in the face of declining demand. Between January and June 1921, oil prices crashed, falling by two-thirds and bringing the average price of oil per barrel down to $1. Later in the year prices recovered moderately, so that by December they reached an average of $1.73.[63] By that time many small producers had gone to the wall, a development Lubbock Oil simply anticipated by some months.

After the great wartime oil boom passed its peak in 1921, the black gold

Easy Money

rush slowed down. As we shall see, however, that did not mean that the American public's desire to speculate in oil was at an end. It was obvious that the nation's future economic growth would be closely tied to petroleum as a source of energy, so it was still possible to think that oil finding would not keep up with the demand generated by the national economy and that the nation would run short of oil. Any of these assumptions made it possible to hope that getting into oil would bring easy money for both promoters and investors. Small failures, like that of Lubbock Oil, did not shake the speculative mentality.

THREE

Selling Shares in a Fortune

F OR THE DIRECTORS of Lubbock Oil, forming a corporation and selling stock were desperate moves to raise money in the later stages of a failing venture, but raising capital for oil ventures through incorporation and stock sales was by no means unusual in the oil industry. The promoters of the well Drake drilled at Titusville, the discovery launching the American petroleum industry, sold stock to finance their venture, and from the first Pennsylvania oil boom on, securities were extensively sold in the East. Thereafter, every new boom brought a fresh wave of petroleum offerings. The eagerness of investors to buy oil stocks during the late teens and twenties of this century, however, made the sale of securities an especially attractive way for small oilmen to raise capital.[1]

The most important reason for growing reliance on stock issues was the oilman's need for greater amounts of capital to pursue exploration. "Poor boy" tactics to drill on shoestring budgets worked well during periods of oil industry recession, but as the cost of leases, equipment, and services rose in boom times it was increasingly hard to cut corners; the income of established operators from producing properties increased, but not as rapidly as the cost of replacing their reserves. The amounts required to drill wells, moreover, rose higher than the sum most individual wildcatters would hazard on a single venture; they also exceeded the amounts most small oilmen could raise within their business circles. Thus, as the boom of the late teens unfolded, soaring costs once again encouraged veteran oilmen to raise funds from the wider public.[2]

Newcomers to the oil industry had even stronger incentives to raise capital by selling securities. They had no income from producing properties with which to pay for operations, and they rarely had access to capital from established business circles. Stock sales not only solved these problems but also were especially attractive to the newcomers because they

Easy Money

demanded none of the expertise that successful field operations in oil required.

The progress of exploration in the United States produced an additional incentive for oilmen to sell stock: the new oil came in at progressively greater depths, requiring a great deal more capital than before to find and produce it. As one industry commentator observed, "The business of drilling for oil in Oklahoma has for several years been growing more and more into a corporate one because of the excessive cost of deep holes, coupled with the ever-present hazard[s], which is too great for any but a multimillionaire individual to assume."[3]

The legendary Tom Slick could still drill "straight-up," entirely from his own funds, when he wished, but most other oilmen would be wiped out by a dry hole or two. In particular, if the new oilman expected to follow the organizational model of Standard and the other major companies, a route to wealth through integrated operations, incorporation and stock sales was the only realistic way to raise the great amount of capital necessary for such operations. There was no way to build a petroleum empire on a shoestring.

It was easy, nonetheless, to start a corporation with little cash in hand, and many oilmen did so. Unless the promoter had legal training or could prevail upon a lawyer to accept stock in lieu of fees, he had to pay for legal help in arranging incorporation, but that normally did not cost much. Next he had to pay a filing fee, $105 in Texas. To grant a charter some states required the projected corporation to have assets or money in the bank to a certain value; in Texas that amount was $5,000. The promoter who was not overly scrupulous, however, could meet this requirement by inflating the value of whatever he had: wildcat leases, played-out wells, junk equipment—anything, in short, that might by some stretch of imagination qualify as an asset. Most promoters met minimum asset requirements with little difficulty. They routinely capitalized corporations for hundreds of thousands of dollars on the basis of assets that were largely imaginary. Indeed, the founders of the Pennsylvania Rock Oil Company, whose promotion led to the Titusville discovery of 1859, did so. Thus it was possible to set up an oil corporation on very slim funds, and the precedent for it was a venerable one.[4]

With his corporation chartered, the promoter could turn to the mechanics of launching his venture. He had to decide on what basis he would sell shares. He might sell "treasury stock," a straightforward sale of equity in the company in which the money paid in by an investor went directly to the corporate treasury. But if he had other objectives, like evading state blue sky laws—statutes aimed at barring sales of securities by companies whose assets amounted to no more than "so many feet of blue sky"—or providing himself with a good part of whatever cash came in from stock sales without openly stealing company funds, he might at the beginning have the company turn a large block of its stock over to him. This maneuver permitted him to sell the "personal" stock that he awarded himself and to keep the proceeds. It also enabled him to evade blue sky regulation in most states.[5]

Once he decided how much stock his company would sell and on what terms, the promoter looked up a printer who could turn out stock certificates. Printers like Chester Bunker, who were experienced at oil field issues, went beyond the standard visual props like screaming eagles and stars surrounded by beams of light to include supposed oil field scenes on stock certificates. Those who bought shares from a number of companies might have concluded that from Pennsylvania to California, one oil field looked much like another. Most certificates showed gushers going over derrick tops, but the settings varied a bit: gushers in valleys, gushers near hills, gushers near tank farms, gushers near factories. The same scenes showed up on certificate after certificate, and regardless of the company's location, most scenes looked remarkably like rural Pennsylvania. One scene that was a favorite showed a gushing well directly behind a building resembling a boardinghouse that fronted on a lake or river; another frequently used view featured derricks and a long line of tank cars. Presumably such visions enhanced the investor's disposition to think of the quick riches that would follow the purchase of a pretty piece of paper.[6]

Certificates in hand, the promoter faced the task of converting them into cash, and that required locating likely investors. This process was often surprisingly expensive. Beginning with the cheapest tactic, promoters often made their initial approaches to the public through advertisements in newspapers. Most daily newspapers printed ads for patent medicines and business promotions, and they seldom showed concern for the truth of their advertising. A few well-placed ads might reach tens of thousands of prospects at low unit costs, but ad campaigns were rarely adequate marketing devices; buyers rarely parted with more than a few dollars in response to paid advertisements, and responses tended to start quickly and halt abruptly. Long-term and large-scale security sales required other approaches.

Some promoters succeeded in locating investors by getting the investors to contact them, either to receive some variety of giveaway or to subscribe to a newsletter or tip sheet. In 1922, for example, Fort Worth promoter R. H. Manning offered a free oil lease to the first twenty people sending him names and addresses of ten friends; those who tried for the giveaway had to send in $1 "to help pay for making your assignment and attorney's opinion." The tip sheet was a very useful device for a promoter because its subscribers were obviously interested in oil investments. Purporting to be an unbiased source of industry information, the tip sheet or "tipster sheet" puffed what the promoter and his friends had to sell while raking rival offerings over the coals. Frederick A. Cook, Hog Creek Carruth, and Chester Bunker were among the many Fort Worth promoters to publish tip sheets. Bunker's *Western World*, for example, pushed oil ventures of Bunker and his associates as well as mining stocks; this puffery mingled with Bunker's own diatribes against conservative bankers, blue sky laws, and the Better Business Bureau, as well as advertisements for oil investments and sexual vigor pills. Bunker thus peddled a wide range of items to the credulous.[7]

The initial identification of potential investors was so vital a part of any promotion that it produced a business of its own, developing and selling "sucker lists," compilations of names, addresses, personal information, and investment history of people who might buy shares. Promoters with experience developed their own files of such individuals, and for a price they would sell them to newcomers. Depending on the extent and quality of a list, its price ran from several hundred dollars to several thousand; one New York brokerage firm was said to have paid $100,000 for a high quality list of 65,000–70,000 names. These lists were sometimes traded, sometimes pirated from clerical workers, and on occasion stolen. Those who lacked the money to buy them were not above rifling trash baskets for envelopes after company offices were closed. A successful prospect list was, in effect, a proven directory of the approachable, if not of the gullible, and it could save a promoter much time, effort, and expense.[8]

Failing a good sucker list, the promoter had to hunt for his own investors, a time-consuming task. Hungry promoters scanned newspapers for names of contributors to charity drives and for people who were written up in society columns. The obituary pages yielded names of widows and potential heirs. Better yet, newspapers in the twenties often published lists of local people who paid income tax and what they paid. In September 1925 the *New York Times*, for example, published such a list for New York City and New York State; it took up eight pages and included mailing addresses. As useful as this list was, however, a promoter did not know which of those people in the paper were good prospects; he could spend a great deal of money on wages, printing, and postage to find out.[9]

Using tip sheets and buying sucker lists took money. So did the professional production of advertising literature, another service experienced promoters commonly used. The most important people in this phase of a promotion were the copywriters, called "pens" by their employers. The promoters of the teens and twenties were willing to pay high salaries for the services of such men as John H. Cain, Walter Keeshan, and the genius of bunkum, Seymour Cox. A good pen could develop a letter or brochure that captured the potential investors' attention and aroused their greed, and that was what the promoter needed.

Once he developed his literature, the promoter sent out plenty of it. A name on a sucker list was worth much more than a single contact, and after several letters some promoters tried telegrams and phone calls. S. Shallcross, for example, besieged the potential investors in his 500 Percent Syndicate with ten letters and three telegrams within three weeks. There were obvious limits to this approach, for it seldom extracted more than $200 from the individual investor, but it paved the way for further exploitation in the form of visits from salesmen. Because that kind of contact could milk far larger sums from the gullible, the pen's work of preparing the ground for others was of great importance. Promoters in large cities, however, favored using the telephone to contact investors; wild promises of instant riches thus left no evidence in print.[10]

When sales failed to take off after cultivation of investors, many promoters resorted to dubious and even dishonest practices. The most common one was the early "dividend," a small payment made shortly after a promotion was launched. The promoter hoped the dividend would encourage shareholders to purchase more shares and to tell their friends what a wonderful stock they had found, thus encouraging additional individuals to invest. Unfortunately, this strategy raised two difficulties. The promoter commonly had no earnings from which to pay dividends, so he made payments Ponzi-style from proceeds of share sales. That led to the second difficulty: paying dividends from money not earned was illegal and often brought federal authorities to investigate the promotion.

Most new promoters progressed to form their own sales organizations after advertisements and mail contacts failed to raise sufficient capital. In-house marketing usually involved the recruitment of salesmen, a difficult process as the directors of Lubbock-Bridgeport and Big Diamond oil companies learned. Usually this approach was not much more successful than newspaper advertisements, and it took much more skill. For that reason many promoters chose to sell stock through intermediaries, brokers and salesmen. Brokerage houses could be the creation of promoters themselves; Frederick A. Cook, S. E. J. Cox, and Paul Vitek were among the many who used their own brokerage operations to rake off commissions for themselves from sale of shares in the ventures they promoted. But there were many other professional brokerage operations like that of Leslie Vincent Company in Chicago, which specialized in selling shares of dubious value. Leslie Vincent's managers, E. V. O'Dowd and Walter Marks, employed a corps of experienced salesmen who traveled through the country; using many an alias, these men were adept at being hard to find when law enforcement authorities took too close an interest in their activities. The salesmen were masters of high-pressure sales techniques and, promising quick returns of hundreds of percent, they wrung thousands of dollars from those they visited. The promoter who retained Leslie Vincent could be sure his shares would sell, but he had to pay the brokers and their employees hefty commissions of three-eighths or more of the revenue from stock sales, and that did not reckon in small amounts of stock to which the salesmen occasionally helped themselves. A promoter short of cash might well be reluctant to hire such expensive professional help.[11]

These techniques of selling stock to fund ventures, so widely used in the teens and twenties, were not novel to the sale of oil stocks. Indeed, as many promoters of oil ventures had previous experience promoting other things, when they moved into oil they took familiar promotional devices with them. There was an especially strong similarity between the techniques used to promote hard-rock mining in the nineteenth and twentieth centuries and the techniques of oil promotion. Mining promoters raised

Selling Shares in a Fortune

capital outside their industry by floating stock. They hired pens to write up prospectuses and other literature; their advertising material made use of celebrity endorsements and of pseudoengineering as well as pseudogeology; they resorted to "stock" exchanges and professional brokerage operations; they used sucker lists; they paid early "dividends." Mining ventures commonly were overcapitalized, and the mineral assets behind such ventures often consisted of used-up properties, properties too small to be profitable, and worthless prospects many miles from production. Such were the financial features of many an oil promotion as well; the devices of one type of promotion worked well in another.[12]

Mining, town site, and real estate promoters set examples for later oil promoters in their use of investor tours of their projects. Such tours, usually accompanied by food and entertainment, were designed to persuade investors that the promoters' promises were as real as the project activity they saw with their own eyes. Promoters also hoped tours would prompt investor excitement, though few attempted as much as Arizona mine promoter Richard Flowers. He planned a tour for his Spenazuma mine investors in 1900 that was to include a genuine western holdup, and had the potential robbers not gotten cold feet, Flowers would have succeeded in robbing his investors twice! Later on, therefore, when oil promoters used tent lunches or barbecues at the well site to promote ventures, they were using time-honored promotional devices. For that matter, many investors who speculated in mining stock fell for the lures of dishonest oil promoters during the black gold rush. Men like Theodore Lamoreaux, the Burr brothers, and Chester Bunker catered to both types of investor-speculator. What they lacked in knowledge of petroleum, they made up in promotional experience and skill.[13]

The use of stock sales to raise capital and the range of techniques used to sell stock are well illustrated by the history of the Big Diamond Oil and Refining Company. Like many another small oil promotion, the Big Diamond venture rose phoenixlike from the ashes of failed promotions. In 1916 a circle of attorneys and businessmen in San Saba, Texas, decided to go into the oil business. The group included Polk M. Faver, an attorney; J. F. "Jimmie" Dofflemyer, a young man in search of a business career; J. R. Polk, a relative of Faver; and George B. Clark, partner in a San Saba menswear store. These would-be oil tycoons organized two companies: the Polk-Clark Oil Company, whose major assets were a drilling rig and

Easy Money

3,000 wildcat acres in Caddo County, Oklahoma; and the San Saba Oil Company, whose principal asset was a 6⅔ acre lease with one producing well in the Humble, Texas, oil field. Neither company made money. San Saba, in particular, ran up debts of $18,000 acquiring and operating the Humble lease, and to meet them Polk and Clark took out personal loans at the San Saba bank. By early 1917 there was simply no more cash in either company till. The San Sabans faced the problem of what to do next.[14]

Desperate for a salvage scheme, Faver and Dofflemyer saw an advertisement which promised deliverance. Oklahoma City promoter Oscar E. Houston offered to "drill out wells for companies that did not have capital." Their companies certainly fit that description, so Faver and Dofflemyer took the train to Oklahoma City for a meeting with Houston and his friends. Houston, attorney and onetime county judge of Custer County, Oklahoma, had promoted at least one company, the People's Refining Company, though with no lasting success; he was much better versed than the two young Texans in the more slippery techniques of promotion. His associates included B. F. King, who traded in Oklahoma leases, and Ed Smith, an Oklahoma City businessman. When Faver and Dofflemyer explained their situation to Houston, he suggested forming a new company on the assets of the earlier ventures. This was a more appealing idea than any Faver and Dofflemyer had thought of, and in mid-July 1917 the group obtained an Arizona charter for the Big Diamond Oil and Refining Company. King was the company's president, Dofflemyer its first vice-president (there was never a second vice-president), Houston its treasurer, and Faver its secretary. Big Diamond, whose name evoked riches, would find, produce, and refine petroleum and market refined products.[15]

When it came to capitalizing their new company, the promoters of Big Diamond showed they had grand designs, for they set its value at $3 million and aimed to sell three million shares of stock at a par value of $1. In reality, however, the assets put into the company were by no stretch of the imagination worth $3 million. Company president King put in two small tracts amounting to 120 acres in McClain County, Oklahoma, and 127 acres near Damon Mound, Texas. This property neither produced oil nor was likely to do so in the near future. Oscar Houston and Ed Smith both contributed $500 to the company treasury. Faver and Dofflemyer put in the drilling rig and Oklahoma acreage belonging to Polk-Clark; they assured their new friends that Big Diamond would receive the assets of

San Saba Oil, as well. Since San Saba's properties included a small amount
of oil production from the Humble lease, that addition would make Big
Diamond an actual oil producer, certainly desirable for a company that
aimed to become a totally integrated operation.[16]

These assets were not only the basis for a grossly overcapitalized company, they were also the justification for some financial sleight-of-hand on
the part of Big Diamond's directors. They began company business by
transferring 750,000 shares to Dofflemyer. He in turn "donated" 250,000
shares back to the company and then divided the remaining 500,000
shares equally among the four Big Diamond directors and Ed Smith. This
interesting maneuver, compensation of the directors for assets they gave
Big Diamond, would let its directors begin to acquire cash before there
was any income from company operations. Some of the revenue from
personal stock sales was supposed to go to the company treasury, but in
actual practice the company never got more than fifty cents on the dollar from such sales. From its very beginning, Big Diamond was thus
handicapped in raising cash for operations, and the stock was one-quarter
"water."[17]

With Big Diamond under way, Faver and Dofflemyer returned to their
Texan friends with the merger plan. San Saba stockholders would ex-
change their shares for an equal number of Big Diamond shares, Big
Diamond would get San Saba's assets, and Big Diamond would take over
the liabilities Clark and Polk had incurred during the San Saba oil venture.
At this point Faver and Dofflemyer ran into an unforeseen difficulty when
George Clark resisted parting with San Saba Oil's major asset. After some
haggling, Clark agreed to sign over income from the production on the
Humble lease to the new corporation in exchange for 125,000 shares, but
he would not sign over the lease itself until Big Diamond paid off the debt
he owed on it. In response to Faver's assurance that Big Diamond would
do so, Clark gave Faver an unsigned deed to the Humble lease, but no
more than that: his signature would be added only when the debt was
paid.[18]

Though Faver did not get what he expected, he did not let his failure
keep him from treating the Humble lease as Big Diamond's property.
Having the deed in hand, albeit unsigned, was evidence that the property
had been "conveyed in blank," as Faver put it. With this bit of creative
legal thinking, Faver was willing to let Big Diamond pay off Clark's

Easy Money

debt—that is, as soon as Big Diamond could afford to do so. He reckoned without his Oklahoma associates. Houston saw no personal or corporate gain in bailing out George Clark; if the Humble lease were to be acquired, as Faver and Dofflemyer had promised, he insisted that the two Texans would have to assume personal responsibility for it. Strapped for cash, Faver and Dofflemyer took out personal loans at the San Saba bank to pay off part of the debt on the Humble lease. They hoped to skim off enough income from Big Diamond's future stock sales to recoup. In short, they counted on future profits, as yet mere hopes, to pay off some very real debts.[19]

Their company organized, Big Diamond's promoters got to work on its promotional literature. With so little cash at hand there was no possibility of hiring a pen; instead, Houston wrote most of the Big Diamond brochure, drawing on what he had used for People's Refining and on the help of anyone who wandered into his office while he was composing it. The result was predictably amateur and undistinguished; it mixed colossally erroneous generalizations about petroleum economics with cynical misrepresentations of Big Diamond's prospects. Big Diamond, for example, could not lose money because it would refine all of the oil it had produced: "No refinery, properly managed, can ever do a losing business that owns its own production." Indeed, far from loss, the investor could expect Big Diamond to yield "profits sure to soar beyond your wildest dreams, a dividend of 1066 percent on the money invested in our refinery alone." How Houston came up with that dividend figure can only be guessed; it owed more to English history than to economics.[20]

The brochure used many familiar and proven lures to investors. Big Diamond's investors would "become associated with reputable businessmen" and be in "partnership with hundreds of the most progressive investors in Oklahoma." It included standard get-rich stories, like that of "M. S. Musselum [*sic*], a poor Syrian," who came to Oklahoma with "ten dollars in Syrian money" and became a multimillionaire; more adept promoters would have had the poor Syrian invest in something offered earlier by Big Diamond's organizers, but the brochure gave "Oklahoma Oil Land" as his source of wealth. Perhaps imitating H. H. Tucker's muckraking approach, Big Diamond told investors it was "The People's Company," a challenge to Wall Street and an obvious appeal to populist thinking. Compared to the sales literature of other companies, the brochure was an amateur effort. A full ten pages, for example, was given over to a tedious overview of refinery operation in the United States. No professional pen would have wasted valuable print on that; professionals concentrated on the appeals to naked greed that swept in dollars.[21]

While they put the finishing touches on their literature, Big Diamond's promoters tried to launch company operations. They put their rig to work drilling a well near Healdton, Oklahoma, and hired one of King's relatives as driller. The company acquired a refinery site at Addington, Oklahoma, and started construction of the plant and of worker housing as well. Lacking cash, the company bought the materials on credit at the local lumberyard and promised to pay construction workers when they finished work. While refinery construction began, Faver and King traveled to Kansas City to open a Big Diamond sales office. After three weeks they ran out of money, gave up the project, and returned to Oklahoma City. It was clear they would need substantial income from stock sales before they could go further, so every effort had to go in that direction.[22]

To push rapid sales of shares, Big Diamond's promoters decided to recruit their own sales force. Faver put together a salesman's kit, consisting of the company prospectus; photographs of gushers, overflowing oil tanks, and vistas of derricks, none of which Big Diamond owned; and sales forms. Big Diamond then advertised for sales personnel in Oklahoma, Texas, and the upper Middle West, hoping to move their shares for less than the 40 percent commissions demanded by established brokers.[23]

The disadvantage of hiring salesmen through such advertisements, of course, was that they attracted a motley group of applicants. Some were only marginally literate. Faver nonetheless responded enthusiastically to all of them. He promised commissions up to 35 percent on sales, and he assured salesmen they could expect to earn between $100 and $750 per week. If they had little experience in sales, Faver told them that they could begin by making rounds with "one of our older boys." And, of course, "with the unabating assistance given our agents from the office, there is absolutely no trouble to sell the stock." Office assistance consisted of supplying the salesman's kit—for which the salesman paid a $5 deposit—and of sending out promotional letters to persons whose names were supplied by the agent. Big Diamond encouraged its salesmen to employ their own agents to speed up sales; if they did so, they could keep a percentage of subordinates' commissions on sales. At no time did Faver

Easy Money

require salesmen to know anything about oil: that was apparently unnecessary. So was experience at sales.[24]

Though most applicants were novices at marketing securities, there were a few veterans. These people proved especially troublesome to manage, for they were quick to detect the inexperience of Big Diamond's promoters. One Oklahoma salesman, for example, actually read Big Diamond's prospectus and wrote Faver that the refinery blueprint in it, supposedly of the company's plant, was the same as a blueprint used by another company whose stock he had peddled; he also noticed that the gushers, tanks, and flowing oil shown in kit photographs all seemed to belong to other companies. Most salesmen were not as embarrassingly observant, but all were slow to forward remittances to the home office. Some never did send in cash; one man absconded with 500 of Big Diamond's stock certificates and was never heard from again. At best, most of these hirelings were not particularly successful at sales. As Faver complained, "It is hard to get the right type of man to work."[25]

Inquisitive, bungling, and dishonest salesmen were bad enough, but Big Diamond's directors fared far worse when they encountered a high-powered expert at grassroots stock sales, R. W. Morgan of Dallas. Late in 1917 they hired this veteran stock peddler and, at his insistence, reluctantly gave him all Texas as his sales territory. A live wire at promotion, Morgan hired ten agents and began pushing Big Diamond stock with considerable success. With a view to making stock move faster, Morgan suggested the use of the early dividend. Since Big Diamond had no income from operations, this step was illegal, but Big Diamond's directors decided to take it anyway in April 1918. By that time they had fallen out with Morgan. Taken aback by their Texas representative's energy and dismayed by the large commissions he was earning, Big Diamond's management decided to modify their business arrangements with him. Morgan balked, complained loudly, and then proceeded to sue. In the end he succeeded in tying up the only production income Big Diamond had, the meager oil runs assigned to it by George Clark from the 6⅔ acre Humble lease, and, by getting the directors to try the "dividend," he ultimately brought them into conflict with the Federal Trade Commission.[26]

Despite the dividend, investors did not rush to buy Big Diamond stock, and by the end of July 1918 only some 41,000 shares had been sold, far short of the promoters' goal of 750,000 shares. One reason for this disap-

Selling Shares in a Fortune

pointing showing lay in the formidable competition for investors' dollars offered by the United States government in its sale of Liberty Bonds. The wartime role of government in the investment arena, moreover, was not limited to bond drives. Any company intending to sell stock had to register with the federal Capital Issues Committee, which then had to approve the company's objectives and decide how much money it could raise. In response to Big Diamond's application, the Capital Issues Committee grudgingly allowed sale of 23,000 shares in order to let it complete its refinery. Because the Capital Issues Committee's guidelines were not strictly enforced, Big Diamond never took this limitation seriously and it presented the committee's action as federal endorsement of the company. Nonetheless, in the field Big Diamond's salesmen were frequently harassed by patriots who demanded to know if they were complying with Capital Issues Committee guidelines and criticized their competing with Liberty Bond drives. That sort of attention did not help sales.[27]

Without steady sales there was neither operating capital nor personal profits. Gross income from the sale of treasury and personal stock was only $25,000; expenditures were nearer $40,000. Increasingly anxious to see money, by midsummer 1918 B. F. King and Oscar Houston decided to try peddling stock themselves. King started selling in rural Kansas and Oklahoma. Houston resigned his company directorship, leaving the office $15,000 in arrears on accounts, and tried his luck in Wisconsin and Indiana. It was reasonable to think that King and Houston would be more highly motivated to sell shares than hired salesmen, and of course they could not be looking for pay for their services. That made it possible to overlook what it would cost to keep them in the field: stock sales would have to pay for travel and living expenses. Once again, that meant less money for the company treasury.[28]

Moving from small town to small town, lodging in cheap hotels and rooming houses, King and Houston soon learned that selling Big Diamond was easier said than done. After a discouraging stay in Lawrence, Kansas, King wrote Faver, "The small dividens [sic] has not put any Enthusiasm in the People and it is Hard grinding here. No matter how hard you fish, they don't bite. The People is so Slow to Decide on Purchasing that I think now that I will return to some point in Okla. . . ." King's sales improved in Oklahoma, though they stayed so small that a $50 sale was cause for jubilation: "Inclosed [sic] Please find check for $50 and if you will Rush the Stock to this old Fellow I will see him again about Tuesday or Wednesday. This is his 2nd buy and he is able to go again. So Boost him for me."[29]

Now president of Big Diamond and in charge of the office, Faver responded to such requests from the field with glowing accounts of company progress. When Oscar Houston wrote "Send us a hot wire regarding developments" in order to negotiate a sale, Faver telegraphed: "Expecting to bring in well Healdton today. Eight-inch casing set yesterday nine hundred eight feet. Water shut out. King talked over phone saying expected to drill in by noon today. Heavy rains last night may delay few hours. Refinery construction being pushed to full capacity. Prospects very bright." Four days later he sent Houston another telegram, suitable for sales work, which proclaimed: "Scrambling for leases. Prospects are fine from two to three hundred barrels. No tanks. Will keep you posted." All this sounded splendid. Virtually none of it was true.[30]

In letters for Houston's own information, Faver made it clear that Big Diamond was deep in difficulty. The well at Healdton was an expensive dry hole. At the refinery, work had slowed to a crawl for want of operating capital, and workers were threatening to stop work altogether unless paid. Worse yet, a carpenter, whom Houston had not required to post a bond, had been paid in full for building a house and had left town, leaving behind a $524 bill at the Addington lumberyard; the yard owner promptly placed a lien on the house. The office of Big Diamond was under "terrific pressure incident to the tremendous bills which had been made," and in short, "We are still having a very hard time to make tongue and buckle meet." He added, "We will still hold a stiff upper lip."[31]

As summer dragged into fall, the First National Bank of San Saba County became anxious to learn when Faver and Dofflemyer would catch up with payments on the debt they had taken over on the Humble lease. Faver begged for time, putting blame on Oscar Houston's lackadaisical management of the Big Diamond office; he predicted the refinery would be completed by the beginning of December and projected that, once in operation, it would yield a net income of $250,000 per year. Despite the implausibility of all of these predictions, Faver's arguments won a little more time from the San Saba bank, but it was clear that unless he and Dofflemyer could begin to make money on stock sales, their financial futures would be as precarious as that of the company they were promoting.[32]

Selling Shares in a Fortune

Then, after so many discouraging months, company affairs suddenly improved. Oscar Houston found an abundant supply of investors in southwestern Indiana, and he began to sell shares for as much as $2. Prospects there looked so promising that B. F. King and Jimmie Dofflemyer decided to join him. What followed was another fumbling hand-to-mouth sales campaign. King had the bad luck to arrive in the area at the same time as the national influenza epidemic. As he told Faver: "The Epidemic of Spanish Flue [*sic*] is something fierce. Quarantine and Everything Shut Down practically." Broke and unable to raise money for living expenses by selling shares, he wired Faver to send him some cash: "I didn't want to do it but no one would cash my check and I was 1200 miles from home, in debt to Hotel and 90 cents in my Pocket. This Probably will never occur again."[33]

But business picked up as the epidemic lifted, and soon King was unloading stock as fast as Houston. As need arose, he found he could use it in lieu of hard cash: "I traded this fellow 400 shares of stock for a Ford car so we could work the Country. A salesman here would be like a one-legged man at a Foot Race if he did not have some kind of a Conveyance." The man who traded the Model T at twice what it was worth for Big Diamond stock would have made a very sharp deal had Big Diamond's stock really been worth anything. Other traders were not as easily taken in, as Jimmie Dofflemyer found out: two salesmen traded stock for "a little worn out Monroe car and the first trip we made in it, it broke down, and it has been in the garage ever since, and I don't think it can be fixed." Despite this mishap, sales were strong.[34]

Back in Oklahoma City, Faver was delighted: "Indiana seems to be a fine field and of course it has no blue sky law and you now have a right to sell Company stock as well as personal stock . . . it is not handicapped with any legal restraints or objections." This development was an unforeseen windfall, and it might even result in capital beyond money to meet bills: "It is not our idea, really, to sell Company stock at all, but if you can prize the people to $2.00 . . . we would all get much more money out of the enterprise." For the first time since its organization, it looked like the Big Diamond Oil and Refining Company might end up with something more than junk acreage, debts, and bills.[35]

Success at sales, however, had the unfortunate result of dividing the company's directors. The Texans, with personal debts they hoped to meet once the company was in operation, felt their Oklahoma partners were not working as hard for Big Diamond's success as at lining their own pockets; King and Houston were slow to forward cash from sales to Oklahoma City. Without that money, completion of the refinery—and Faver and Dofflemyer's satisfaction of their banker—was indefinitely postponed. Dofflemyer complained, "You know selfishness and greed have kept this [the refinery] from going over long ago, and I'm not claiming a salary or commission, but I am determined to see the refinery built and running, & it never will be done if we depend on a bunch of leeches." Like Dofflemyer, Faver looked forward to the refinery's operation: "If we go to taking in money it will be no trouble whatever to use all this money in finishing our refinery." Both Texans had, in effect, promoted themselves on Big Diamond's glittering future.[36]

The high point in Dofflemyer's upper midwestern sales push came early in 1919 when he happened across a gentleman who had $2,000 to invest and was willing to take Big Diamond seriously. Here was someone the promoters of the $3 million company desperately wanted to cultivate, and Dofflemyer suggested the familiar device of the tour of the company's holdings. Faver was as eager to please the investor as his friends, but he had some practical misgivings: "Of course it will be perfectly satisfactory to bring people down here, as we have always invited attention to every holding and operation . . . but would suggest that you have the party subscribe for the stuff before coming." As it turned out, that would have been a better plan. After seeing Big Diamond's office, refinery site, and acreage, the investor only parted with $1,000. In Big Diamond's hands the tour device, like so many others, misfired.[37]

By February 1919 Big Diamond's directors and agents had worked southern Indiana and Illinois thoroughly, and stock sales again sagged. B. F. King and his sidekick Joe Mitchell tried their luck in Sioux Falls, South Dakota, where investors were cannier. Much to Faver's disgust, King and Mitchell ended up having to wire Oklahoma City for money. Dofflemyer tried to peddle shares to friends and relatives in North Texas, but with scant success. Worse yet, letters from restive investors began to arrive, inquiring about promised dividends; even these "dividends" were not likely to be paid unless stock sales picked up. Faver fell back on the standard repertory of promotional tactics to soothe investors and jack up sales. In a general letter he told investors that if they would only invest $25 more in Big Diamond stock, the refinery could be completed and operating by spring: "A refinery, when once in operation, pays the biggest in-

come of any investment known in the country." He offered a stock dividend of 50 percent. Faver also told sales personnel to let investors know
that Big Diamond's stock would shortly be sold through brokerage offices
in New York, and that would make the value of shares go up. Of course,
Big Diamond shareholders were assured that "the prospects of this company for the year 1919 could not be better."[38]

In reality, prospects were more dismal than ever. It was clear by March
1919 that Big Diamond's largely amateur sales force was not going to
peddle many more shares, and what they sold was exclusively personal,
rather than company, stock. Remittances to the treasury were made tardily
or not at all. Faver finally decided that the only way to revive sales was to
seek out professional brokers. He found a brokerage firm in New York,
about which he knew nothing, that seemed eager to do business. Meanwhile, the office lacked cash to pay daily bills. Within two weeks of Faver's
assuring stockholders that company prospects for 1919 could not be better,
he had to turn down Dofflemyer's urgent request for $50: "Heavy liabili-
ties coming in Saturday and this morning have run us to where we have
nothing left." Merely to keep the office open, it was necessary to sell Big
Diamond's drilling rig.[39]

It was increasingly hard to see how the lights would stay on in the Big
Diamond office, but Faver and Dofflemyer had not given up on their
dream of a petroleum empire. Despite having to sell the company's drilling rig, they proposed investment in another well, this time on proven
acreage. Dofflemyer naively assured Faver that they could find such
proven acreage through answering newspaper advertisements and making
a deal to put down a well; they could arrange to pay for the well as they
sold stock. Faver liked the idea but he was inclined to find someone who
would drill on part of Big Diamond's own wildcat acreage in return for a
lease, a strategy that would require no up-front cash. Faver's wildcat pro-
posal drew a protest from B. F. King: "It looks to me like if the Big
Diamond ever expected to do anything besides sell stock it's time we was
getting down with our feet on the ground and stop wildcatting. We are
not in any position to wildcat." King's observation was entirely correct:
Big Diamond was in no position to stake everything on a high-risk wildcat venture. King failed to see, however, that without capital to invest in
proven acreage, Big Diamond had little choice but to take on wildcatting
if it were to drill at all.[40]

As Big Diamond grew more discouraging, the Texans began to plan

Easy Money

new promotions. Dofflemyer suggested a company that would quarry marble for tombstones, and Faver thought of a company to manufacture cotton picking machines. The latter venture, named the Boll Weevil Company, became particularly attractive to them. They found a mechanic who designed a plausible enough looking machine, and they tried to acquire a factory site in exchange for Big Diamond stock. They were sure they could launch Boll Weevil stock by promoting it heavily in the rural South at a price "that would appeal to most anyone." Dofflemyer even proposed giving away shares of Boll Weevil to anyone who bought Big Diamond stock, but Faver thought this device might be illegal.[41]

The hitch in all these plans was lack of money, and though Faver and Dofflemyer schemed at length, they could not get around this barrier. By August 1919 Dofflemyer lamented, "I am ready to start the Boll Weevil campaign, just as soon as I can get a [Texas] charter but you know it will cost one hundred and five dollars, all of which I have not, and then too, we will have to make sworn statements that the Co. either has a certain amount of money in the bank, or assets to a certain amt. [amount], and we unfortunately have neither." Nor was it likely that the impatient directors of the San Saba bank, familiar with the promoters' finances, would help them concoct a statement that the would-be Boll Weevil Company had assets amounting to $5,000. In this quandary Dofflemyer fell back on Big Diamond: "If we can't get the charter any other way, we can sell enough [Big Diamond] stock to actually have the funds in the bank and then we can transfer it to where we need it so badly." But this suggestion once again raised the main problem facing Big Diamond: its stock did not sell.[42]

The course of 1919 proved that Big Diamond's situation could indeed go from bad to worse. April brought the arrival of Schedule A from the Federal Trade Commission. As soon as King caught wind of the FTC's interest in Big Diamond he sent in his resignation from the board of directors, but Faver refused to oblige him by accepting it. In July Faver received the unpleasant news that the agent of the New York brokerage firm selling Big Diamond stock had peddled 25,000 shares and vanished with the proceeds; angry purchasers pointed New York police officials in Big Diamond's direction. In September Big Diamond lost the lawsuit brought against it by its onetime salesman Morgan. In October Addington creditors sued to collect debts from refinery construction. And in

71

Selling Shares in a Fortune

November investigators from the FTC paid a lengthy visit to the Big Diamond office.[43]

After the harrowing events of previous months, Faver found the FTC's inquiry surprisingly easy to accept: "All in all, Jimmie . . . I consider the visit one of the best things that has ever happened to the office, as it has been one of the things we have all looked forward to with some degree of uneasiness, and it is over now and they went away highly pleased with conditions, personally, I have no fear." Faver was sure federal authorities could do nothing to Big Diamond, since it was not "passing stuff through the mail not allowable." Better yet, after what he told the FTC agents of King and Houston's dealings, it looked like the two Oklahomans might be in hot water.[44]

Despite Faver's impression that Big Diamond was unscathed by the FTC inquiry, the company had no viable future. In May 1920 the Big Diamond Oil and Refining Company entered receivership; its receiver found that its only asset was the half-completed refinery with its site. The following year, on September 2, 1921, the FTC issued a formal complaint against Big Diamond and its directors. It held hearings on Big Diamond in the spring and summer months of 1922, and in March 1923 it concluded that Big Diamond's practices were in violation of federal law. On March 16, 1923, Big Diamond was served with an order to cease and desist, but it had long since ceased to do business.[45]

Why did it fail? One of Big Diamond's liabilities was the tendency of its directors to think in grand terms and overlook small practical details. They did not just aim to get into the oil business; they aimed at an integrated petroleum empire modeled on the Standard Oil companies. They set out to find oil, produce it, refine it, and sell products—without experience at any of these objectives. Thus they spread the meager assets they had far too thinly to be of real effect. Like Lubbock Oil, they encountered the rising costs and competition for services prevalent during boom times; as with Lubbock Oil, want of cash ruled out effective competition.

But even if Big Diamond's stock sales had gone more successfully, it is unlikely the company would ever have been profitable. From Big Diamond's inception, too many dollars from stock sales went to pay the directors and support the sales effort; too few dollars ever found their way into the company treasury. Worse yet, Big Diamond's directors could not

Easy Money

manage efficiently the money they did raise, for they did not even plan and provide for the expense of selling shares, much less the expenses of real operation. They were not skillful businessmen, much less skillful oilmen. If its directors had been completely honest, Big Diamond's shareholders would still have fared poorly.

As the company's history makes clear, Big Diamond's directors were far from completely honest. But viewing the company from the FTC's perspective, as a fraudulent enterprise, raises the question of why its directors could not even make money the old-fashioned way, by stealing it. Here again, Big Diamond's promoters were handicapped by lack of experience and cash. Unable to afford professional help, they bungled the devices that other promoters used to raise money from investors. They wrote their own advertising copy and emerged with material likely to put an investor to sleep. They hired their own salesmen and ended up with cranks and misfits. They tried the device of the "dividend" without enough money to pay out sums that might have prompted additional investments. They tried the device of the investors' tour, and their only traveler halved his intended stock purchase. Finally, they placed stock with a bogus brokerage house and were robbed. As dabblers in fraud, they were like the gang that couldn't shoot straight.

The history of Big Diamond shows a mixture of aspiration and deception characteristic of many promotions, past and present. Its directors, like many other promoters, had some legitimate objectives. When they ran up against problems of raising money during boom times, however, they fell back on deceptive practices to further their plans. Because they lacked both experience and cash, the venture they put together always had a high risk of failure; no knowledgeable investor, told the truth, would have put money in Big Diamond. Big Diamond's directors, therefore, had to sell to naive investors and were obliged to exaggerate potential return and minimize risk. They entered a game in which they held no high cards, and they tried to respond by cheating. But for Big Diamond, as for so many other underfinanced oil promoters, it took more than dishonesty to make money in oil.

1. "General" Robert A. Lee is displayed prominently in this trust certificate, created by Charles Sherwin and Harry Schwarz in 1922. By permission of the Southwest Branch of the National Archives.

2. The promoters of the Revere Oil Company exploited history and patriotism and misrepresented the actual working capital of the company by more than 1,000 percent. Authors' collection.

3. Paul Vitek's oil certificate was typical of those issued between 1880 and 1930 and includes the common view of a gusher. Authors' collection.

4. Seymour and Nelda Cox in Big Spring, Texas, in 1920. Both built their public images on their status as aviators, and Nelda flew the "Texas Kitten" to Seymour's newest project. By permission of the Permian Basin Petroleum Museum, Abell-Hanger (S. D. Myres) Collection.

5. Dr. Frederick A. Cook is surrounded by evidence of industry in the offices of his Petroleum Producers' Association in Fort Worth, Texas, in 1923. By permission of Bettmann Newsphoto.

6. Dr. Frederick A. Cook (right) and his attorney, former U.S. senator Joseph Weldon Bailey, in front of the Federal Courthouse in Fort Worth, Texas, during Cook's trial in 1923. By permission of Bettmann Newsphoto.

7. A controversial "doctored" photograph, distributed by the Vetek [*sic*] Oil and
Refinning [*sic*] Company, by Paul Vitek in 1923. By permission of the Southwest
Branch of the National Archives.

8. A promotional photograph of H. H. Hoffman in front of his producing property in the Humble, Texas, oilfield. Only the nearest well actually belonged to Hoffman's company. By permission of the Houston Metropolitan Archives, Houston Public Library.

9. Chester Bunker (center) supervises the replacement of a flat tire on his touring car near his World Oil Company property in 1923. By permission of the Permian Basin Petroleum Museum, Abell-Hanger (S. D. Myres) Collection.

FOUR

Money in Trust

NLIKE UNDERFUNDED novices, promoters who successfully raised money in large-scale campaigns planned their cultivation of prospective investors with great care. They captured the investors' attention, won their trust, and roused their greed; they did not hesitate to rely on expert help to do so. Most of them operated from large urban centers, near the skilled craftsmen so useful to their trade—advertising copywriters, tip sheet publishers, securities brokers, stenographers, and printers. Ambitious oil promoters gravitated to the financial districts of New York and Chicago, and to Denver, Houston, and Fort Worth, which were near regional oil activity. They formed business communities of their own, in which they kept up with the latest and hottest oil action, traded properties, swapped sucker lists, pirated sales gimmicks, and collaborated in ventures.

Familiarly known as "cowtown," Fort Worth developed as a regional center for finance and the cattle business in the late nineteenth century. In the 1880s it had an area reputation as a "gamblers' mecca," a place where cowboys and country folk looking for action could find excitement they did not want to be seen enjoying back home. With the banker and the cattle dealer, the cardshark, the plunger, and the gambler for high stakes were familiar figures in local life; they all brought dollars into the local economy. A businessman expected to pursue his affairs without interference from his neighbors. After 1900 the development of meat packing plants and light industry gave Fort Worth the look of a modest-sized western city. It was less a cattle and horse-trading town, but it retained the distinctive "live and let live" attitude of its past.[1]

By the time of the First World War, Fort Worth experienced problems common to American cities. Industrial growth brought labor unions to town and, as in 1922, clashes between labor and management were bitter. Race relations were troubled; the Ku Klux Klan had a large and energetic

Easy Money

following and was a force in local politics. Local government was tainted by repeated charges of corruption, the subject of a federal grand jury investigation. Rapid growth from regional oil development exacerbated these problems.[2]

Oil first affected Fort Worth's growth in 1911–13, when discoveries near Wichita Falls opened a new oil-producing region in Texas. Fort Worth, with its railway nexus and a growing population, was an attractive regional industrial site, and the Gulf and Pierce oil companies built refineries there. Five years later, the great west central Texas boom began with discoveries in Eastland County; it affected a large area whose transportation network consisted mainly of railroads that came west from Fort Worth. Anyone or anything bound for "Roaring Ranger" was likely to pass through Fort Worth, which became the regional headquarters for a wide range of oil businesses.[3]

By mid-1918 Fort Worth showed many of the familiar signs of a community in the midst of an oil boom; all that was missing were the derricks and gushers. The *Fort Worth Record* reported that "an army of oil operators" had come to town. The *Saturday Evening Post* described an invasion of "the soldiers of fortune, the pathfinders, the trailblazers, the scouts, big and little, attached and unattached, . . . lease sharks, grafters and grabbers, operators, speculators, and gamblers." So intense was activity that at the beginning of 1919, Pathé Weekly's film crew arrived from California to film boom-time excitement. The Californians assured Fort Worth reporters that crowds on Main Street could not be outdone in size "by any city in the United States."[4]

Oil brought highly visible prosperity. As the horde of newcomers swamped existing hotels and office facilities, hotels set five-day limits to guests' stays; they let those for whom they had no beds sleep in chairs along corridors or in their lobbies. The latter, however, were continually thronged with people trading, dickering, striking deals, and doing business that would have been conducted in offices had any been vacant. Fast-pitched trading spilled out of hotel lobbies and to adjacent sidewalks. A storefront on the corner of Fifth and Main streets developed into an informal curb market for oil issues. Known as "Mack's Oil Board," this operation filled a room about fifty by one hundred feet with sales personnel and stenographers; a blackboard listing hot local oil stocks stretched across the rear wall. Speculators from all income brackets swarmed in and out of the establishment throughout the day. Like so many others, they hoped to make their fortunes from oil, and hectic activity made that hope credible.[5]

Not surprisingly, heightened business activity spurred rapid real estate development, and within four years the former cowtown became a city of skyscrapers. The grandest of them was the Farmers and Mechanics Bank Building, a twenty-four-story structure whose base was Ohio granite and whose corridors were trimmed with Vermont marble. It became the most impressive business address in town, and any promoter with grand designs aspired to afford an office suite in it. In 1922 alone, buildings worth $12 million went up; they represented many new employers and many new jobs. Much oil promotion took place through the mail and gave work to hundreds of office workers, printers, and postal employees. Oil thus gave a massive boost to the town's economy.[6]

Clearly a desirable base of operations for the promoter aiming to launch a nationwide sales campaign, Fort Worth had only one drawback as a location: so many promoters flooded the nation with mail postmarked "Fort Worth, Texas," that by 1920 public sales resistance had developed to oil schemes generated from the town. For that matter, so many oil companies like Lubbock Oil and Big Diamond had peddled shares around the country that the public was warier of oil deals than it had been three years earlier. It was increasingly necessary to find new means to win the confidence of investors. Promoters had to convey the message that, unlike their unscrupulous brethren, they would not lead trusting investors astray. Speculators may have been plucked before, but they would win now.

One device promoters used to enhance their credibility to investors was that of an appealing company name. Promoters who wanted to rouse gambling lust opted for names evoking chance: Lucky Ten Oil, Straight Eight Oil, Double Five Oil, Magic Eighty Oil. The direct appeal to greed was obvious in names like Shallcross's Smackover 500 Percent Syndicate, Will Heard's Paymaster Syndicate, and Paul Vitek's Bonanza. But to instill confidence, something more staid was called for. Names like First National Oil, Pilgrim Oil, Uncle Sam Oil, and Revere Oil sounded eminently respectable, trustworthy, and patriotic, though the promoters of all these companies were indicted on fraud charges. Such names not only played on patriotic emotion, but they also were easy to remember and were likely to catch investors' notice.

Easy Money

Promoters also bid for investor trust by using celebrity endorsements: if the famous were involved, surely the ventures must be reputable. Thus Seymour Cox got a former New York City police commissioner, a former Oklahoma governor, and a magazine publisher to endorse Universal Oil and Gas. Similarly, C. N. Haskell, a former governor of Oklahoma, and Dr. Frederick A. Cook traded on their own modest celebrity. But perhaps the most audacious and imaginative use of the celebrity device was carried out by two young Fort Worth promoters, Charles Sherwin and Harry H. Schwarz. They chose a dead hero, General Robert E. Lee, as the foundation of their appeal and used his credibility as an asset, thus blending patriotism and fame.

Like so many oil promoters, Sherwin and Schwarz joined the crowds that looked for easy money in Fort Worth. They had no experience as oilmen; Sherwin's work for five months in oil fields near Wichita Falls was the closest either man had come to oil. Both were eager to cash in on oil fever, however, and in 1920 they managed to raise a small capital stake by borrowing from contacts in California. With this stake they launched at least one modest promotion, but the dollars failed to pour in. Two small fish in a big pond, Sherwin and Schwarz discovered that they needed a special gimmick to attract attention and to compete successfully for investor dollars. They found it in December 1921, when a fellow Fort Worth promoter, Walter Pelletier, introduced them to a stocky little old man in his seventies who sported a white beard not unlike that worn by General Robert E. Lee.[7]

His name was Robert A. Lee. His family had migrated from Tennessee to a farm in Denton County, Texas. Robert was not content to stay on the farm, but the grand dreams of his youth came to nothing over a lifetime. He led a drifter's life in the northwest, working as a janitor from time to time. Now in old age, he amused his relatives by trying to find oil on their farmland with a divining rod. He was the kind of harmless eccentric no one really had time to listen to, except for Charles Sherwin and Harry Schwarz.[8]

Sherwin and Schwarz saw in Robert A. Lee a superb marketing device, a figure supremely suited to win public confidence, akin to Uncle Sam, Lydia Pinkham, or the newly devised Betty Crocker.[9] Here was a man who could plausibly pose as a relative of the great southern hero and who even looked a little like General Lee. The two promoters saw his promotional possibilities in a flash of inspiration: they would turn the threadbare janitor into "the Miracle Man of Oildom," and reap the profits of the transformation.

And so, as Lee told Sherwin and Schwarz of his past adventures and present financial embarrassment, the two promoters made him an offer. They would organize an oil company with Lee as its figurehead. If he would sign letters and let them use his name, they would pay him $50 per month, plus 10 percent of any production revenue their company received. They would organize the venture as a trust estate, and Lee would join them as a trustee. Lee, however, would have no right to ownership or management of properties; only Sherwin and Schwarz would sell beneficial interest shares in the trust, and only Sherwin and Schwarz would be entitled to money from such sales. The role they created for him was less impressive than his family name, but it was the best offer anyone had ever made the old man, and he accepted with great enthusiasm. To him the promoters were "mighty good men who knew that an old man's misfortunes are not always of his own making."[10]

When Sherwin and Schwarz organized their venture as a common law, or Massachusetts, trust, they followed the example of many contemporary promoters. The trust had several compelling advantages. It was easy, quick, and inexpensive to organize; in Texas, for example, all the law required was a simple declaration of intention filed by three trustees at the courthouse nearest their business address. There was no red tape comparable to that of getting a corporate charter, nor were there regulations concerning the amount of assets in the venture or the amount of capital in it. Trusts were not covered by laws regulating corporations; many promoters saw this as freedom from both state and federal regulation of any kind, which was not altogether far off the mark in terms of practical law enforcement. The term trust could be expected to have a certain amount of investor appeal, as it sounded suitable to high-powered finance; when the oil stock swindles began to generate adverse publicity, moreover, the trustees of an oil promotion could righteously show that their "units" or "interests" or "certificates" were not securities. The impression promoters hoped to convey was that the trust offered more security for the investor than other types of organization.

In reality, investors in the trusts possessed even less security against mismanagement of their money than under corporate organizations chartered in Delaware, and that was another feature of the trust's appeal to promoters. The standard trust declaration gave the trustees "absolute power to manage, control, hold, and dispose of" any money, property, or assets the trust had or might receive; the trustees had full discretionary power over what came to the trust, as if "they themselves were the sole and absolute owners of the properties." They could do business where, when, and as they chose, and they alone determined the amount of their compensation for managing the trust. They could have the trust sell interests or units and legitimately pocket all proceeds from the sale. They could sell the trust their own worthless properties for grand sums or make it assume costs incurred by other ventures. In short, they could do very much as they pleased with whatever investors gave them.[11]

By contrast, the rights given investors in a trust were meager indeed. They were entitled to a share of the profits or income generated by the trust, but the trustees decided the size, form, and frequency of that payment. If the trust was liquidated, they were entitled to a share in the proceeds of liquidation. But they had no legal right to the trust's property while it was in existence, no right to call for a dividend, no right to call for an accounting of trust management, and no right to call for a dissolution of the trust. As one veteran of petroleum law reflected on the trust, "It gave the participant little if anything to hang his hat on."[12]

With Lee on the payroll, on January 3, 1922, Schwarz and Sherwin organized a common law trust capitalized at $25,000. For the trust's assets, they bought leases on 200 acres in Limestone and Navarro counties in Texas from Sherwin's sister-in-law, K. A. Kain, who had paid $1,000 for them; they announced that they would sell 1,250 beneficial interest shares in the trust, General Lee Interests, and make big profits by selling the leases when oil development took place around their acreage.[13]

Once the legal papers were filed, Sherwin and Schwarz hired Walter Keeshan to write letters and circulars at the rate of $100 an item, and it was Keeshan who developed their major asset, "General" Robert A. Lee. From Keeshan's pen, the General emerged as a scion of one of the South's most venerable families, a man who was first a southern gentleman of the old school and then a thoroughly modern geological genius, a man whose idealism and spirit of self-sacrifice utterly ruled out the pursuit of a fast buck. The General had found gold in the Klondike and California, and oil in Oklahoma and Texas, but he always worked for others and hence was

Money in Trust

not rich himself. Now, however, he would work for his investors. In Keeshan's hands he became a success: he had never located a well that turned out a dry hole or bought acreage that "did not prove productive." Of course, that was true: Robert A. Lee never located wells or bought acreage.[14]

The General, as Keeshan constructed him, did not confuse his potential investors with talk of assets and liabilities. Instead, from the first promotional letter onward, he talked of his ideals and his family history. This led to a gripping family anecdote in his first letter:

> I was only a bit of a lad when General Robert E. Lee used to visit my father, back in Chattanooga, Tennessee. Tears would well up in his eyes as he trotted me on his knee and told and retold the story of the great Civil War, and the South he loved so well. It was on his last visit before he entered that Haven of Eternal Life, that he called me to him and said, "Bobby (he always called me Bobby), before I go back home I want to give you one word of advice, as I may never see you again. THE NAME OF LEE IS ONE OF HONOR. It has never been dishonored and stands without a stain. Keep it so, Bobby, as long as you live. Be square and honest for there is a reward for clean dealing that cannot be purchased with wealth. If you do this you will always be happy, and Bobby, you will always be successful."[15]

As the reader wiped away the inevitable tear in order to focus on the General's pitch, he learned that all this great and chivalrous geologist wanted was the chance to share the "gigantic wealth" he was going to make in Texas's developing Mexia oil field. He would permit only 1,250 people to join him, taking shares of $20 each. They had to act fast because the small sum he was raising would be oversubscribed rapidly. To stress once again that he had never been a money grubber, he ended with the postscript, "Do not send your wires collect, as this is not a promotion scheme, and I cannot afford to pay these charges."[16]

The fictitious figure of the General was splendidly calculated to appeal to just the sort of investors whose names cropped up on Fort Worth sucker lists. Such people usually knew nothing about oil, but what did that matter if they could trust the General? The General's communications were full of talk about honor and honesty and square-dealing; surely a man with these old-fashioned values would not cheat investors. And it

Easy Money

was reasonable to think he had such values because he was a Lee. Like so many investors, moreover, the General was not rich; like so many, he had worked long for others, had seen them grow wealthy, but he himself was far from affluent. As created by Keeshan, the General was in much the same circumstances as the would-be investors he appealed to—which should have given them pause!

Though they had hit upon an excellent promotional device in the General, Sherwin and Schwarz found that their General Lee Interests promotion was not an overnight success. It brought in checks and money orders for $20 or $40, and very occasionally $100 arrived in the office, but only $15,000 came in before the momentum of the promotion was expended.

Prepared for such a contingency, the two promoters launched a follow-up, General Lee Interests Number Two, on February 4, 1922. They capitalized this venture at a more modest figure, $18,000, to be divided into 900 shares of $20 each. Once again the source of profit would be lease speculation in the Mexia field area; the trust acquired three more tracts, 140 acres in all, from K. A. Kain. These tracts were supposedly over "the Great Mother Pool," which was "Due West of the Monster Mexia Gusher Area," and because they were surefire money-makers, subscriptions to interests were limited to twenty-five per applicant, "TO PREVENT THE LUCKY ONES FROM TAKING ALL OF THESE INTERESTS."[17]

This "precaution" was entirely unnecessary, for General Lee Interests Number Two also failed to sell out. Schwarz and Sherwin tried advertising more widely in the *Houston Chronicle* and other newspapers, but with little result. Accordingly, in April 1922 they organized a third trust, the General Lee Development Interests. Under this new arrangement, Lee, Sherwin, and Schwarz agreed to buy 6,163 acres in Denton and Tarrant counties, Texas, from Schwarz, Sherwin, and their associate, Abe Lebenson, for a price of $250,000—a massively inflated figure for acreage scorned by conventional oilmen. In return for the acreage and in lieu of cash, Schwarz, Sherwin, and Lebenson were entitled to take whatever money came in from the sale of 250,000 beneficial interests. Since it was capitalized at $250,000, they therefore had prior claim to the total capital of General Lee Development Interests in exchange for the junk leases.[18]

General Lee Development Interests marked some important modifications in Sherwin and Schwarz's operations. Most obviously, the promoters decided to raise much more money. Previous ventures, floated for small amounts, had moved slowly, however, and higher capitalization required an adjustment in their marketing strategy. Following the examples of more successful Fort Worth promoters, they decided to make use of professional securities salesmen to peddle their interests, and they reached an agreement with Walter L. Marks, partner of E. V. O'Dowd in the shady Chicago brokerage firm Leslie Vincent Company. Marks agreed to sell 100,000 General Lee interests in return for a commission of three-eighths of all of the money he took in. Marks's price was high, but his operation was experienced and efficient, and he could guarantee results. Sherwin and Schwarz were willing to pay for that.[19]

After two disappointing lease-trust promotions, Schwarz and Sherwin also discovered that gushers had more emotional appeal for investors than leases; they decided that it was time for their geologist general to drill ten wells, though they promised investors that they would be charged for only one well. Thus, on the new General Lee Development Interests stationery, opposite the emblem of the crossed American and Confederate flags, stood a scroll with the motto, "To drill Ten Wells in the Heart of Texas." As their artists depicted it, the heart of Texas was conveniently located in Denton and Tarrant counties, within the bounds of the promoters' acreage. Equally fortuitous, it was on what the General assured investors was the "Roanoke Uplift," near the small settlement of Roanoke, whose name brought additional Virginian associations to the minds of investors. Wealth greater than that of the famous Tidewater planters would follow shortly because the General assured investors, "I positively guarantee to get production."[20] The General might make such a guarantee, but certainly Sherwin and Schwarz could not. Nor did they have money from oil production uppermost in mind.

Sherwin and Schwarz made one more change to make their certificates easier to sell. Adopting the street peddler's philosophy that a fast nickel is better than a slow dime, they lowered the price of an interest to $1, one-twentieth the price of what they had previously offered. At $1 nearly anyone could buy an interest from General Lee. Of course, if the promoters were to make the kind of profits they hoped for, they would have to sell more than one interest to each investor; each investor would have to be cultivated assiduously by the General to insure a steady series of investments. Once hooked, the investor had to be kept on the line.

To keep their investors sending in money, Sherwin and Schwarz had the

Easy Money

General bestow abundant attention on them through the mail. As soon as an investor made his first payment, he began receiving special tokens. The first was the General's photograph, picturing a beaming Robert A. Lee sporting a Confederate officer's hat. This missive came with a letter conveying the General's motto: "Do Unto Others First." There followed a pamphlet, "The Honor of the Lees, 1649–1922," ostensibly by the General, and an explanatory note: "I don't remember whether I sent you one or not, but anyway I want you to have one before they are all gone again." Near July 4, investors got a pamphlet on the Declaration of Independence; as the General said, "Financial Independence is what I am striving to get for you." In all, the investor would receive at least one item from the General each week, signed with the clear if somewhat shaky signature of an aging man. Robert A. Lee earned his $50 a month.[21]

If the volume of mail received from General Lee made the investor feel important, so did the content of the General's communications. Though mailings went out from Fort Worth to thousands of potential investors from coast to coast, what the General sent rarely read like conventional form letters. Keeshan and the promoters contrived to write their material in an intimate chatty tone, in the sort of language one would use to a close personal friend. Visions of personal contact between the reader and the General were frequently conjured up by such phrases as "If I could take you out into the field with me," "If you could sit here in my office, so that I could tell you my plans," and "But that I could clasp you and others by the hand and have a word in person with you." Emphasis was on the personal touch. When Schwarz and Sherwin made a show of getting down to business by spudding in a well in Denton County in June 1922, investors received invitations to a barbecue at the well site, a gesture that reinforced the images of personal contact and southern hospitality. Better yet, from the promoters' perspective, the barbecue cost little, despite the lengthy guest list, because few investors lived near enough to attend.[22]

The General was not only hospitable, he was personally solicitous of his investors. Those who could not travel to Fort Worth to clasp him by the hand were frequently encouraged to write to him. They received prompt and apparently thoughtful answers to their letters. The General, for example, wrote Alice Kane, an elderly Massachusetts hairdresser: "I certainly enjoyed reading your letter, and am glad to know that you feel you could confide in me." Then followed advice given many another correspondent:

Money in Trust

"Do not hesitate to write just the way you feel. Just anything that you want to know, I assure you, will be explained to you in detail." The General was willing to sacrifice his time on the investors' behalf: "If it requires that I write a book to answer your questions, then you may expect one in return, for you are my partner now, and when I want anything of you, I am going to write you, and I expect you to do the same." The General was eager to assume the role of confidant. He was an avid pen pal, and so were many of his investors.[23]

The pleasantries of correspondence, of course, were always directed toward extracting cash, but even in pursuit of dollars the General kept his courtly manner. He did not tell investors that they had to buy interests; he said he personally wanted them to have them. Thus, he advised Miss Kate Telford of Sierra Madre, California, "I am going to reserve 100 interests for you until I hear from you again." Once he had an investor in the bag, however, the General kept the drawstring tied with strong encouragement to buy more than his prospect had initially bargained for. A $100 check for 100 interests was acknowledged as the down payment on a far larger block of interests—300 or 500, for example—and the General was always accommodating about taking the balance several months later or in installments.[24]

The kindly General appealed to both pride and trust: "A $10 bill, a $20 bill, or even $100 is not going to break you. In fact, this amount of money will not even help me, [but the investment] may be the means of affording some of the luxuries that this life affords and of which you and yours are entitled." He confided to another investor, "The majority of people who write me are poor people and cannot afford to lose their money. Several people have written me that they are even borrowing the money they are investing with me as they have such faith in my ability to find oil." When this small investor sent in a $200 check for 200 interests, she received a certificate for 300 interests and a generous extension of the time to pay the balance. The General was taking care of her.[25]

Sherwin and Schwarz's creation of the General as the generous and sympathetic mentor to those somewhat down on their luck was especially effective in appealing to people whose names they found on promotional sucker lists. The promoters knew not only that their targets were gullible but also that they had been other promoters' victims. The General's investors needed—and received—constant reassurance that the General would

Easy Money

not be like the rest. And for their part many investors could admit, at least privately, that they had trusted unwisely in the past. What a relief it was finally to find an unselfish and knowledgeable financial adviser, a man whose character was above reproach, to tell them how to place their money safely. To let him understand why they could not send him the additional amounts he suggested, they often poured out their financial woes to him. P. G. Wooster, a self-described "old man" living in Pasadena, California, confided that he looked to profits from General Lee to over-come losses in earlier oil investments: "I may conclude to send you more. I am a little timid. I have just lost in the Mexia Extension Synd. I am afraid those boys stopped drilling too soon. What do you know about that location? Was it good to your mind? I am in several other wildcats down in Texas and am waiting to see how they are to pan out." Wooster did not want the General to take his hesitation for want of confidence: "I have great faith in you, you as being of the line of the famous Lees." Nor did he wish the General to see him as selfishly hankering after riches: "I want to win to give away my winnings to worthy friends."[26]

For investors like Wooster, the General seemed to offer security in a bewildering financial whirlpool that had already proven full of snags for the unwary; he was a longed-for mentor. For others, snagged too often, he was a last chance, a savior who would throw them fiscal life preservers as they were about to sink for a third time. I. H. Kirkland, a businessman from Brunswick, Georgia, had to scrape together the money for 1,000 shares of General Lee Development Interests: "Money is short with me at this time, as with most everyone else and it is a struggle to pull thru and if I did not believe you could make good and be fair and honest with me as well as all others I would not make an Effort to take any more interests with you now." But Kirkland did believe in the General: "I have been stung as others But believe in you." After Leslie Vincent salesmen told him how greatly General Lee interests would appreciate in value, he was desperate to purchase more in order to realize the quick profits promised: "If there ever was one that needed help, I am the one." Resorting to an alternative that may well have been very familiar to him, Kirkland asked if he could offer his personal note in part payment. Most regretfully, the General demurred: "As much as I would like to, it would be impossible for me to accept your note."[27]

The extent to which Sherwin and Schwarz won the trust and support of

Money in Trust

their investors is well demonstrated in the promoters' dealings with N. J. Cary, a retired banker, of Utica, Illinois. Mr. Cary was given careful attention from the first General Lee promotion onward, and he received the same sequence of letters and mementos as the other investors. But, like many other investors, he could not be coaxed by mail to part with really large sums. General Lee waited patiently. When Cary sent in $10 on January 16, 1922, with a promise to pay the $20 balance due within a month, the General wrote, "I appreciate you taking one interest with me as much as I do the man or woman who purchased fifty interests." At the same time, however, there was a suggestion that one share was not enough: "If this is all that you can afford to carry, it is certainly with much pleasure and satisfaction that I realize the trust you have placed in me, but let me state to you that should you be in a position to purchase more, do so without a moment's hesitation."[28]

Cary hesitated, but after a steady barrage of letters and souvenirs during February, he mellowed enough by March to purchase an interest in General Lee Interests Number Two. Once again he sent in $10 and promised to pay the balance at the month's end. Two weeks later, however, he decided to plunge for an additional interest. He was clearly circling around the promoters' lures, but at so slow a rate that he was scarcely worth the high cost of personal cultivation by mail.[29]

At this point Schwarz and Sherwin correctly reasoned that Cary would part with his cash more readily in face-to-face sales. On May 6, 1922, the General wrote his friend Cary to say that his personal representatives would pay him a call. The personal representatives were, in fact, two of Walter Marks's ace high-pressure stock peddlers, Max Hirsch, alias Max Haas, and Phillip Goldstein, alias Phillip Gibson and Ralph P. Gibson. On May 19, the two salesmen visited Cary and dazzled him with visions of overnight riches: General Lee Development certificates, purchasable at $1, were really worth $6 each; in a few weeks they would be selling for $20. On June 15 the interests would be listed on the New York Stock Exchange, unmistakable evidence of success and respectability. All of this was more than Cary could resist. There was no comparable path to quick riches in Utica, Illinois.[30]

Even with this inducement, however, Cary would not part with cash. Instead he gave Hirsch and Goldstein securities to hold as collateral on a $3,000 purchase, and he promised to pay in full within one year. Confident they had Cary well and truly hooked, the salesmen contacted another Leslie Vincent employee, Nathan Sang, alias Nathan Lang, who paid Cary a visit five days later. Fully ripe for the plucking, Cary now pledged to buy another 12,000 shares, "thus making a Full Block of 15,000 shares." Once again, he offered securities as collateral instead of cash: 3,500 shares of Colorado Collieries, a $500 gold note of the same company, a $1,500 note on the American Sumatra Tobacco Company, 1,104 shares of Kansas and Gulf stock, 10 shares of Bowes Postage Meter stock, and 40 shares of Page Detroit Motor. These securities were sent without delay to Leslie Vincent Company in Chicago.[31]

So skillful were O'Dowd's salesmen that Cary's reaction to agreeing to part with $15,000 was akin to euphoria. He wrote a long letter to the General to express his gratitude for being allowed to place more money in General Lee Development Interests: "Again, I want to thank you Dear General for your many kindnesses and courtesies to me and your many stockholders, and to tell you how much I honor and respect you, and what entire confidence I have in you and the Companies and interests bearing your name you are connected with. It is a rarity indeed, in these days of 'frenzied finance' to meet and do business with a man of your character and ability, and I truly hope to meet you in person one of these days 'ere long." General Lee went beyond inspiring confidence; he inspired devotion.[32]

By mid-June Cary's euphoric mood gave way to doubt and suspicion. He feared that he had been hoodwinked—not by the General, of course, but by his sales representatives. If the General had been so grateful for his earlier $20 investments, why had the General failed even to acknowledge the $15,000 purchase? Had the salesmen given his shares to the General? Then Cary learned that his Kansas and Gulf shares, which Leslie Vincent Company was supposed to hold as collateral, had been sold. He wrote Sang in care of the brokerage firm, only to be told that no one named Sang worked for the firm. This news led him to write a worried letter to the General: "It begins to look a little as though I might be the victim, though I can hardly believe it."[33]

Sherwin and Schwarz lost no time in responding to Cary's complaint; a $15,000 investor was worth keeping happy, and reassurance arrived by return mail. Though he knew that Leslie Vincent Company usually cashed in securities as soon as it received them, Sherwin made a show of telegraphing Walter Marks to find out what had been done with Cary's property. Then, on June 29, the General wrote Cary that the salesmen "took it upon themselves" to sell Cary's stocks; the situation was regrettable, but it would work out well: with the twenty-to-one profit Cary would make on General Lee Development Interests, he would be able to buy back his former portfolio "and have many times the amount it is actually worth in the bank." Cary was mollified. He replied, "It was just as I supposed, *you* had nothing to do with the selling of my collateral."[34]

Though Cary exonerated the General, he was still unhappy and suspicious, a frame of mind incompatible with the continuing investment the promoters sought. Sherwin and Schwarz knew Cary was most susceptible to face-to-face solicitation, but sending someone else from Leslie Vincent was now out of the question. It would take personal effort to wring more money from the old man. Accordingly, on July 6, the General telegraphed Cary that his private secretary, Mr. Schwarz, would call on him soon, and several days later the adroit promoter arrived. After abundant pleasantries, he softened up the retired banker for another touch. He convinced Cary that despite past misunderstandings, the General would "take care of him," because a Lee was always a man of his word. Harry Schwarz was at the top of his form.[35]

Even Schwarz did not realize just how persuasive he had been. Cary not only recovered confidence in General Lee Development Interests, but he also decided that the buoyantly optimistic Schwarz was a perfect investment counselor, just the man to ask about all the opportunities that came in the mail from the southwestern oil regions. As he wrote Schwarz on July 14, "I wish to again thank you most kindly Harry for your kind offer to help me in any way you can in giving me information as to oil properties and concerns in Texas. As you know, the 'Woods are full of them,' good, bad, and indifferent, and a fellow has to be on his guard all the time nowadays if he expects to escape the snares set for him in the 'Oil Game'." What, asked Cary, did Harry think of Lester Petroleum or of the Mexia-Wortham Oil and Leasing Syndicate? "They all have very attractive offerings to make, but as to the financial or moral responsibility, I know little or nothing." Not surprisingly, Harry knew of no investment as safe as General Lee.[36]

As adept as Schwarz was at promotion, during the summer of 1922 the professional stock salesmen—Hirsch, Goldstein, Marks, and Sang—were

Easy Money

chiefly responsible for the revenues rolling into General Lee's coffers. They commonly traveled in two-man teams, a tactic that gave them important psychological advantages in face-to-face sales as their skillful patter interwove themes of trust, low risk, and vast riches in a colorful verbal tapestry. Targeted investors like Cary always received telegrams announcing the imminent arrival of the General's personal representative. Not uncommonly, investors were more wary than Cary when the salesmen showed up on their doorsteps. Many, like Dr. J. E. Davis of Atlanta, Georgia, wrote the General to ask if the people who came to sell interests were in fact the representatives the General told him to expect, which indicates how common visits from securities salesmen were in some parts of the country. On receipt of reassurance from the General, however, most customers were happy to buy hundreds of dollars of interests.[37]

If the salesmen had moderate to good success on their first contacts with investors, colleagues made follow-up visits. After buying $200 in interests by mail, for example, Toledo hardware manufacturer C. F. Throm received successive visits from Hirsch and Goldstein, and Sang and Marks. Each time, he bought more interests, so that by June 1922 he had invested $15,578. Like Cary, he parted with securities to do so: 480 shares of Marconi Wireless and 480 shares of RCA. An experienced businessman, Throm had clearly used some discretion in his previous investments. When confronted with high-pressure salesmanship and the Lee image, however, he threw discretion to the winds.[38]

In their eagerness to scoop in commissions, the salesmen told investors virtually anything that would sell interests. The kind of promises made to Cary were modest compared to what they could say, and during the course of 1922, the salesmen's pitches grew steadily more exaggerated. They told one investor in Lexington, Kentucky, for example, that she could expect a 20 percent dividend check on September 1, and 5 percent a month thereafter; in reality there were no plans for dividends, nor were there any profits from which payments could be made. Salesmen assured another investor that a "syndicate" was about to buy whatever interests in General Lee it could get for $2.50 each and thereafter no more would be available. In a variation on this theme, a gang of brokers was supposedly planning to seize control of the company and drive up the price of interests. Whatever the scenario, however, the investors were always assured that the interests were already worth far more than the $1 par value; the salesmen

Money in Trust

often claimed that they could be re-sold immediately for $6 each. These promises induced investors to buy interests at prices well above par value.[39]

Such techniques moved large blocks of interests at high prices, but they soon created problems for Sherwin and Schwarz. The promoters often did not know when the salesmen made their calls or what prices they extracted from investors. It was embarrassing when a customer who had bought interests at $2.50 received a letter from Fort Worth several days later, offering them for $1. An exasperated Harry Schwarz wrote Walter Marks in October: "In nine cases out of ten, when we get a squawk it is caused by one of the men calling on a customer and making a sale and the same customer receiving one of our letters or telegrams and securing more interests at par. Many of these kicks could be eliminated if you will wire as we requested you some time ago when these sales were made."[40]

Investors also complained that they had paid salesmen for interests that they never received. These complaints were most common when they traded in securities for General Lee certificates, because the securities were sent to Leslie Vincent Company for sale and not to Fort Worth. Payments of less than $100 were often pocketed by salesmen, who did not report them to either Chicago or Fort Worth. Any sum paid above the $1 par was also kept by the salesmen, without a report. In all of this double-dealing, Schwarz and Sherwin could do little: they depended upon the cooperation of men who shared their perspectives and business ethics.[41]

Difficulties with salesmen were not the only problems Sherwin and Schwarz faced as the promotion went on. In mid-July Federal Trade Commission investigator John Southworth dropped by the office and demanded to know much more about the venture than they wanted to tell him. They had ignored an earlier FTC questionnaire; now Southworth threatened them with jail and fines if they did not supply information to him. The FTC's interest in their business came as an unwelcome surprise to the promoters, for from the beginning they assumed that common law trusts, virtually unregulated by Texas, were outside federal jurisdiction. Under pressure, however, Schwarz and Sherwin cooperated. Two weeks later, postal inspectors arrived, to ask many of the same questions. When they departed without indicating the possibility of further action, the promoters returned to business as usual.[42]

Unfortunately for the promoters, they soon faced fresh problems. The

Easy Money

Fort Worth Press took an unfriendly interest in them in October 1922. In November one of the Californians from whom Sherwin borrowed money two years earlier grew tired of waiting for payment and sued to place him in bankruptcy. N. J. Cary reached the limit of both his trust and his funds and sued for an accounting. Plunged into legal hot water, Sherwin and Schwarz could not watch over their front man, Lee, and the General took fright and consulted his own attorney. Alarmed that his $50 a month salary might have placed him in a vulnerable position, the old man placed some distance between himself and his colleagues; he decided to let investors know that he, Robert A. Lee, had not taken their money. He was not responsible![43]

Thus it was that investors received a letter of a very different sort from the General. There were no cheerful promises or flights of idealistic sentiment. The General's latest letter was signed with green pencil rather than the usual blue-black ink. He revealed that Sherwin was having legal problems and suggested that investors might wish to consider litigation of their own. How the General's followers reacted to this sudden and dismaying news can only be guessed, but at least one of them, P. G. Wooster, asked for a fuller explanation. He got much more than he expected. For the first time, the real Robert A. Lee replied, in a penciled, barely coherent note: "Swarz and Sherin Has Handeln all the money and wooden let me No Nothing So theas Jews is trying to get a way with about $100,000 So I am trying to proct th Stock Haldrs I will Rite you more fuly as sune as this is seteld." Gone was Walter Keeshan's eloquent Miracle Man of Oildom; here was Robert Lee, semiliterate retired janitor. The company's major promotional asset turned himself into a liability. This was a problem the creators of Lydia Pinkham and Betty Crocker never had to face.[44]

Sherwin and Schwarz were now down, but they were not out of the game. By the end of December 1922, they had wriggled free of their legal difficulties and set about reviving the promotion. Since no one else was interested in paying Lee, they bought him back into docile silence. The General wrote investors to admit that there had been some slight "misunderstanding" among the trustees, and there had been a lawsuit. But, as the General assured everyone, "Now it affords me much pleasure to be able to again write and tell you that everything has been settled, and the company affairs will run along just as smoothly as ever." Schwarz and Sherwin, he continued, had just posted a bond to drill all the wells promised investors, and they would try drilling next at Smackover, Arkansas. Despite the adverse publicity surrounding the legal problems, the General urged investors to consider whether they had as many interests as they should have when the golden profits began to flow in. The Virginia juggernaut rolled on.[45]

Though Schwarz and Sherwin resumed their promotion, their brushes with federal investigators led them to modify their promotional strategy. Letters to investors were less frequent, and their tone was more restrained. Gone were the General's family anecdotes and sweeping promises; in their place were blander generalities about oil prospects for the year ahead and sober reflections on how much the Roanoke well, now admitted to be dry, had cost. Along with these attempts to sell more interests to investors, Schwarz and Sherwin defended their past actions. They offered a singular justification for apparently having put so much money in a dry hole: "When one takes into consideration that we have, with no little amount of diligence and care, drilled this well to a depth around 3,000 feet with not the slightest indication of getting a well, but every sign that would indicate anything else but an oil well, we think that we are due credit for performing our duty." In other words, tenacity in the face of overwhelmingly negative information ought to count for more than merely finding oil.[46]

Sherwin and Schwarz did not quit readily, but by the end of the winter of 1923, it was clear that the General Lee promotions had gone as far as they were likely to go. Over two years the three schemes brought in as much as $165,000, a handsome amount on paper. It was less, however, than what the promoters had originally aimed for, and it had been raised with the costly expedients of mail-order publicity and hired professional help. Thus, though there is no way to determine exactly how much Sherwin and Schwarz made, it is reasonable to think that they were able to make crime pay—but not very well. Their promotional device of the General had been successful in winning investor confidence. On the other hand, using General Lee gave Sherwin and Schwarz notoriety and made them subject to unpleasant exposure in the *Fort Worth Press*. General Lee's novelty made them, in effect, too conspicuous; Sherwin and Schwarz were good targets for crusaders, as they were to learn.

92

Easy Money

While Charles Sherwin and Harry Schwarz created a celebrity to appeal
to the public in their promotion, Dr. Frederick A. Cook traded on his
own modest renown. Unlike Sherwin and Schwarz, whose overriding
motivation was chasing a fast buck, Cook wanted to be a promotional
tycoon, outdoing all the rest. A more practical person might have thought
that objective unrealistic for a man with no working knowledge of oil, but
Cook, who spent a lifetime pursuing dreams of fame and fortune, was
rarely troubled by practicality. He found fantasy far more congenial than
reality, and its pursuit justified any expedient. Cook aimed to be incompa-
rable, but he usually succeeded only in being implausible.

Cook's early life had the dramatic elements of an American rags-to-
riches success story. His parents, Theodore and Magdalena Koch, were
German immigrants, and Theodore was a country doctor in Sullivan
County, New York. When Cook was only five years old his father died,
leaving Magdalena destitute with five young children. She moved the
family to Brooklyn; with a daughter's help, she eked out a living as a
seamstress, while young Frederick and a brother worked long hours for
pennies at Brooklyn's Fulton Market. Under such bleak circumstances,
Cook's formal schooling was necessarily sketchy. Still, he dreamed of
achieving something extraordinary. He saved enough money to buy a
second-hand printing press and wrote, designed, and sold his own line of
greeting cards; this little business enabled him to enter medical school at
Columbia and, later, New York universities. An early morning milk route
helped him pay additional bills. He was a poor boy determined to make
good.[47]

By 1890 Cook had completed his medical training and married, but he
was dogged by misfortune. His medical practice in Manhattan failed—he
treated only three patients in a half year—and his wife and infant died
following the baby's birth. It was natural that he dreamed of escaping his
wretched situation; years of hard work and saving brought him only frustration, poverty, and desolate grief. Cook looked for an outlet in high
adventure, so he signed on as physician for Robert E. Peary's Greenland
expedition of 1891–92. Though the expedition was unsuccessful, Cook
performed well. He won praise from Peary and recognition among the
wealthy coteries of would-be explorers back in New York.[48]

During the rest of the decade, Cook struggled to make a living. He led
tourist trips to Greenland in 1893–94, but that business was not successful.

Money in Trust

He worked up a modest medical practice, which gave him a living but did
not make him rich. In 1896 he married his first wife's sister, but she died
three years later. Through it all, Cook sought new adventures. In 1898 he
signed on as physician for an unsuccessful Belgian expedition to the South
Pole, an experience he described in *Through the First Antarctic Night*. In
1901 he went on another Arctic expedition. Clearly, frustration in his career and grief in marital life spurred him to dream of fantastic adventure
and encouraged him to seek fame as an explorer, but, though he had built
a reputation in geographic circles, he was not yet a celebrity.[49]

Cook's luck began to change when he met Marie Hunt, wealthy widow
of a Philadelphia surgeon. With Marie's money, income problems were
temporarily resolved, and he could give much more attention to exploratory feats. Thus, in 1903, with a subsidy from *Harper's Monthly*, he made
an unsuccessful attempt to scale Alaska's Mount McKinley. No quitter, in
1906 Cook tried again; this time he said he made it. If one believed him, a
middle-aged doctor with one companion had succeeded in climbing a
hitherto impassable face of a mountain, with little equipment and no
support group. On such terms, it was a stunning feat.[50]

Naturally, many experienced climbers did not believe Cook. They argued that his photographs of the summit were doctored, and that what
could be seen with certainty was not the peak of the mountain. However,
though Cook's claim to fame was challenged, he gained enough celebrity
through this exploit to promote modest funding for his own expedition to
the North Pole, a venture that would compete with one in formation by
Peary. More experienced and better known, Peary raised funds for a massive expedition; Cook traveled light.[51]

Cook and Peary both set out for the pole in 1908, but shortly after he
reached Greenland, Cook disappeared, and, as long months passed with
no word from him, it was assumed that he was dead. That made his
reappearance in September 1909 all the more sensational. Cook made his
way to Copenhagen and declared that he had stood at the North Pole.
The Danes gave him a hero's welcome, and he was feted by royalty, university faculties, and an adoring public. At last, the limelight he had
sought for so long was his; he reached fame and fortune. Unfortunately
for Cook, as soon as the spotlight was shone on his incredible exploit, it
began to look implausible. Cook could produce no log of compass bearings, no sightings of geographical features; he said he left all his records

at an undisclosed site in Greenland. Nor were there any witnesses to his feat, save for two Eskimos, also somewhere back in Greenland. If he had reached the North Pole, what evidence proved he had done so? Journalists, especially those writing for the *New York Times*, pointed out that Cook's story about the pole resembled his story about Mount McKinley: there was no solid evidence he had done what he said. They were inclined to credit Cook's rival, Peary, with victory in the race for the pole.[52]

In the face of widespread skepticism about his achievement, Cook's hopes for fortune evaporated, and his fame turned to notoriety. Once more strapped for cash, Cook turned to the lecture circuit, describing his adventures to paying audiences. At this, Cook was quite successful. Personally charming, he appealed to audiences as an underdog, as an unassuming man done out of his just recognition. The lecture circuit paid Cook's bills: he made as much as $80,000 in a year. But with the misfortune that tracked him, Cook found that as he charmed audiences, the press grew increasingly hostile to him and wrote him up as a fake, "a magnificent liar." His response to unpleasantness, once again, was to run from it. He and his wife traveled incognito in Europe and South America for more than a year. As soon as the polar controversy was stale news, Cook went back to the lecture circuit, from which he made a good living until 1915, when he made an unsuccessful attempt at another mountain climbing expedition, this time in the Himalayas. Now fifty years old, Frederick Cook was still not ready to settle for a conventional life. He continued to pursue fame and fortune, but they eluded him.[53]

Over the years, however, Cook had developed a group of loyal friends and supporters, and in 1916 Dr. Frank P. Thompson offered him a chance at a completely new endeavor. Thompson owned some oil leases in the newly active oil regions of Wyoming and asked Cook to participate in developing them. That led to the formation of the Casper-based New York Oil Company and, in 1917, to the chartering of the Cook Oil Company. In the latter venture, capitalized at $1 million, Cook received a block of stock. Though the company bore his name, Cook Oil was in fact the creation of Frank G. Curtis, the president of New York Oil. Cook spent his time traveling about in western Wyoming, staying in Thermopolis and visiting potential oil leases. In later years he said he identified good prospects in Hamilton Dome, Hidden Dome, and Red Rose Dome, "three fields that are more or less to my credit." *Less* was the correct designation,

Money in Trust

for, as with his claims in geographical exploration, no reliable evidence supports Cook's claim to successful prospecting in any of these places. But if Cook had little impact on Wyoming oil, it had a telling effect on him. Surrounded by the bustle and excitement of an oil boom, Cook scented a new future as exciting and expansive as mountain climbing and polar expeditions. He would still win fame in exploration: this time he would look for oil.[54]

He found the trail of it in Fort Worth, Texas, where he launched his first Texas oil promotion, the Texas Eagle Oil and Refining Company, in January 1919; the venture was organized as a common law trust. As oil prices rose, he rushed to acquire properties for his fledgling venture. His first transaction was the purchase for $50,000 of a five-acre lease, offsetting a producing lease at Burkburnett; to this he added leases near Desdemona, in proven but declining territory. These purchases, made while the price of oil was soaring, absorbed most of the capital Cook and his partners placed in Texas Eagle, and when he tried to hire a rig and crew to drill a well, Cook found that boom-time prices exceeded what he could scrape together.

Cook and his associates thus decided to raise additional capital by incorporating Texas Eagle in Delaware, capitalizing the new company at a grand $2.5 million. Cook, by contributing his trust certificates, obtained at least one-quarter of the shares, which he held for sale as personal stock. He also contributed 182 acres of junk leases to Texas Eagle, in return for additional stock.[55]

Confident that the company's money problems were solved, Cook tried to develop properties in five counties, built derricks, paid to rig them up, and drilled dry holes on excessively expensive leases. Pouring out money faster than it came in, he had to step up his promotional efforts, so he tried a massive mail-order appeal to his investors. His chief asset was his fame as an explorer, so Cook made constant use of the publicity he had received in earlier years to try to inspire investor confidence. Circulars to shareholders were mailed along with personalized letters from "Dr. Frederick A. Cook, World Renowned Explorer, President." One brochure identified Cook "not only as an explorer and scientist, but a geologist and finder of oil." Of its leases, Texas Eagle promised that "every acre has been personally examined and approved by him," a claim that was probably true, because though Cook was no geologist, he was hardworking and he

Easy Money

represented his own opinions on all subjects as "scientific." Presumably that was close enough to geology to please anyone.[56] The good doctor also gave his investors a steady stream of assurances that money placed in Texas Eagle was safe. Texas Eagle stock was an investment, not a gamble. It had "a 99 percent chance to make good," and as a sure sign of success, the value of the preferred shares would "be advanced at least 50 percent" in the brief span of a few weeks. All of this was fiction, but it is possible, even likely, that Cook believed these claims in 1920. He was fully aware, however, that serious misrepresentations were made to sell Texas Eagle stock. Though he had received a sizable bloc of shares in exchange for junk leases, for example, he wrote, "There is no watered stock, no promotion stock—it is a fair clean-cut company, organized by Dr. Frederick A. Cook." Nor did he object when his brokers added their hype to his. The Fort Worth Oil Exchange, Incorporated, advised its clients that Texas Eagle "appears to be an excellent company," based on the claim that less than half of the company's leases alone had "a public appraisement" of $3,500,000. The completion of a refinery and further development of company properties would soon boost the value of company assets by severalfold.[57]

The truth about Texas Eagle was far less encouraging. Like so many promotions of its kind, the company had no income from operations; all of its income came from the sale of about $800,000 worth of stock. This was a healthy sum, but after sales commissions and selling costs were covered, Cook had less than half a million dollars in working capital. What he acquired with this money, at peak boom prices, was a collection of inefficient equipment, wildcat leases, and declining producing properties. Unless one assumed that mounting speculation triggered by continually rising oil prices would enhance the value of these assets, there was no reason to think they would generate profits. In Cook's hands they did not do so, despite the record high oil prices of 1920. When oil prices plunged in 1921, therefore, Cook was hard-pressed to pay his bills, let alone build a petroleum empire. A veteran of the oil fields might have avoided these problems by buying properties more carefully, but Cook was still relatively new to the game. An easy mark for those who wished to unload junk at premium prices, Cook was hurt by his lack of experience.[58]

By midyear 1921, when oil prices began a slow recovery, Cook had sunk not only the proceeds from the stock sales but also $50,000 of his own

Money in Trust

capital in the company, with no apparent return. It was clear that Texas Eagle would never soar. At the end of the year the company was under attack by its creditors and went into receivership. Unlike geographical exploration, in the oil business failure produced no heroes.[59]

Cook's investors lost their money and Cook lost most of the assets he brought into Texas Eagle, but the venture was not a total loss for him; he had learned three valuable lessons. The real money in the oil game as he had played it was made by promoting investors; his attempts to drill wells and produce oil came to nothing. It was also more profitable to sell goods and services to other promoters than it was to explore for oil. Finally, he realized it was better to take risks with other people's money than with his own. He applied this costly knowledge in his third venture, the Petroleum Producers' Association, named grandly after the important Pennsylvania trade association of the 1860s and 1870s.[60]

Like the initial version of Texas Eagle, Cook's PPA was a trust, and he exercised full and sole control of its assets. The two other trustees of record never met to transact PPA business, and one of them later denied that he knew his role in the venture; the other offered preliminary advice but was never regularly consulted by Cook thereafter. Cook intended to be absolute ruler in his new business empire. In April 1922 Cook began selling PPA certificates, either directly or through three brokerage operations that he owned or in which he held an interest. This tactic not only lined Cook's pockets with commissions on sales, but also sidestepped a major obstacle to expansion, the refusal of most reputable brokers to handle PPA interests.[61]

During May Cook assembled the assets of PPA, working and royalty interests in producing properties and undeveloped leases. He purchased a half-working interest, for example, in a thirty-one-well lease in the Petrolia field in north Texas for $30,000. In reality, only three wells yielded any oil, and they pumped no more than five barrels per day between them. In Cook's mind, however, they were potentially prolific: he expected the lease to produce at least 2,000 barrels per day when additional oil-producing horizons were brought into production. At that rate, PPA would have its money back in about one month, and everything thereafter would be profit. Or so Cook reasoned. In fact, Cook, the self-identified "petroleum technologist," deceived himself, for the Petrolia property was not worth even the expense its operation entailed. There was no realistic prospect of

Easy Money

producing from new horizons at that time. Had there been such a possibility, the property would not have been on the open market. Cook, the dreamer, was trapped by a more clever promoter who knew full well that the doctor did not know what he was getting.[62]

In any event, the money PPA would make was not derived from the sale of oil but from milking investors. Cook's main device to appeal to them was the merger scheme, a favorite ploy of the fraudulent promoters in Fort Worth. He offered investors in other oil companies, mainly failed ventures, the opportunity to convert their holdings into PPA certificates with the payment of a 25 percent fee. The investors were told that the new company would thus acquire the assets of earlier companies and realize a profit by operating and developing them more efficiently. Investors could believe this move would save them from the losses incurred from earlier speculation. What investors were really doing, however, was paying additional money for shares as worthless as the ones they were giving up. Since the "assets" PPA was taking over were generally worthless, it had no more chance of turning them to profit than its predecessors. To have done so would not have been management but magic.[63]

In order to locate disappointed investors eager to trade with PPA, Cook bought about 300 lists of investors from other promoters, most for $200 to $300 each. In some instances he purchased stolen lists from former employees of other companies. Either way, he had one of his own employees write to the investors in the guise of "special trustee" or "Stockholders' trustee" with the conversion offer. These "trustees" ordinarily knew even less than Cook about the oil business. O. L. Ray, for example, who served in this capacity for fifty-eight companies and as Cook's front man in a brokerage operation, was the driver of a bakery wagon when Cook recruited him.[64]

Cook's merger campaigns were nearly identical. They began with a postcard teaser, telling investors in failed oil ventures that they would soon hear from someone whom they would perhaps misunderstand—and that a new opportunity was beckoning. A few days later, a letter over Cook's signature, or that of Ray, contained bad news: "As your stock now stands it has no market price whatsoever." Then the conversion pitch was made: "When you convert the stock of your company into Association shares, you will acquire an interest in 88 wells already drilled, and your advantage will grow as this organization spreads its activities." Thus an earlier mistake would miraculously lead to bonanza.[65]

Money in Trust

Letters, circulars, and visits by Cook's salesmen followed. Yet, for all of Cook's effort, the results were disappointing. Cook mailed out at least 200,000 pieces of literature, but resultant income was barely adequate to cover costs. Poor timing was part of the problem: there was simply too much effective competition from other promoters for the dollars of mail-order investors. This was especially true in 1921–22, when the flood of mail-order promotion in oil, real estate, electronics, and the auto industry produced sharp competition for investors' dollars. It took more and more money to raise money.[66]

If Cook had followed the usual practices of promoters, he would have let PPA subside into receivership, like thousands of failed oil promotions before and after it, and launched an entirely new venture. PPA's creditors would have been put off, and, with relatively little at stake, frustrated investors would have either accepted their losses and backed away from oil or tried their luck in new ventures. But defying conventional wisdom, Cook revived PPA in September 1922. He looked for new merger targets, pursuing distant companies in New York and California. He expanded his work force, ultimately leasing more than one full floor of the new Farmers and Mechanics Bank Building, the most expensive office space in Fort Worth, and installing a full-service printing department. This new department of PPA had five full-time employees and ran two shifts per day, using two multigraph machines; it was capable of turning out 24,000 to 30,000 pieces of promotional literature per day. Two addressograph operators and a full-time mail boy handled mailing. The cost of this operation was offset in part by Cook's offering printing and mailing services to other operators. He provided copy, and printed and mailed letters and brochures, for a percentage of their gross income. By late 1922, material Cook turned out for himself and others swamped the PPA mail room with as many as 300,000 pieces per week. At this time Cook was employing as many as fifty-three full-time typists to keep up with the contract work and the correspondence of PPA. Cook thus committed himself to mail-order promotion on a grand scale.

The key to the revival of PPA was not only a strong mail-order effort, but also a new sales campaign, beginning with Cook's recruitment of the equally ambitious and unprincipled Seymour E. J. Cox to write dazzling letters and persuasive brochures. Cox moved from Houston, where he had been acquitted of mail fraud charges, to a four-room hotel suite in Fort Worth and began to work long hours for PPA. Cook and Cox planned sales strategy and devised pamphlets and letters in the office, over meals, and late into the night. Early in the mornings, Cook went over the text of the previous day's literature and edited it to suit himself, while Cox worked on new material at a desk in Cook's private office. When Cox finished a piece, Cook approved it for printing and distribution. As soon as one of their "highly polished apples," as Cook referred to their promotional literature, went through the printing department, it sped through the mail to potential investors. Working in close collaboration, Cook and Cox turned out several dozen brochures, scores of form letters, and many columns of hot copy for Cook's tip sheets, newsletters that purportedly carried unbiased industry information but in reality served only to boost investor enthusiasm for Cook and his clients.[67]

The promotional literature showed Cox's imaginative genius and his favorite phrases. He revised the standard fill-in-the-blanks subscription form to exude positive thinking and confidence in Cook. Investors were asked to sign the following statement: "I believe in you . . . Doctor, I hope it won't be but a few months until you mail me larger and greater dividends running into hundreds [of] percents every month, and under your plan, I believe you will." The form letter that accompanied this blank contained one of Cook's favorite lures, the possibility of buying into PPA as part of the preorganizational syndicate, a privilege ordinarily reserved for the rich and well-connected bankers and brokers of the East.[68]

Cox and Cook played upon investors' anxieties as well as on their hopes. Cox was especially adept at preying upon the fears of elderly people: "Consider the welfare of yourself seriously, because in a few years your earning capacity will be impaired and unless you provide now by making profitable investment, you may suffer during the years you should be happy. . . . You owe it to yourself and loved ones in providing for those who are dear and near." The two promoters argued that future security was worth present sacrifices: "Even if it becomes necessary for you to borrow the money, the conditions entirely justify the sacrifice." In an age before Social Security, this approach was particularly effective—if thoroughly unethical.[69]

The basis of the promised security was the fabulous assets Cook had acquired for PPA: "more than 100 actually producing wells, and many more under process of drilling in the most profitable oil fields in the entire world." These assets included royalties on more than 14,000 acres in Stephens and Eastland counties, "a lease in the Petrolia field with 31 producing wells—and room for 200 more!"; and 350 acres in the Smackover field, "near where the Texas Company paid $2,000,000 for 40 acres," a property that would produce 200,000 barrels of oil per day and that would be worth $25 million in sixty or ninety days. "A thirty acre lease, with a well down to 1800 feet" was "almost certain to be a great producer and it alone may be worth enough money to pay the security holders of this association several thousand percent on every dollar invested."[70]

All these promises were liberally covered by Cox's colorful prose. PPA's oil came not from mere geological formations, it flowed "From the Bowels of Mother Earth and direct from the Reservoir of Nature's Eternal Gift." It gushed forth in vivid descriptions of oil fields, noisy with the blast of whistles and derricks "grinding and churning." Cox's imagination soared when he described the PPA's prize holding, extensive acreage over a vast secret oil field, "a place where many of the big oil sands converge, forming a basin of oil so much larger than anything yet discovered that bringing in the first well will startle the oil men of the world and start a stampede for the district such as has never been heard of."[71]

Though PPA's assets, so strikingly described, produced negligible income, the collaboration of Cook and Cox brought record subscriptions— as much money in less than two months as Cook had raised in nearly a year. In all, PPA took in about half a million dollars. About 5 percent of it came from Cook himself in the form of cash advances that PPA never repaid. Where did all the money go?

When he decided to revive PPA Cook spared no expense, and he made no effort to control costs. Postage and envelopes alone took more than 10 percent of the PPA sales income; altogether wages, printing, stationery, office supplies, and office operation used up half of all the money paid in. In only three months, Seymour Cox received more than $15,000 in salary and commissions; the amounts Cox received through internal transfers of funds cannot be determined. The show properties and field operations, all acquired at top dollar costs, used about one-fifth of the capital. In all, at least three-quarters of the gross income from stock sales was required to pay the costs of selling the stock. The money seemed to melt away as fast as it poured in, because Cook was an inept manager. PPA always lived beyond its means, and those means were generated by sale of worthless paper.[72]

Easy Money

The fragile nature of Cook's paper empire was not obvious to other businessmen for it seemed the very picture of success, a paradigm of boom-time prosperity. PPA became one of the largest employers among independent oil companies in Fort Worth. Cook dressed and lived well, so it was natural to assume he was a rich man. By the end of 1922, the apparent success of Cook's promotion brought him favorable notice in Fort Worth business circles; he was unquestionably a figure of local prominence. There was, however, a price to pay for such a high profile: it also brought the unwelcome attention of federal authorities. The Federal Trade Commission and the Post Office Department, moreover, had been on Seymour Cox's trail for more than three years. Though they had become aware of Cook's activity by early 1922, their interest in him quickened when "Lucky Cox" signed on for work at PPA. There was no question that Cook achieved his objective of outdoing all others in the promotion game, but that very achievement made him vulnerable.

Federal investigators began intensive scrutiny of PPA in the fall of 1922, but Cook's investors were unaware that he and PPA were under investigation. Even as FTC and postal investigators were working in PPA offices, Cook wrote "I am with you with clean hands to the end of the world" and warned his investors against the snares of fraudulent promoters. When federal agents completed their work and withdrew to analyze their findings, Cook finally told his stockholders that PPA had been under study, but he added that federal authorities had given it a clean bill of health, even something of an endorsement! Like so many others, he did not expect much to come from federal attention, let alone that it would destroy both his prospects and reputation.[73]

How successful was Cook at making a fortune by going into oil? Though his aims were more grandiose than any of the other Fort Worth oil promoters, his adventures in the oil business followed a familiar pattern. Like so many promoters before and after him, he entered the oil industry during an upturn and tried to make his fortune in a complex and volatile business, lacking both basic business experience and specific expertise in oil. During the upswing, the brilliant prospect of quick riches blinded him to the financial realities of everyday business, leading him into extensive and costly purchases and high overhead operations. Texas Eagle and PPA never generated real income; the work Cook did for other promoters brought in cash but that was eaten up by office overhead.

103

Money in Trust

When his dreams of easy money were dispelled by an avalanche of unpaid bills, Cook fell back on sharp and deceptive practices to acquire the capital he needed to reverse his fortunes. In doing so, he reinforced the charges of his many critics that his castles in the sky were built of hot air. Critics aside, he was both dishonest and incompetent. In the oil business he was a striking but pathetic figure, blinded by his dreams, largely ignorant of the practical steps necessary to their realization, and lacking in enough moral sense to stay on the right side of the law.

For the thousands of investors in PPA, however, this side of Cook was obscured by his public celebrity. He was a noted explorer, a man of science, a medical professional—all that should have meant he could be believed when he promised easy money. What his admiring public did not realize was that Frederick A. Cook was always better at building dreams than building incomes, his own included. He came closest to making a fortune when he helped other promoters in the work of fleecing the gullible. In oil, however, as in polar exploration, legitimate success stayed beyond his grasp.

FIVE

The Napoleon of Promotion

N THE ANNALS of oil promotion there are few who ever mastered techniques and devices for raising money more thoroughly than S. E. J. Cox. By any standard, Cox was a virtuoso of the art. The *Financial World* singled him out as its prize "blue sky pilot," and the Federal Trade Commission labeled him "the most seductive and unreliable promoter in America." These dubious accolades were well deserved. In the course of his career, he tried virtually every promotional strategy, and, for the most part, he executed them flawlessly. Yet Cox was so caught up in the techniques of promotion, in creating the appearance of wealth, that he overlooked the reality of business success: accumulating income from operations. A genius at promotional illusion, Cox was an utter failure at coping with business reality. Cox's career is a lesson in how promotional skills taken without business or management acumen lead to financial loss. Cox took in millions of dollars, but he failed to build a fortune. For him, as for his investors, easy money was an illusion, one he himself created with consummate skill.[1]

Seymour Ernest Jacobson Cox was an inveterate promoter. In less than two decades, he created about thirty separate ventures, none of them exactly what they seemed to be. Before World War I he promoted a "miracle" carburetor company in Michigan; peddled bogus virility pills and useless female contraceptives through his Strong Chemical Company; promoted locomotive and engine companies, none of which ever left the station; launched two bucket shops in Manhattan; and organized a wallpaper manufacturing company and the Kangaroo Sales Company of Chicago, Illinois. "Alphabet Cox," as he was commonly known, was no specialist. He was ready to peddle anything that would sell.[2]

In 1916 he turned to securities, and in 1917 he obtained a Delaware charter—used by many promoters as a license to steal—for the Prudential

Securities Company, obviously trading on the name of the famous insurance company. Using Prudential Securities, he exploited the strong demand for mining and oil stocks for part of the year, and then in November he rode the front wave by founding the Prudential Oil and Refining Company in Chicago. After he launched the sales campaign for Prudential Oil, Cox decided to take a closer look at the oil business; he traveled through Oklahoma, Texas, and Louisiana to locate a base of operations closer to the scene of the booming oil business. Near the end of 1917, he moved to Houston and launched three more companies, Louisiana Oil and Gas, Bankers' Underwriting Syndicate, and Ranger-Texas Oil Company. During 1919 he took Prudential Securities public by selling shares in it and floated the General Mines Underwriting Syndicate, the Opportunity Publishing Company, and the General Oil Corporation; the last was a Texas corporation that absorbed Ranger-Texas and Prudential Oil and Refining.[3]

Of all these ventures, General Oil was Cox's first significant success, and he made the most of it. In 1920 he took out a full-page ad in the *Houston City Directory* that touted General as "Oil Producers, Oil Refiners, Marketers, and Shippers of High Grade Petroleum and Its Products." Among its major assets, the company listed producing leases in the Burkburnett, Humble, and West Columbia fields of Texas, an interest in a fabulous gusher in Louisiana, and a producing lease in Eastland County. Cox expanded the company's operations still further by picking up leases for it in Howard and Glasscock counties in western Texas. General looked like a petroleum empire in the making.[4]

Under Cox's direction, General actually drilled for oil and completed four wells in the Red River field, bringing it production of about 1,000 barrels per day. General also developed its west Texas properties by selling leases and drilling wells. Cox began by leasing about 86,000 acres and sold five-acre leases for $50 each, raising about $440,000 in the process. He then went on to drill several wells on the unsold leases, with what he described as astounding success. General's first well, McDowell Number 1, was "unquestionably one of the largest oil wells in the world." By his calculation, its success proved the production potential of at least 40,000 acres and made the holdings of General and the small leaseholders worth at least $100 million.[5]

Cox followed his promotion of General Oil with another giant venture, the Cox Realization Company. Like General, Cox Realization acquired a

Easy Money

refinery, producing properties, and a large block of leases in west Texas, this time in Martin County. Cox also sold portions of these leases to close to 1,500 clients, raising about $220,000 for the company. The original thrust of this promotion was oil, but by midyear of 1921, with oil in recession, it took a new direction, for Cox announced the discovery of a massive deposit of high-grade potash on the Martin County land. Thereafter the company drilled to confirm the claim, and Cox made plans for mining, the construction of a narrow-gauge railroad, and processing facilities.[6]

With this whirlwind of business activity it was hard for most observers to keep up with Cox; the rate at which he created new ventures was dazzling. In Houston, where small oil companies came and went with predictable speed and regularity, Cox's proliferation of ventures set him apart from the pack of small promoters. He emerged as one of the most up-and-coming young men in a town that respected drive and ambition.

Cox was fully aware of the value of his favorable public image, which he carefully constructed. The quick succession of his new ventures and their apparent success gave the impression that Cox was a towering genius, both to his investors and to the Houston business community. He was very much a man on the way up! Cox reinforced this impression by leading a glamorous public life. He and his wife bought a large, comfortable house in the affluent Montrose Addition, drove fast cars, and dressed well. Both were highly photogenic—Seymour, tall with wavy dark hair and an engaging smile, and Nelda, "my little partner," as Seymour was fond of calling her, small, shapely, and with the face of a star of the silver screen. They were the perfect provincial jazz-age couple, young, attractive, adventurous, and affluent.[7]

Nor was Cox content to cut a dashing figure in his new hometown. He frequently flew to airport openings and aviation competitions throughout the West. In 1920, for example, he made a highly publicized flight to Oklahoma City with his dog, "Jack London," and was hailed as "an oil millionaire." More distant travel was also a useful element of his public image, and he always made certain that local newspapers carried word of his business trips to New York City and of his family vacations in Europe. Tom Slick and Josh Cosden had made their grand tours of the Continent, and so did Seymour Cox. Like many another promoter, Cox understood the business value of a high public profile, and he enjoyed celebrity.[8]

The Napoleon of Promotion

Cox's best publicity came to him as an aviator. Both of the Coxes exploited current interest in aviation by engaging in highly publicized races and distance flights. He raced *The Texas Wildcat*, so styled in his own honor, and *The Cactus Kitten*, named for Nelda. Cox even claimed to have broken air speed records, though his accomplishment was unobserved and his claim was never recorded in the official record books. He gained national renown in 1920, when he entered his airship *The Oracle* in the Gordon Bennett air races in France, competing for the Aero Club of Texas. He made a game try for the trophy, and though his airplane malfunctioned and he dropped out of competition, his reputation as a sportsman remained intact and impressive. Not to be outdone, Nelda drew the attention of newsmen by flying Seymour Junior to prep school in the East—in her own airplane. Their aviation feats made both Coxes seem to embody the spirit of youth, daring, and courage. And, of course, the pursuit of aviation as a hobby implied both wealth and success.[9]

If all this were enough for any promoter's aspirations, the Coxes had an additional asset: both of them made friends easily. Seymour's smile, enthusiasm, and self-confidence were infectious. He did not live in Houston long before he attracted the favorable notice of wealthy and important socialites, among them John Henry Kirby, one of the richest and most influential men in Texas. Kirby's fortune was vast even by Houston standards. He controlled banks, lumber operations, the Kirby Petroleum Company, a printing company, a real estate corporation, a brokerage house, and, for that matter, the Republican party of Texas. Cox cultivated Kirby not only for his connections but especially because the aura of respectability that came with their association reinforced public confidence in Cox's ventures. For that reason this friendship was more valuable to Cox than business relationships with most other men in the petroleum industry.[10]

Cox did not stop at becoming prominent in the Houston social whirl. As he continued to expand General Oil and other operations by acquiring producing properties, leases, refineries, and retail outlets, he orchestrated a press campaign to spread the word of his burgeoning empire. He announced that he was going to move from the seven-story office building he then occupied to a twenty-story tower he was planning to build on a prime site in downtown Houston, across from the City Auditorium. He purchased the property for $35,000, evidence of his intentions and pros-

Easy Money

perity. At this juncture, however, legal problems began to slow his mete-oric business growth and dull his glittering public image.

After a brief lull in entrepreneurial activity, he moved to Fort Worth in 1923, organized the Industrial Finance Company, a new securities firm, and launched the Continental Oil and Casing Company, the Amalga-mated Petroleum Company, and the Rodgers Production Company. His meteoric career as an oilman ended with a jail term that began in 1923. After several years in the "Banker's Institute," as Leavenworth Federal Prison was popularly known, Cox's pace slowed, but by the end of the decade he had participated in the founding of the Original Developer's Pool, the Universal Oil and Gas Company, Securities Services Corpora-tion of Kingston, New York, and Securserve Corporation in Manhattan. His middle-age career ended with the creation of the Compañía Minera La Proveedora in the Pachua mining district of Mexico, about sixty miles from Mexico City. This effort was short-lived, and Cox abandoned it when he returned to the United States in October 1932. After World War II he made a brief comeback with another Oklahoma promotion, which folded after less than one year.[11]

In all, then, Seymour Cox launched about thirty separate ventures. Had federal authorities not interfered with his progress, he would certainly have done even more. As the list shows, he came to specialize in oil, securities, and mining activities, but there is some evidence that he also investigated real estate and motion picture promotion in California, as well as real estate in Houston. As diverse as Cox's interests appear to have been, he had one consistent and overriding purpose in all of them—the sale of stock and certificates of interest. From the beginning, his approach was largely financial.[12]

The key to Cox's operations was his network of securities companies: Prudential, S. E. J. Cox Company, Securities Services Corporation, and Securserve Company. He sold shares in the various other ventures largely through these agencies, which he owned until they had played out. At that point, the Prudential and Cox companies went public. In the meantime, he used all of them to rake off large proportions of the paid-in capital. Selling Ranger-Texas and Bankers' Texas Oil Company, for example, paid Prudential 40 percent of the money they took in, plus the costs of sales. Securserve received a modest 5 percent commission, but it was permitted to retain half of the income from stock sales to cover sales expenses. After

The Napoleon of Promotion

the practice of the times, Cox ran a fast-moving skimming operation and thereby deprived his oil companies of at least half of the operating capital paid into them by investors.[13]

Cox also used his position as organizer to increase his return on his ventures. When he established the General Oil Company, for example, he awarded himself 580,000 shares out of a total authorized distribution of 1,100,000 in exchange for one worthless oil lease. His shares were thereafter considered "personal stock," and were sold by his securities company at no charge; the cost was thus born by General's 8,000 paid-in stockholders. When he created Amalgamated, its capitalization was supposedly based on sole ownership of a 1,000-acre oil lease, but Cox actually kept a 50 percent interest in the property. In most of his ventures he elevated overcapitalization to an art form, but he did not stop with that.[14]

Cox's salaries, about $28,000 per year, were drawn on General Oil and the other publicly owned companies; he drew no salary directly from the securities companies until they went public, because he was their sole proprietor, entitled to all of the net income from operations. He routinely charged the expenses of private ventures, including his adventures in aviation, to the public companies. Thus, though Amalgamated Petroleum paid to drill two wells during the early 1920s, it owned only a small interest in one of them and Cox personally held all of the interest in the other. When it came to skimming from and looting his own companies, there were few angles that Cox did not explore to his own advantage.[15]

As Cox's companies followed each other in rapid succession, the assets of one company were carried over to a successor and stock was folded from one venture into the next, in exchange for a conversion fee that ranged from 10 to 25 percent. Some companies were linked because Cox paid dividends to the investors of one company with the stock of another corporation. Thus, when Prudential Securities went public, he paid a 200 percent stock dividend in shares of Prudential Oil to boost sales of Prudential Securities. When he promoted Ranger-Texas, he began with a "contest," awarding $5,000 in Prudential Securities stock to the winners. Thus it was often hard to say where one Cox venture ended and the next began. Similarly, Cox carried stockholders over from one venture to the other. When he launched General Oil, for example, Cox offered Prudential Oil investors one share of General, par value $10, for each $50 that had been paid into Prudential. With this fold-over as with others, many of his investors accepted the conversion and purchased additional shares of the new venture. Some of them followed him for more than a decade. Martin Jachens, a disabled World War I seaman, stayed with Cox through all of his promotions until 1923. By that time Jachens had acquired 8,325 shares of General, Amalgamated, and other issues, par value $1 and up, for $525.[16]

Individuals like this faithful follower enabled Cox to build up a fairly extensive sucker list, which he sold to other promoters and to securities companies. As his ventures multiplied, he purchased lists as well. In 1922, for example, he negotiated with a representative of Carlo Ponzi, the Boston pyramid-scheme artist, for his list. As it turned out, however, Ponzi asked too high a price, and Cox balked at that and at its having been sold to too many other promoters, especially those who worked the New York Curb Exchange.[17]

Cox was particularly fond of the early dividend as a device to stimulate stock sales. When he launched Prudential Oil, for example, he paid a 2 percent cash dividend and announced that it was merely the first of many monthly dividends. At the time, Prudential had no income apart from the sale of stock, but Cox promised that operations would sustain further payments equal to at least 24 percent per year. Though this was the first and last cash dividend from Prudential, he followed it six months later with a 900 percent stock dividend and promised that the cash dividend would be resumed based on the par value of the new issue. As any eager investor could calculate, the new rate of return would be 18 percent per month or—as Cox was quick to point out—216 percent every year![18]

Cox's real genius, however, lay in advertising, and few investors were not swayed by his way with words. One of the ablest pens in the oil fields, he learned rhetorical style from his preacher father, adapted it to sales for printing companies, and applied his developing skill as a manipulator of words in his early promotions. He found suitable models in Chicago, where he came to know Napoleon Hill, one of the most successful advocates of positive thinking in salesmanship. Cox recognized Hill's talent and hired him to write for Prudential Oil and other ventures; Hill also helped Cox polish his own craft.[19]

Cox described the Hill-Cox approach to selling in a number of ways. He told his sales force that they should begin with facts and then put "the sunshine on them." By the time Cox finished with the facts, they were, in his own words, "pretty well decorated." Another promoter described them

The Napoleon of Promotion

as "painted up some." In practice, Cox relied on time-honored techniques: appeals to the greed and naïveté of his readers combined with gross distortions of reality, all conveyed in highly inflated language.[20] When General Oil drilled a noncommercial well, one with only slight shows of oil, Cox described it thus to his investors:

> Fascinated by the oil flowing into the slush pit and by the constantly arriving crowds of people who are arriving to see the McDowell well, I am dictating this letter from a corner of the derrick, and I trust that all who receive it will get some of the spirit and thrill that comes to us who are here watching the development of this, the first well in Texas' greatest oil field. I hope to have five hundred men working on the lease before ninety days more have rolled around. Here is certainly evidence to prove that we have at Big Spring not only the largest oil field in Texas but one of the largest and best oil fields in the world.[21]

Though the well was a financial failure, Cox wrote that it would soon produce "at least 2,000 barrels a day according to the best and most conservative opinion." Winding up his pitch, he claimed "there is no doubt in the world but that the McDowell well will be a gusher with a daily capacity of from 2000 to 5000 barrels, and possibly more." Cox's visions were so optimistic that the production of the soon-abandoned well increased even as he wrote. He concluded by inviting the shareholders in General and the people who bought nearby ten-acre leases for $100 from Cox Realization to a barbecue: "There will be a grand old-time western round-up and barbecue at Garden City, the town nearest the McDowell well to celebrate the bringing in of McDowell No. 1, and I want all of our stockholders and leaseholders possible to be present at that celebration."[22]

Cox's two-day fete was one more example of his borrowing on the time-honored promotional devices but doing them up more grandly than usual. He leased all of the rooms in the Cole Hotel, where he kept the local lady who operated the Big Spring Chamber of Commerce busy for days arranging housing and meals. To bring investors to this remote part of West Texas, he chartered a train from Dallas, the "Houston Oil Special"; some shareholders came from as far as Canada to celebrate "the end of the rainbow." Cox spread oil fever throughout Big Spring, Texas; as one journalist recalled, "He closed his eyes as he proclaimed a vision of miles upon miles of derricks." Cox created so much excitement about his project that local citizens even raised $8,000 to pay for the celebration.[23]

When the celebration began on August 7, 1920, Cox introduced his heavy caliber orator for the day, former U.S. senator Joseph Weldon Bailey, who had hired out for the occasion. Bailey's florid oration was followed by the much advertised free barbecue. In the afternoon Cox provided a rodeo, horse races, an auto exhibition, and aero demonstrations. The day ended with a dance under the stars, with music provided by a band from Houston.[24]

The hard sell came on Sunday. Cox led a motorcade from town to the well site. Then that pied piper of promotion staged a brief flow of oil by swabbing the well to make oil run into the tanks. Spectators, kept at a distance, were told that the well was flowing freely and that it had proved up to 40,000 acres of leases held by Cox in the area. That single well would produce from 2,000 to 10,000 barrels of oil per day when it was completed, and it would be followed by "a line of derricks seventy-five miles long." Cox would make Big Spring a thriving metropolis, and all of his investors would join the exalted ranks of rich oilmen.[25]

Cox used the two-day celebration to peddle more leases at $10 per acre both to those present and those far away. He sent enthusiastic telegrams to his copywriters in Houston, giving them what they would pass on to investors. The McDowell lease would produce 1,000 barrels a day. "Its potential is 22,000 to 30,000 barrels of oil per day! The McDowell well is absolutely the biggest thing this country has ever known. We have here one of the largest oil fields in the world." His newsletter proclaimed: "McDowell Well Worth $100,000,000!"[26]

Cox, of course, did not limit his rhetorical talent to oil. Six months later, when the price of crude oil declined, he turned his promotional energy to potash and alerted his investors to "the discovery of the greatest potash bed in West Texas where we have many thousands of acres of mineral leases which gives our stock a value that can hardly be calculated as the finding of potash is probably THE MOST IMPORTANT MINERAL DISCOVERY IN AMERICA SINCE COLONEL DRAKE DEVELOPED HIS FIRST OIL WELL IN PENNSYLVANIA."[27]

Cox said he found a potash bed 1,300 feet deep on land leased in Martin County, west of Big Spring. America would be the better for it: "There are no potash beds of any dimensions in the United States at the present

The Napoleon of Promotion

time. The whole nation depends upon Germany and Peru for its principal supply and it is very important the Government should have a large supply of potash to supply the Army and Navy with materials necessary for the protection of our citizens." As Cox put it, potash had a strategic value that surpassed petroleum. For their investments Cox's patriotic investors would be rewarded with a return of "something like 3,000% per annum in dividends." Seymour Cox was just as adept at putting the sunshine on potash as he was at decorating oil investments.[28]

Cox was equally successful at coloring the facts for other promoters. Butler Perryman, the self-described failed pig farmer who organized the Blue Bird Oil Company with H. H. Hoffman and others, paid him nearly $40,000 for two months' work as a pen, and he was not overpaid. As Perryman recognized, the facts concerning Blue Bird were in urgent need of painting and decorating because Blue Bird's initial capitalization rested on the assets of about a dozen failed companies. Their unfortunate stockholders were offered an opportunity to recoup losses by turning in their shares in exchange for shares in Perryman's Blue Bird venture. The scheme, an example of the "reload" technique, required that the shareholders pay a 50 percent fee, based on the par value of the stock they turned in, to receive shares of equivalent value in Blue Bird. Perhaps the cost discouraged potential investors. For whatever reason, investor response was slow, and Perryman hired Cox to coax investors along: "Can it be that they do not understand that I am trying to do something for them? Is it because they are quitters? DO THEY LACK THE MORAL COURAGE AND STAMINA TO BACK UP THEIR OWN JUDGMENT?"[29]

As Cox hammered home, it was no time to quit! There was a gusher on a company lease at Goose Creek that would permit the paying of a large dividend, 300–400 percent, in the near future. Blue Bird's lease would be worth $3 million when it was fully developed and Blue Bird could then sell it and declare a 2,500 percent cash dividend. Blue Bird was on its way to becoming one of the largest and strongest oil companies in Texas! No investor could pass up a chance like that.[30]

In this promotion, Cox drew on one of his favorite themes: the mantle of righteousness. The device of promoting one's own venture by charging that those run by others were dishonest swindles was not new, but Cox took it to more splendid lengths than most promoters could have dared. In one Blue Bird circular he described "The meanest man in the world:

Easy Money

He robs the investing public not only of their cash, not only of the money which they might use themselves to build a competence for their old age, but robs them of a vastly more important thing—he robs them of civilization's greatest asset, he robs them of a belief in human nature and their fellow man."[31]

The copy was familiar: Cox had used it one year earlier when he wrote to his own stockholders. But the earlier material served him as well as ever in writing for Perryman. In one long, rambling letter, he had Perryman wax moralistic on the theme of swindlers:

> Most of these men are looking for a chance to get rich quickly on the promotion—an opportunity to make a great deal of money from the investments of those who placed confidence in them and trusted them with their hard-earned cash. And this, according to my idea is the lowest form of business brigandage and legal highway robbery that exists.
>
> The man who would take your money to develop a big idea—his idea—and then put that money in his pocket, or a large portion of it, instead of using it for the development of the proposition in which you were buying stock, is my idea of the meanest man in the world.

No wonder Cox could wax eloquent; as he knew, he was writing about his employers and himself.[32]

Like Perryman, Dr. Frederick Cook recognized Cox's genius as a pen, hiring him in 1923 for $2,000 per week and a commission on sales. Again, Cox was worth it. He affected a folksy style to appeal to pensioners:

> Say old timer—are you one of the crowd that jumped in ankle deep—head first—on this Smackover Petroleum deal with me? If so—congratulations—or do you still belong to the army of skeptics who skulk the alleys of small effect—who cringe at the sneer of the warning friend—who live in the judgment of free advice—and learn through the school of bitter experience—only after it is too late? If so, tear off the shackles! Drain the last dregs of the bitter cup of defeat and resolve now to bring yourself and your loved ones, the happiness, pleasures, and luxuries of which you have so long dreamed.[33]

This was psychological manipulation at its promotional best, a technique at which Cox displayed particular artistry. In effect, Cox preyed on the investors' secret fears and lack of self-confidence. He insinuated that the investors were cowards and shirkers, gutless creatures who were poor because they would not take daring action, doomed failures because they cared too much about what others thought of them to stand on their own feet. These were jibes that were likely to hit home, for the people in search of easy money all too often had not succeeded in making fortunes on their own. And Cox implied that timorous investors did more than simply condemn themselves to failure: they were also denying their loved ones the good things in life that they all deserved. In short, they were contemptible to themselves and to those around them.

To these failures, Cox offered economic salvation, an evangelistic business appeal comparable to the spiritual uplift offered by Billy Sunday. All the investors had to do was have faith and reach for their checkbooks. And to make this conversion more tempting, Cox offered the usual bait of a big, quick dividend, 100 percent and more to follow: "I aim to pay 2,000 percent or even more before I am through, and the longer you put off joining me the more apt you are in the next few days to think and regret because of what you might have done." The source of these regal dividends was "Four Ceaselessly Flowing Gushers pouring forth their liquid wealth at the rate of approximately 40,000 barrels of oil each day." Reaching a new height in cynicism, Cox urged his correspondents to "strain your borrowing capacity to the very limit," to borrow money to buy interests in Cook's Smackover Syndicate![34]

Cox knew that the investors in the Smackover Syndicate had invested in previous promotions because Cook obtained their names from sucker lists. He could be reasonably sure that they had lost their stakes, and he put this knowledge to effective use in masterful manipulation of investor psychology: "If some security you have invested in fell by the wayside, then it is more the reason why you should invest in one that has stood, and now is able to endure the acid test, for it is now you may recover your losses, and bring yourself pleasures and luxuries you have not yet enjoyed."[35]

From Cook's offices, Cox wrote letters and brochures for Smackover, PPA, the El Dorado Oil Trust, Revere Oil, the Trapshooter Development Company, and Vitek Oil and Refining. Paul Vitek, according to Cox, "is living up to his promise to stockholders in carrying out his drilling plans, and etc., and it is only a question of time until we feel that Vitek will be leading the entire field in oil production." Cox reached his pinnacle of

Easy Money

optimism while he wrote for Cook's tip sheet, *The Oil Tribune*, which continued to carry his copy months after he had left Cook's payroll. Only Napoleon Hill could have done better at inflating the facts with positive thinking, for Cox told tip sheet readers: "DAY BY DAY, IN EVERY WAY, THE OIL INDUSTRY IS GETTING BETTER AND BETTER."[36]

Hope for riches, of course, was Cox's favorite theme, and he returned to it again and again: "It takes faith and enthusiasm and confidence in oneself to win any of the battles of life and if you haven't confidence in yourself, you might as well go around to the old down-and-out club and rap on the door and ask for admittance because sure enough, that is where you are going sooner or later." In other words, failure to invest revealed self-doubt, not prudence.[37]

Cox's most splendid prose efforts came with his final oil promotion, Universal Oil and Gas, an integrated company based in Oklahoma. He drew on his full quiver of cliches and come-ons for Universal. Letters to potential investors featured headings such as: "CAN YOU QUALIFY TO BE A MILLIONAIRE?; WHY INVESTORS LOSE IN OIL; YOUR INVESTMENT PROBLEM SOLVED; THE KEY TO WEALTH; ARE YOU SUCCESS TIMBER?" The first mailing urged recipients to read "Why Investors Lose in Oil," which was ghostwritten by Cox; it explained that this advice "was not dashed off in an hour; it was not the result of an afternoon's idle writing, but rather the result of years of study and many months of careful analysis." The prose had indeed worn well: Cox originally wrote the booklet in 1921 for another promotion.[38]

In the Universal Oil promotion, Cox's appeal was once again a potent mixture of his own brand of psychological manipulation and the sort of "scientific" analysis offered by Napoleon Hill. Thus, Cox wrote, "wealth may be and often is obtained by accident; that much must be granted. But the broadest road to wealth you may travel only if you are willing to devote the time necessary to develop the qualifications required to follow this road. The road to wealth is defined by scientific analysis." Then, as he so often did, Cox preyed on his prospects' self-doubt: "If you would attain great success, this is the question you must meet and answer in every detail of life's work. Are you able to qualify for the duties which unusual success in any direction demands of you? If you would be a pharmacist, an automobile speed-king, or an aeronaut you must qualify." Presumably, the test of qualification would be money in the mail to Universal.[39]

The Napoleon of Promotion

To promote Universal, Cox also fell back on the timeworn promotional device of celebrity endorsement. Hitherto he used his own fame as a draw to investors, but by the time of the Universal promotion, he had spent some years in prison; he was more infamous than celebrated. That led him to assemble a famous, if not notably competent, roster of backers, as front office men for Universal. Jack Walton, a former governor of Oklahoma, headed the list. Though he had been impeached, few investors in the East and Middle West were aware of that, and Walton played his role well. He showed visiting investors around the oil fields and recruited additional window dressing. Walton's best catch was the Reverend Henry Knight Miller, an erstwhile Methodist clergyman from Brooklyn and publisher of *Psychology* magazine, who came to inspect Universal's properties. Walton, Cox, and others gave him a "potemkin tour" of wells and refineries in central Oklahoma. Delighted with the tour and his clever new friends, Miller returned to New York to tour the Manhattan financial district with Cox, whom he introduced as Mr. White, and tout Universal. Miller's greatest service, however, was his recruitment of Universal's most useful front man, former New York City police commissioner Richard Enright. Enright, Miller's old political ally, was a most useful name to have associated with the company. Cox used it when he mailed out "Your Last Opportunity" over Enright's signature.[40]

Cox built handsome rewards for the celebrities into the Universal scheme. Walton received 300,000 syndicate units while Miller and Enright each received 30,000 units. Each unit was convertible to five common shares at $10 par. If they succeeded in selling all of their shares, the governor would have grossed $15 million and his confederates $1.5 million each. That would have made him the most expensive window dressing in the history of American promotion; as ever, Cox worked on a grand scale.[41]

With the early dividends he sent to investors in Universal Oil, Cox also brought the promotional device of the free handout into play. Two weeks before Christmas 1929, Universal sent $20 checks to the people on its sucker list. The accompanying letter asked: "Will you accept $20 as a Christmas gift from us?" Of course, there was a hook in the worm: the checks were redeemable only as partial payment toward $100 in syndicate units. Still, it looked like something for nothing, if one assumed Universal's units had a value.[42]

Behind the scenes, Cox made Universal look important and profitable.

Easy Money

By the end of 1929, it claimed production income of $20,500 per month. If one believed the company's balance sheets, assets outweighed liabilities by $1,110,401.27. Universal displayed an impressive spread of leases, including 1,800 acres in Texas with two flowing wells on them. One of the wells, Quincy Corbet Number 1, was described as a discovery well worth $5 million to $50 million. A photo of this great producer gushing was used often. The vigorous company expanded to purchase an 800-barrel-per-day lease in "the Saltdome District" of the Texas Gulf Coast. It even diversified by acquiring 56,000 acres of royalty interests, and it purchased 8,000 acres of land in fee in Hudspeth and Williamson counties in Texas. Its largest single asset was its Oklahoma refinery, valued at $435,000. In all, this was an impressive array of properties, which former police commissioner Enright assured investors that he had spent two weeks inspecting. With the lawman's emphatic guarantee of the extent of Universal's assets, investors bought syndicate units during the uncertain times of late 1929 and early 1930; their confidence in Enright, Walton, and Miller permitted Cox to sell 150,000 units at $10, less the 52 percent commissions paid to his brokerage operations. Notwithstanding the ruin of Wall Street speculation, Cox carried on.[43]

As was usual with Seymour Cox, nothing about Universal was as it seemed, and that was especially true of the company's assets. The Oklahoma refinery was obsolete and inoperative; 1,500 acres of the company's leases consisted of virtually worthless leases in Stephens County; Universal never held as much as an option on any salt dome properties; the gusher photo, actually of a Cox dry hole of 1922, had of course been doctored to add the gushing oil. Total income from Universal's oil production was only $6,742.20 from April 1929 to April 1930. Universal, like Cox's earlier ventures, was no more than a stock-selling scheme, but it was his most spectacular effort.[44]

Yet with all this energy, Seymour Cox no more succeeded in building a fortune than his investors. It is clear that he was highly skilled at selling securities; his commissions on sales in his own companies probably exceeded $750,000. Earnings as a pen might well have earned him enough additional income to bring his gross income to at least $1 million by 1932. But by that time his family was reduced to living out of one rented room in the Fort Worth YWCA, and his wife made their living by selling books. In terms of long-run success, most of his companies fared no better than

The Napoleon of Promotion

Cox did. Only General Oil proved to be viable after it was taken over by trustees; it was out of debt by 1928, a major accomplishment in view of Cox's early management of it. Cox's other ventures went nowhere.

In practical terms, it is not difficult to understand the failure of Cox's companies. Overcapitalization made it unlikely that they would ever make a reasonable return on invested capital. Cox's subsequent skimming and looting of the companies made survival impossible. In fact, his practice of folding one failure into another creation required that successive ventures fail.

But why didn't Seymour Cox get rich quick? Why couldn't he make money by stealing it? Cox's personal failure is more problematic. In part it is explained by his failure as a manager, a trait he shared with the promoters of Big Diamond, Lubbock-Bridgeport, and hundreds of other ventures. Cox's companies rarely kept reliable records of expenses and income. The most carefully operated, General Oil, even lacked an accurate list of stockholders. This deficiency, with Cox as with other promoters, was largely the result of an ad hoc approach to the conduct of business; there were rarely plans, budgets, and balances. The problems of the day were met with the insights and resources of the day. There was flexibility, but at the expense of control.

For the fraudulent promoters who raised funds quickly, folded their ventures, and disappeared, such a disorganized approach was workable because there were few major expenditures beyond the initial expenses of promotion. Everything gathered in thereafter was reasonably taken to be net income. If such promoters actually purchased properties as window dressing, the properties could be sold if they were of value or simply abandoned because the promoters never anticipated operating income from them. Fast-moving operators could walk away from each separate promotion with easy money.

This avenue to personal wealth was closed to Seymour Cox because he pursued the roll-over strategy. One venture flowed into another, and investors were carried along over an extended series of separate ventures. Junk properties merely accumulated without producing operating capital for Cox's growing paper empire. His companies, already under-funded because of his deep skimming operations, incurred considerable operating expenses, and even Cox was obliged to cover some of them. He put off some costs on suppliers of goods and services; contractors waited for payment and in several instances were never paid. But Cox had to find real money to pay for the four wells his various companies actually drilled; he also had to pay the post office, his landlords, the utility companies, and his growing office staff. After the cash ran out, as it typically did early in every promotion, Cox had no choice but to cover daily expenses from his own resources. In only one instance did he actually borrow funds to cover a cost, the payment of a bogus dividend, necessitated by a flagging promotion. In the end, Cox dissipated much of his gain, realized at the expense of his investors, to keep his pyramided empire alive. That meant that, in essence, he promoted himself, but so gradually and over so lengthy a period that he seems to have been ignorant of the fact.

Like many other promoters, Cox paid little attention to the costs and values of the properties he acquired, perhaps because he assumed that they were virtually worthless, perhaps because he assumed he would make profits so great that costs did not matter. The logic was the same in all instances: though valueless in reality, acquisitions could be touted on paper as significant assets, to move more shares on which a handsome commission was paid to Cox. He quickly learned, however, that at the height of an oil boom even negligible properties were expensive. Thus he paid $40,000 for a small lease in the Red River, the disputed border between Texas and Oklahoma. At the time of purchase, income from the lease was minor and it was tied up in escrow pending settlement of the states' boundary dispute. The story was much the same with Cox's Eastland County lease: production declined rapidly, and General Oil never received much more than 5 percent of the purchase price in revenue from the sale of crude oil. Similarly, Cox paid several times the market value for a Wichita Falls refinery because it was immediately useful in supporting his claim to having built an integrated petroleum operation, from derrick to gas pump. In Houston he signed an expensive contract with Columbia Oil for the purchase of a chain of forty to fifty ramshackle gas stations for the same reason. With his focus on selling shares, income from actual operations—producing and selling oil—did not enter into his planning.[45]

Cox compounded his strategic errors by leveraging the purchases of his show properties with relatively large down payments. His purchase of the prime downtown lot in Houston required $7,000 initially and six additional payments in the same amount. His purchase of gas stations from Columbia Oil cost $100,000, one-tenth of it up-front, and his leases for three more sites set him back $95,000, one-third of it paid at the time of the signing. When he purchased an obsolete and inactive refinery near Houston, it set him back $52,000, with $5,000 down and the balance covered by 8 percent notes. In all, from these purchases alone, over a three-year period Cox laid out $55,000 for properties that produced no income.[46]

It is likely that Cox never calculated this cost, because he saw his purchases as stage props for specific promotions. They had no larger purpose, and it is unlikely that Cox ever saw them in the context of a long-range business plan, because he had none. His strategy was to create a succession of ventures, skim them initially, fill them with useless assets, let them fail, and then fold the ventures and the stockholders into new ventures.

The logic of the strategy, of course, broke down when Cox lost his bearings and began to fancy himself an oilman, cut from the same cloth as Tom Slick and Josh Cosden. That happened in 1920, with the false hope of the McDowell well and significant new discoveries in the Red River area, near General's properties. These developments led Cox to think that he might actually make a go of conventional business. In any event, Cox decided to operate General's properties to sustain his ventures, forgetting that, apart from the Red River lease, they were nearly worthless. He put more of his own money into the Wichita Falls refinery, though it was still incapable of operating at more than 10 percent of its rated capacity. Even after he reopened it on this reduced basis, Cox could not keep it running because his company fell behind on pipeline payments and lost its supply of crude oil. His solution required more money: he signed a contract for tank cars, another notable addition to the empire, but the tank car salesman pocketed his down payment and died. Cox never recovered the money from the estate. When it looked as if his companies might actually produce and refine oil, Cox decided to retain the Columbia Oil gasoline stations and paid an additional $60,000 toward the purchase. The paper empire was being transformed into an operating company at a high cost to Cox personally. Cox had begun to believe the illusions he had peddled to tens of thousands of investors. In the end, he conned himself.[47]

Like so many grand schemers, Cox had neither instinct nor training in efficient management. He shared this fault with reputable businessmen in oil and other industries, especially during boom times. In common with other oilmen, he found it difficult to find competent workers, and the ones he did find made expensive mistakes. His land man was a former barber and his field superintendent was an erstwhile shoe salesman; neither knew much about oil until he went to work for Cox. The field superintendent ran up vast expenses in connection with the Big Spring promotion and then seems to have misled Cox into expecting a big discovery well where only a theatrical display had been planned. Cox's heightened expectations led him to approve costs that far exceeded his resources.[48]

It also seems to have escaped Cox that his flashy life-style was another high cost of doing business. Expensive cars, fashionable clothes, foreign vacations, and airplanes ate up the proceeds of his theft from stockholders at a rapid rate. When he finally recognized the high cost of air racing, he tried to charge it off to General Oil, a move that brought several Houston stockholders to force the company into receivership, out of Cox's hands.[49]

Allowing for some expensive mistakes, by 1930 Cox should still have had several hundred thousand dollars left from the estimated million dollars he received from his numerous promotions. He did not, because of another cost he failed to calculate: the unavoidable high legal costs of doing business in his style. Stockholders, especially those of General, tied him up in costly legal wrangles. When he lost control of General, he had to pay his own legal expenses. Even more important, Cox's habitual recourse to fraudulent practices led to five separate criminal fraud cases in federal courts. By 1930, when the last trial was over, Cox had only enough money to flee to Mexico and launch a new promotion. When it failed, he had no choice but to return to the United States and serve out a sentence for mail fraud. At that point, he seems to have been flat broke. By the time his career ended, he had raised $2 million, stolen half of it, and lost the lot. That "Lucky Cox" could make easy money had always been an illusion, but, like thousands of the investors he short-changed, he spent years pursuing it.

Promotion on Trial

THOUGH SUCKER lists contained names of people who lost their money time and again in get-rich-quick schemes, not everyone who failed to land on Easy Street took losses stoically. Skillful promoters usually tried to pacify investors who "squawked" with hasty reassurances, extra personal attention, and, occasionally, refunds of money. But sometimes these efforts did not head off further complaints, and irate investors looked to the law for vengeance. Particularly as the great speculative boom of the twenties continued and a growing number of investors believed they had been bilked, there was mounting pressure on law enforcement authorities to crack down on fraud artists. That pressure led to several well-publicized cleanup campaigns, some showy prosecutions, and some short prison sentences, but it produced few barriers to promotion, honest or otherwise. Overall, the ability of federal or state authorities to put dishonest promoters out of business was almost as much an illusion as the quick riches investors hoped for. No one could keep the gullible from chasing rainbows.

When aggrieved investors looked for sympathy, they found it in a variety of quarters. Local bankers, for example, did not wish to see savings flow out of their institutions into the pockets of promoters in Chicago, Denver, or Fort Worth, and they were happy to join the hue and cry against mail-order fraud. Journalists saw the antipromotional cause as excellent copy; thus, after only a year of feverish oil speculation, the *World's Work* ran its "Pirates of Promotion" series on oil and other promoters, and there were similar exposés in *Scribner's Magazine, Current Opinion,* and the *New York Times.* The Associated Advertising Clubs of the World joined the campaign in 1921, largely in the interest of protecting the shaky reputation of their craft and avoiding restrictive legislation. The clubs gathered data and stirred up public interest through their National

Easy Money

Vigilance Committee, which worked with local and regional subcommittees across the country.[1]

In the face of mounting complaints, federal prosecutors began desultory action against fraudulent oil promoters. In midyear 1919, as oil speculation grew ever more hectic, a federal grand jury indicted the promoters of two companies, the Panuco and Gulf Oil Company and the Black Diamond Oil Company. The former was the creation of two Manhattan promoters who sold $855,000 worth of stock and turned over a bare $45,000 to the Texas operations of the venture. The latter opened offices in New York and Chicago and made a strong appeal to women investors. Among other assets, the company claimed to own Padre Island off the Texas coast. General public ignorance of geography made this believable; the *New York Times* described the property as "an islet of approximately 120 feet by 40 feet in the Gulf of Mexico."[2]

During the following year, federal attorneys in Kentucky and Texas investigated ninety oil companies and ten brokerage houses, but only four cases were tried. In the oil-producing states there was remarkably little legal action. In Houston, for example, federal prosecutors tried only twelve cases of mail fraud from 1917 through 1922. Dallas rarely had more than half a dozen cases per year; federal law officers there much preferred to try violations of the Mann and Volstead acts. Still, public demand for action grew, and by mid-1922 federal authorities had increasing reason to find a way to make a public demonstration of energetic enforcement of fraud statutes as they applied to oilmen.[3]

In large part, the Justice Department sought opportunities to demonstrate its effectiveness in the face of growing scandals in the administration of President Warren G. Harding. In 1922 a sensational story of high-level corruption in the Veterans Bureau rocked Washington and touched the Justice Department, which was widely accused of deliberate inaction. On the heels of it came growing congressional pressure for an investigation of the noncompetitive leasing of the Naval Oil Reserve in California and of federal lands at Teapot Dome in Wyoming. Secretary of the Interior Albert B. Fall resigned under fire on March 4, 1923, and appeared as the leadoff witness in the congressional investigation of Teapot Dome on October 24, 1923. In this case, as in the Veterans Bureau scandal, the Justice Department was accused of discouraging inquiries, if not of actually covering up wrongdoing. Clearly the department had immediate need of a diversion

Promotion on Trial

from the Washington scandals; it needed to demonstrate its probity and efficiency in the most conspicuous way, in court.[4]

Doing so required a target with a reasonably high public profile, and for that role, S. E. J. Cox was eminently qualified. Apart from Cox's own public posturing, the *Financial World*, an industrial and municipal bond tip sheet published in New York, had spotlighted Seymour Cox's activities for several years. In 1917 it advised that "the prudent investor will keep away from this Prudential overnight producer of wealth," and ridiculed his claim to have located a Texas hermit "whose knowledge of geology and mineralogy was so accurate as to make it certain his company had discovered a great lake of oil." Two years later it exposed the come-on used by Cox's short-lived Ranger-Texas Oil Company: "He writes to his prospective dupe the blithesome tidings that the recipient of the letter has been selected as the leading citizen of the community to participate with him in the large profits sure to come from this enterprise." When Cox announced that prizes totaling $5,000 (in Prudential Securities Company stock) would be awarded to Prudential Oil stockholders, the *Financial World* protested, "It is a crying shame that this financial mountebank is permitted to so openly work the public." The journal kept up a steady barrage against Cox, making him well known among its readers as a bunco artist.[5]

Through these articles and from complaints from Cox's investors, his promotions came to the attention of the Federal Trade Commission in midyear 1919. In September the agency issued a formal complaint, the first step in the administrative process, against him. Cox was not cowed by the distant paper tiger. His immediate response was "Tell the Commission and the people at Washington, God damn them, to go to hell!" Six weeks later Cox's attorney responded more temperately, and the case dragged along, causing no sensation in Houston and bringing no interruption in Cox's fund-raising. After a delay of close to a year and a half, the FTC held hearings in Houston, but the agency's cease and desist order did not receive judicial confirmation until June 1923. By that time, "Lucky Cox," as he had persuaded local journalists to call him, had gotten deeper into trouble.[6]

While Cox was in France for the Gordon Bennett Air Races, dissident stockholders of his General Oil Company convinced Texas District Judge J. D. Harvey to place the company under the direction of trustees because of "mismanagement." The judge also accepted the sizable claims of Chi-

Easy Money

cago lenders and other unpaid creditors; he approved the financial charges against Cox prepared by a stockholders' committee.[7]

Certainly this was an unforeseen setback, but it did not stop Cox from promoting Cox Realization and potash leases. With these developments, however, Cox entered a period of chronic legal troubles. Instead of thanking Cox for finding the potash that would guarantee American security, an ungrateful federal government indicted him for mail fraud on the ground that the whole Cox Realization promotion was dishonest. The government had learned that Cox's driller said that there was no potash, that Cox's refinery was inoperative and had never worked, and that Cox's meager oil production came nowhere near amounting to what he said it did. Investigators also found that Cox never owned the various properties in Arkansas and Louisiana that he had advertised as company assets.[8]

As legal clouds gathered, Cox refused to run for cover. Even while federal investigators amassed evidence against him, Cox continued to promote his ventures. With postal inspectors scrutinizing his mail-order business, he turned again to securities brokers to peddle his issues, and in March 1922 he rode the train to New York to find vendors who operated on the curb exchange. As usual, in Manhattan he cut a grand figure, but he nonetheless found few allies because the word was out on the street—the law was after Lucky Cox. It caught up with him in the theater district of Manhattan in mid-March, but he managed to garner publicity by turning his arrest into a humorous occasion, pulling the legs of the New York reporters who covered the event. He called their attention to his elegant leather puttees, which he insisted "all prominent businessmen in Houston affected." In Houston, however, his arrest was front-page news and no laughing matter. The *Houston Chronicle* called attention to Cox's large following: "Placards with Cox's philosophy and his photograph adorn thousands of homes in the United States and many Houston offices."[9]

Cox waived extradition hearings, and after two nights in the Tombs, he was escorted to Houston by a deputy United States marshal. The charges against him were formidable: the indictment, a fifty-four-page document, alleged fourteen separate counts of fraud in the sale of $41 million of securities. In the face of it, Cox never lost his confident air. He told Houston reporters, "I am not worried in the least. I have violated no law." No doubt some of his self-assurance was based on his understanding of the political realities of the situation: however massive the government's evidence, its victory depended on effective prosecution. The postal inspectors and examiners for the FTC might gather evidence by the carload, but Cox's friends weighed more heavily in the balance of justice in Houston.[10] His greatest political asset was the support of John Henry Kirby, who along with J. W. Gillespie signed as surety for Cox's $25,000 bond. Kirby also enlisted the aid of H. F. McGregor, Republican National Committeeman for Texas and patronage referee for Justice Department positions in Texas. Thus, as it happened, the United States attorney for the Southern District of Texas, who owed his appointment to McGregor, placed the Cox prosecution in the hands of an inexperienced young assistant. When the trial finally got under way, the diligent but inept young man effectively buried the government's case with an avalanche of undigested evidence. Hour after hour, he plodded through his task, reading highly repetitive examples of Cox's prose to an increasingly restless jury. He called scores of witnesses, including former employees and associates of Cox, to the witness stand, where they supported the government's case in elaborate detail. In all, the government called forty-one witnesses who supported the charges against Cox and identified the tall stacks of exhibits as literature that Cox had written and mailed.[11]

Through it all, Cox did not seem the least perturbed. He was "immaculately attired," responsive, and animated. He exuded energy and, above all, confidence. He even laughed when the assistant district attorney questioned E. A. Trombley of Flint, Michigan: "Would you sell your [potash] leases for $5,000?" "I'd sell them for a good cigar!" Cox was amused when Judge Joseph Hutcheson asked one of his potash investors: "Do you know anything about potash?" "No, sir." "What made you invest in something you knew nothing about?" "Well, I just thought that I might make money easier than by farming." Cox remained unruffled when L. B. House, his "noted geologist," admitted that he was really a barber, but that he had "once read a book about geology." To judge from Cox's reactions, the proceedings were a pointless farce.[12]

In effect, Cox promoted another audience. On the final day of the trial, the crowd in attendance was conspicuously friendly to him. It murmured approval when his attorney compared him to "old man Lucas," the discoverer of the Spindletop field, and to Henry Ford. Cox's lawyer depicted him as "an optimist by nature," and reminded jurors of the great contribution made to America by men like Cox: "The world owes its progress to the adventurous spirits who took a chance and not to the misers who hoarded their gold." Most of those present were thus in a frame of mind sympathetic to Cox when Judge Hutcheson presented a conventional summary of statutes covering fraud.[13]

The statute Cox was accused of violating was one allowing considerable latitude of interpretation. As Hutcheson explained, the accused

> might have had a belief that these companies would sometime and somehow in the providence of God or in the passage of time come to complete fruition, yet if in bringing that about he made false statements, the law denounces the act as an offense and it is not affected by the general ultimate purpose or hope of success. On the other hand, if he made no false statements or if he made none knowingly and if he had a belief in the statements that he made, in the organizations that he set on foot, in the practices that he adopted and authorized, the fact that they in the course of time collapsed and his hopes turned to ashes, would not justify a conviction.

After twenty-four hours, the jury had not reached a verdict. One day later, they acquitted Cox.[14]

Cox made the occasion a public relations event: "Too happy for words when the verdict was announced, Cox shook hands with his lawyers, joyously kissed his wife and then thanked the jurors profusely, shaking his [*sic*] hand." He even had a quotable comment ready for the occasion: "With malice toward none, I am going to hit the line hard and build up my companies." Covered with the verbal mantle of Abraham Lincoln, Lucky Cox was promoting as he left the courtroom. For his part, the young prosecutor tried to put a good face on loss. He insisted that after the expenditure of $50,000 on the trial, "We could have done nothing more." Perhaps Cox's investors, the government's witnesses, and others who read this defense believed him, but even before the verdict was in, a reporter for the *Houston Chronicle* discovered that the prosecutor had knowingly permitted a fishing buddy of Cox's and several of his fellow lodge members to be impaneled. Judge Hutcheson, intelligent, sober, and widely respected, was furious; the crusading journalists raised the charge of mismanagement against the government, and the Post Office Department and Federal Trade Commission decided not to let Cox off with his acquittal. After their embarrassing defeat in Houston and a growing number of allegations about corruption in the Department of the Interior, the Harding administration was highly motivated to show better results in the campaign against fraud in the oil fields.[15]

Promotion on Trial

In response, the Post Office Department dispatched several veteran investigators to Fort Worth in August 1922 to work up evidence for other prosecutions. Reinforcements arrived during September. In October representatives of the National Vigilance Committee and Federal Trade Commission investigators joined postal inspectors in their scrutinizing of more than one hundred concerns. By the end of the year, the federal government had leased a large suite of offices, expanding to more than one full floor during the early months of 1923. It was clear by the end of March that Fort Worth was to be the scene of a spectacular judicial display.[16]

The local federal attorney, Henry Zweifel, took the results of government investigations to the federal grand jury in April. After deliberating one week, it returned indictments against ninety-two people and fourteen separate companies, among them Seymour Cox, Dr. Frederick A. Cook, and both a former Tarrant County attorney and a former sheriff. Even the Republican nominee for the postmastership of Fort Worth was on the list, though the charge against him was later dismissed. Managers of the various merger schemes at PPA, Pilgrim Oil, and Revere Oil were pursued with considerable zeal because national media had already focused on their activities. These cases were followed by more than one hundred others, all of them adding up to what gave every appearance of being a major crackdown, perhaps even a clean sweep.[17]

Before the cases went to trial, federal officials exploited the press coverage for all it was worth. Prosecutor Zweifel led the way, claiming that the stock sold by the indicted parties totaled $200 million and that 2,064,000 individuals had been victimized. Postmaster General Harry New presented somewhat lower claims—$100 million in stock sold to 500,000 investors. Both these estimates assumed that promoters actually sold most of the shares or units in their organizations, an objective seldom realized. The point, nonetheless, was the same—that the government was acting decisively to stamp out fraud. Investors were protected, and the reputation of the advertising industry had been saved. It was even safe for Americans to invest in oil again: Henry Zweifel claimed that he had closed down "approximately 85 percent of the worthless oil companies . . . and we are fast after the remaining 15 percent." Oil's Augean stables would be spotless by the time he was done.[18]

In reality, the clean-up was not as thorough as federal authorities indicated it would be, for they did not have the manpower or time to pursue every shady promoter. In the interests of economy and drama, federal strategy concentrated on the most spectacular cases; the more obscure promoters, therefore, were permitted to bargain guilty pleas for light fines, or the cases against them were simply dismissed. The local federal judge, James C. Wilson, known to be sympathetic to entrepreneurs of most stripes, was willing to accommodate Zweifel with bargains and dismissals.

Having narrowed objectives, the second element of the federal strategy dealt with Judge Wilson's attitude; with a large investment in the Fort Worth investigations, federal prosecutors could not risk having Wilson on the bench for the key trials. Accordingly, Henry Zweifel's assistants worked up enough additional indictments to flood the court's docket, thus creating an obvious overload for the kindly judge. In Washington, Chief Justice William Howard Taft obligingly assigned additional judges to hear the Fort Worth oil fraud cases. In all instances, the outsiders had some previous experience with oil fraud prosecutions and were known to be hard on convicted offenders.[19]

The third element of the government's strategy lay in singling out those most vulnerable to local prejudice from the crowd of promoters indicted and trying these scapegoats before the remaining sheep. Federal prosecutors scanned the list for newcomers who had few local connections. They looked for people whose operations were more flagrant than those of the majority. And, in a town where the Ku Klux Klan had a large following, they were especially interested in those whose religious or ethnic backgrounds were likely to make them victims of bigotry. The Jewish promoters of General Lee, Charles Sherwin and Harry Schwarz, filled all these requirements. They were the first stars of the Fort Worth promotional crowd to go to trial.

For Sherwin and Schwarz, indictment for mail fraud and conspiracy was not as immediate a setback as seeing postal authorities stop deliveries of mail on May 8. Nonetheless, the two promoters determined they would not go down without a fight, and on May 14 they filed the conventional motions, challenging their indictments. In addition, they claimed immunity from the prosecution on the grounds that FTC representatives had promised them such immunity in exchange for cooperation. With this understanding, they had released damaging information, which became the heart of the government's case against them. They had, moreover, operated as a common law trust, and they thought the federal authorities

131

Promotion on Trial

had no jurisdiction over such an organization. Visiting federal judge Ben-jamin Bledsoe of California dismissed their objections, and Sherwin, Schwarz, the General, and their salesmen went to trial in Fort Worth on May 28, 1923.[20]

At the commencement of the trial, it was clear that the government intended showmanship as well as prosecution, for some seventy-five wit-nesses from all parts of the United States were brought in to testify. There were preachers, merchants, widows, Confederate veterans, and invalids. G. T. Lee, a real nephew of General Robert E. Lee, was on hand with the Lee family genealogy, from which Robert A. Lee was conspicuously ab-sent. Not all the witnesses were fully aware of legal niceties; Mrs. Violet R. Bowen, a General Lee investor, told a reporter, "I haven't any idea which case I was called to be a witness in; I invested in so many oil companies I can't recall them." But everyone expected a good show; the mood in the crowded courtroom and adjacent hallways was, to quote one journalist, "as if all were anticipating a snappy ball game."[21]

From the outset of the trial, the professional salesmen—Walter Marks, Phillip Goldstein, Nathan Sang, and Max Hirsch—had no intention of contributing to the government's entertainment. They would make no commissions in jail and had no wish to drag matters out by fighting the charges. It was better to cooperate with the government, plead guilty, pay their fines, and go on their way. After all, they had not thought up the promotion; let Sherwin, Schwarz, and Lee save themselves, if they could.[22]

And so the government began its parade of witnesses against the three promoters. There was Miss Alice Kane, the seventy-year-old hair-dresser who lost $3,000. There was the erstwhile correspondent of Harry Schwarz, N. J. Cary, who lost $15,000. Mrs. Mary Strowbridge had put up $4,000 in securities belonging to a widowed and dying sister, and Kate Telford and P. G. Wooster came to Fort Worth from California to tell how they lost their savings. The government even brought in J. N. Lee of Denton County to ask if he was Robert A. Lee's brother; he grudgingly replied, "I suppose so. My parents told me I was." He knew of no family connection to Robert E. Lee. The government's show continued unre-hearsed in courthouse hallways during adjournments. One elderly woman buttonholed the General on the first day of the trial to air her feelings: "So you are General Lee, are you? I thought I knew you from your picture.

Easy Money

What did you mean by writing me what a good man you were and how you would help me? . . . It was nearly $2000, all the money I had in the world. I believed what you told me—that it would provide for me when I got too old to provide for myself." A delighted reporter watching this episode unfold told his readers that the General would not look her in the eye. It all made wonderful copy.[23]

On June 5 the jury not surprisingly returned the guilty verdicts the government sought. Charles Sherwin and Harry Schwarz each received a ten-year sentence and a $15,000 fine; the General, a pawn but a willing one, drew a two-year sentence and a $6,000 fine. As they had expected, the hired salesmen escaped prison, though Judge Bledsoe told the press he regretted their exemption. Still, they drew unusually heavy fines: $15,000 for Marks and $10,000 each for Goldstein, Sang, and Hirsch. Indeed, the fine was more than Hirsch could raise, and he spent a number of months in the Tarrant County jail. The other salesmen went on their way to indictments in other courts. Walter Marks, for example, was indicted on similar charges in Houston in September and again in Fort Worth in November. Marks and his associates made their way into federal docket books through the rest of the decade. As for Lee, Sherwin, and Schwarz, their paths finally diverged. The General, who had been represented separately from Sherwin and Schwarz, arrived at Leavenworth on June 19. But Sherwin and Schwarz filed for an appeal, were released on $30,000 bond, and fled to Mexico with their sucker lists.[24]

The main event in the round of trials was that of Frederick A. Cook and his confederates. In the months following Cook's indictment, the prosecution had whetted public interest with a long series of press releases and interviews; the principal defendants responded with renewed claims of innocence. By the time proceedings began on October 15, 1923, a sizable national and regional audience was assured for what became the show of the decade in Fort Worth.

The principal actors were well cast for their roles. Cook appeared in a dark suit, carrying an expensive-looking black leather briefcase. He would have looked more like a lawyer than the attorneys present were it not for his overlong, stringy hair. His dark, deep-set eyes lent a visionary air to his appearance. By all odds, he would be the star of the show, but there were rivals for public notice. The prosecutor, Henry Zweifel, presented a striking contrast to the dignified and cultivated image conveyed by Cook. Short, stocky, wiry-haired, Zweifel looked every inch like the oil field tank builder he had been during his earlier years. He was pugnacious and stubborn, not a man to be bowled over.

Nor was Judge John M. Killits, B.A., M.A., LL.B., LL.M. Wittier and more polished than Zweifel, Killits ordinarily sat on the federal bench in Ohio, and his assignment to Fort Worth was unexpected. The prosecution had awaited the arrival of a senior district judge in the Fifth Circuit, but he went on the circuit court of appeals to replace an ailing colleague. Both prosecution and defense assumed that he would be succeeded by visiting Judge Bledsoe, until it was clear that Bledsoe's Fort Worth docket was already full through 1923.[25]

The result of all of the judicial maneuvering and shuffling was important because it brought in a judicial celebrity. Killits was billed as "one of the most fearless judges on the Federal bench." The *Fort Worth Star-Telegram* claimed that he had defied death threats when he presided over a series of "black hand" cases. Even more to the point, Killits had extensive trial experience, dating from service as a county prosecutor in 1888. Since 1910 he had served on the federal bench, traveling to Cleveland, New York, and California to preside over fraud trials.[26]

Judge Killits also knew a bit about oil apart from his legal training and experience, for he was a disappointed investor in the stock of a number of oil companies. He told a reporter at the trial that he was ready to sell what he had "at a very nominal percent of what I paid for it." It is also likely that he was keenly interested in Cook's merger scheme; during the trial he received notice that one of the companies in which he invested had been merged. From the beginning of proceedings, the judge took a strong interest in the substance of the trial, and he would pursue an active role in its progress; justice would not be left to the contending attorneys.[27]

The attorneys were almost as numerous as the defendants. In addition to Zweifel, the prosecution included two special assistants, both Washington lawyers and one of them a retired federal judge. The obvious investment in legal talent reflected accurately the government's determination to win convictions in the Cook case. The defense attorneys were more numerous and less experienced. Seymour Cox and another defendant were represented by their own attorneys—Cox by a team of three. The twelve other defendants, including Cook, were represented by Herbert G. Wade and Joseph F. Greathouse, both promising young attorneys, and by Joseph Weldon Bailey, former United States senator from Texas.

The participation of Bailey, who was paid by Cook, guaranteed that the trial would indeed be a show, though not of the variety arranged by the prosecution. Bailey was eminently newsworthy, at least in Texas. Entering Congress in 1890, he was elected to the Senate in 1900. Bailey specialized in dramatic poses, parliamentary maneuvers, and eloquent rhetoric, making effective use of his melodious voice, tall frame, and handsome face. He looked every inch the senator; long after styles had changed, he continued to wear the stereotypical broad-brimmed hat and long frock coat. Clever and aggressive, he was highly self-assured. As one historian put it, "The junior senator never questioned his own brilliance."[28]

By 1923, however, Bailey's political star had lost its luster. His reputation suffered when the public learned that while he was fulminating against Standard Oil on the floor of the Senate, he received a sizable loan from a Standard subsidiary. When he retired from the Senate in 1913, he still had wealthy and powerful friends, including Cox's friend, John Henry Kirby, whom Bailey represented for many years, but he never returned to elective office.[29] He attempted a comeback in Texas in 1920, but he lost the Democratic gubernatorial nomination by a wide margin. Thereafter he practiced law in Dallas. The Cook trial gave him a moment in the limelight, another chance at a comeback. His florid oratory, ripe with references to Jeffersonian ideals, would once again move the hearts of Texans— or at least those of the twelve men who sat on the jury.[30]

The government's strategy, clear when the indictments against Cook and the others were returned, was to build an overpowering mass of evidence against the defendants. By the time of the trial, therefore, the prosecution had enlisted more than 200 witnesses and had assembled hundreds of separate exhibits. One large table was conspicuously piled high with envelopes, filled with Cook's promotional literature and correspondence. The government's army of postal inspectors had done its job well. In the face of this mountain of physical evidence, the defense could not maintain the innocence of the defendants. Shortly after the grand jury returned the indictments, Cook and four other defendants offered to plead guilty in exchange for an assurance from Henry Zweifel that he would recommend that they be spared prison terms. Cook had little success; Zweifel refused to settle for less than a full guilty plea, a hefty fine, and a two-year prison sentence, and that would have been an impressive victory for the government. Cook vacillated, but Senator Bailey insisted that he and the other defendants hold to their pleas of not guilty. Bailey

Promotion on Trial

assumed that kindly Judge Wilson would hear the case and, in the event the jury found against Cook, hand down more lenient terms than Zweifel had offered.[31]

This strategy ran aground when the government arranged the displacement of Wilson, leaving Bailey and the other defense attorneys in need of a new approach. On the opening day of the trial, it was clear immediately that they had devised one: they would object and obstruct on every occasion, hoping for either a mistrial or a reversal on appeal. At the very least, the government's steamroller would be slowed, perhaps enough to make the whole proceeding tedious for the jurors; they might react against the prosecution's drawn out campaign, especially if effectively swayed by Bailey's oratory.

Thus on the opening day Senator Bailey and Joseph Greathouse stopped the federal steamroller in its tracks by insisting that each of the government's exhibits would have to be read into the record verbatim. This tactic made it inevitable that the trial would last a month and not one week, as prosecutors had planned. Bailey, for his part, interrupted the prosecution's opening remarks so many times that the prosecution rarely uttered two sentences in sequence. Killits remarked that the prosecutor's argument, "if it is to be considered an argument, will hardly be effective." That was just what Bailey intended. Bailey's other tactic was to provoke responses from prosecutors or from Judge Killits that might warrant a mistrial or a reversal. Thus he repeatedly baited the judge. When his objections were overruled—and they were in most instances—Bailey took an exception for the record, a common procedure, but he then continued by arguing in support of the exception. As Bailey knew, and as Judge Killits reminded him at least daily, argument after a ruling was out of order.[32]

Legal sparring continued for four weeks. Bailey attacked the rules of evidence that applied in federal courts, using the occasion to launch into an oration on Jeffersonian democracy and federal tyranny, as well as to taunt Killits. Bailey stretched to his full height and roared that federal judges had broken down one rule after another, "until we have no rule." He concluded by arguing that Cook was being tried in much the same way as Jesus had been centuries before, and that Killits was, by implication, in the unflattering role of Pontius Pilate![33] The judge asked Bailey to limit his remarks to the argument at hand; Bailey's response was swift—he moved for a mistrial. When Killits denied his motion, he disputed the decision with an argument lengthy enough to take up four pages of trial transcript.[34]

Nor was Bailey content with verbal aggression directed at the bench. Throughout the trial, Bailey baited Killits with his manner as well as his arguments. The senator repeatedly argued his case, and even addressed the court, with his back to the bench. Killits objected to no avail: Bailey declined to face him squarely even when he was being admonished.

After two weeks of verbal skirmishing, Bailey pressed Killits so hard that, after a heated exchange, the judge sent the jury from the courtroom and responded. He charged that "there was an effort to bait the Court" and that the intention was to mount an appeal on the claim that the court was unfair. He continued: "I can say to Senator Bailey . . . that I have never had such an unpleasant experience since I have been on the bench, in the atmosphere which some of the counsel for the defense have created in this case." Bailey and Greathouse were attempting to "brow beat the court." Killits was keenly aware that the defense carefully contrived to stop just short of providing clear grounds for disbarment.[35]

Still the government's case plodded on as, one by one, 200 witnesses spoke. They were chosen with the main view to their effect on the jury. Thus Mrs. Mary Phillips, a Civil War veteran's widow from Coshocton, Ohio, limped to the witness stand to tell that she had even sold the rugs on her floor to raise the money she sent Cook. As her tale unfolded, she broke down in tears and Judge Killits ordered a brief adjournment. After this delay, she concluded her testimony, left the stand, and berated Cook before a startled judge and sympathetic jury.[36] For the most part, the witnesses merely identified their letters and correspondence from Cook and the PPA. The process, often long and tedious, was also carefully managed by prosecutors to establish Cook's duplicity, often in humorous ways. On one especially tiresome day, John Pratt read one of Cook's letters into the file and elicited laughter from the jury when he came to Cook's dramatic conclusion: "Old-fashion hell is too good for a faker."[37]

Apart from Bailey's predictable goading of Killits, the defense of Cook and his codefendants was decidedly random. Alphonse Delacambre's attorney, for example, argued that his client was unaware of the falsehoods contained in PPA literature and that he had sold interests in good faith, largely on the strength of Cook's public celebrity. Seymour Cox's attor-

Promotion on Trial

neys tried to disassociate him from deliberate fraud; Cox merely wrote up
the facts that Cook provided. As if to emphasize his separation from PPA,
Cox absented himself for a two-week stretch during proceedings. Lesser
defendants, most of them salesmen, were also gone because Senator Bailey
had assured them that the government had no case against them and that
their presence was unnecessary. In their absence, Bailey offered no defense
for them; his assurances merely kept them from testifying against Cook.[38]

When he was not exercising his ego, Bailey's efforts were spent on
Cook's behalf. The substance of the defense rested largely on the vagaries
of the oil business and on the narrow rebuttal of specific points. In response to the charge that the companies merged into PPA were dead, he
argued that the companies had real assets; when pressed, he identified the
assets as lapsed leases, which could have been taken up again. The absur-
dity of the assertion that properties to which PPA had no legal claim were
assets was too much even for Bailey, and he used the argument only once.
He was fonder of enlarging on the difficulties of the oil business. He
prompted one prosecution witness with this view: "You know that a few
men make great fortunes out of it, and that nine men out of ten who
invest in it lose money, do you not?" His secondary line was the inveterate
optimism of oilmen. Midway through the trial, Bailey waxed eloquent on
this theme: "The poet says that hope springs eternal in the human breast,
but never in a breast like it does in the breast of an oilman." Both arguments were truisms, presumably acceptable to jurors, but effective only if
they believed in the good intentions of the defendants.[39]

During one full month of heated battle, however, Bailey did little to
erode the government's case. He completely ignored all his clients except
Cook, and even Cook's interests were secondary to Bailey's grand ego.
Rather than defend Cook, the senator spent his efforts dueling with
Killits, whom he said was trying "to discredit me before this jury and
before this community." Thus, what began as a criminal trial for mail
fraud finally evolved into a twelve-man referendum on the senator. The
verdict on Cook, in Bailey's view, was a judgment on his attorney as
well.[40]

In an effort to elicit a last hurrah, Bailey threw himself into his closing
argument, mustering all the florid phrases in his repertoire. Before a full
courtroom, he equated Cook's fate and the future of American democracy.
In a stem-winder peroration, he once again transformed Cook into a Jesus

Easy Money

figure: "It is the same old story: crown the victor, crucify the loser." Then, on the thirtieth day, Bailey rested, his creative work accomplished.[41]

By contrast, the prosecutor's closing argument and Judge Killits's summation were pedestrian. Killits allowed that oil was "a line of business in which chance and luck have an unusually large place." He urged the jury to remember that "sincere optimism is allowable even if it should seem to us foolish." The jurors' decision should hang on their assessment of the written literature and on Cook's intention. The judge reminded the jurors that as sole trustee, Cook was responsible for the actions of all of his employees and colleagues, and that they would have to weigh his claims of ignorance against their judgments of his character.[42]

In all, the jury had a considerable burden. It had to consider 168 counts against fourteen separate defendants. It did so rapidly, in twenty hours, and the results of its deliberations were devastating. Cook was found guilty on all counts; he was to pay a fine of $12,000 and serve fourteen years and nine months in the federal penitentiary at Leavenworth. With the exception of a salesman who received a directed acquittal, the other defendants were all convicted. Seymour Cox, found guilty on seven of the ten counts in the indictment, was sentenced to eight years in prison.[43]

Cook was visibly stunned by the outcome and the sentence. He might well have stood mute: the sentence was exceptionally severe—several times longer than those meted out in most other cases for similar offenses. As if to justify the sentence, Judge Killits delivered a dramatic oration, easily the equal of Bailey's best performance and suitable for extensive quotation in newspaper accounts of the trial. With the erstwhile explorer and oilman standing before him, Killits intoned: "This is one of the times when your peculiar and persuasive hypnotic personality fails you, isn't it? You have at last got to the point where you can't bunco anybody. You have come to the mountain and can't reach the latitude; it is beyond you." The judge warmed to his task: "First we had Ananias, then we had Machiavelli; the twentieth century produced Frederick A. Cook. Poor old Ananias, he is forgotten, and Machiavelli; we still have Frederick A. Cook." Staring down at Cook, the judge damned the pirate of promotion: "Cook, this deal of yours, and this conception of yours, and this execution of yours, was so damnably crooked that I know the men who defended you, defended you with their handkerchiefs to their noses; rank smelling to high heaven." He reminded Cook of his ill-gotten gains: "Every penny of it was robbed from orphans and widows, and credulous old people; people in the depths of poverty; people anxious to get money enough to ensure a decent burial." Killits rose to a thundering climax: "Oh God, Cook, haven't you any sense of decency at all, or is your vanity so impervious that you don't respond to what must be calls of decency to you? Aren't you haunted at night? Can you sleep?" Cook sat down in silence. Seymour Cox sat nervously, muscles twitching during the sentencing. When the trial ended, he raced to the water cooler, tossed down a glass of tepid water and slumped in silence. Matters had not gone as the promoters expected.[44]

As soon as Cook was sentenced, federal officials raced to use their victory to political advantage. The victory in Cook's show trial was front-page news in the national press. Assistant Attorney General John Crim told reporters that the federal campaign against promoters had shut down oil fraud; he likened it to the federal "war" against the railroads during the Roosevelt administration. In Fort Worth, Henry Zweifel played it to the local audience, asserting that he had dealt "a death blow to fraudulent oil stock selling in Texas. The fakes who use the mails to send broadcast from Fort Worth fraudulent literature, written to get the money of the people of poor means throughout the country into their hands, have received notice that Texas no longer tolerates them." Zweifel's boast was not altogether hollow. Fort Worth postal receipts fell 36 percent from the level of the previous year in the fall of 1923, reflecting a decline in local mail-order business.[45]

Following the Cook trial, the government moved against two other merger schemes, Pilgrim Oil and Revere Oil. Both were trust estates registered in Texas, and both offered their stockholders unparalleled opportunities to trade in their shares in dormant and defunct companies if they purchased shares in Revere and Pilgrim equal to one-quarter of the value of the traded-in securities. But the thirty Revere case defendants, including Dr. Frederick A. Cook, had the good fortune to be tried before Judge Wilson, and their sentences were light. One-third of them, including Cook, got off scot-free when Wilson dismissed the charges against them. Only John C. Verser and Albert H. Shepherd received jail terms, nine and six months respectively. John G. Guerin, Revere's pen, got off with a $2,000 fine. In the end, local authorities permitted Verser to evade both fine and prison, and he continued to promote companies in Texas and Oklahoma for at least one more decade.[46]

In the meantime, Seymour Cox sat in the county jail in Fort Worth, unable to post his bond: fortune frowned on Lucky Cox. On January 15, 1924, federal marshals took him back to Houston for his second appearance before Judge Hutcheson. Once again Cox faced charges of writing deceptive promotional materials and engaging in mail fraud, this time on behalf of the Blue Bird Oil Company, promoted by Butler Perryman and others. There were no well wishers to greet Cox on his arrival back in town. John Henry Kirby was no longer hovering in the wings to rescue him, because the Fort Worth trial had demolished faith in Cox's character and business operations. Lacking friends and money, Cox was without counsel, and he represented himself during the proceedings.

From the beginning, it was clear that more had changed in Houston than Cox's circumstances. The new trial would not be a repeat performance of the first one. The government no longer employed the young prosecutor who had let Cox escape its clutches, and it took the case out of the control of the local United States district attorney by appointing a special prosecutor, George B. Peddy. Peddy, a professor at the University of Texas law school, proved cautious and thorough. Both he and Judge Hutcheson quizzed prospective jurors to ferret out friends of Cox and the other defendants. This time Cox would not be saved by fishing buddies and lodge brothers.[47]

Cox's defense consisted of claiming that his wife, and not he, had written for Perryman; when she had done so, he was sick and out of town. Perryman, his secretary, and other defendants, however, contradicted Cox's statements, and in the end, the jury found Cox and the lot of them guilty after only two hours' deliberation. Judge Hutcheson handed down relatively stiff terms; Cox drew the hardest, five years in Leavenworth and a $15,000 fine. Perryman received a short term in the county jail and a light fine, but he objected to even this punishment on the grounds that he had been deceived by Cox. Judge Hutcheson dismissed his claim as "Adam's defense: he was guilty and so are you."[48]

The judge saved his choicest remarks for Cox. Still rankling at Cox's earlier acquittal, Hutcheson began: "When you were charged in this court two years ago, I believed you guilty." He continued by quoting from the writings of John Milton and John Dryden, explaining, "I speak to you in poetry because that's the language you understand and live in." He had the full measure of Cox's character: "You are a victim of your own egotism, your own self-importance. Your trouble is megalomania, a desire to do great things. You are suffering from the most over-developed egotism I have ever seen. As soon as you see a thing and believe it, immediately that thing is allright and all who disagree with you are wrong." Hutcheson told Cox that he would have been better off if he had faced his shortcomings, confessed, and pleaded guilty. He added, "An honest confession is good for the soul—and good for the courthouse!"[49]

With concurrent sentences from Judges Killits and Hutcheson, Cox was bound over to serve five years in Leavenworth. His fate was newsworthy in Houston, Fort Worth, Chicago, and New York. One of the leading "pirates of promotion" was off the streets and investors could rest secure. At least, this was the impression that the federal government was anxious to convey.[50]

There were scattered oil fraud prosecutions thereafter, in Omaha, Cincinnati, Houston, Dallas, Texarkana, and other cities. In Fort Worth, twenty-two people were indicted in July 1923, but prosecution was dilatory; twelve indictments were dismissed, and only two men were sentenced to jail. At the end of the year, there were eight more indictments in the city, but no jail terms were assessed. During the following year, there was another show of a crackdown: fifty-nine people were indicted in one sweep, but thirty-two were dismissed and the remainder drew jail terms of no more than ninety days. At the end of 1924, there were thirty-four additional indictments, eleven of which were dismissed; ten ended with light jail terms. It is clear that with the end of the Cook trial, the heat had been turned down on Fort Worth promoters for the time being.[51]

Three years later, four postal inspectors returned to Fort Worth and produced evidence to support twenty-four new fraud indictments, but public attention was focused on Los Angeles, where the more sensational Julian Oil Case was in the headlines. This elaborate case involved inside trading, stock rigging, and the creation of high-yield investment pools as a part of a refinancing scheme. The major charge was that C. C. Julian had promoted the Julian Petroleum Corporation by overissuing stock and obtaining money under false pretenses. Julian, his bankers, brokers, and other confederates were supposed to have issued 3,650,000 shares of watered stock, with a par value of $150 million, to over 40,000 investors, mainly in the Los Angeles area. The press was drawn to the case largely because several Hollywood celebrities, including director Cecil B. DeMille and producer Louis B. Mayer, had invested in the investment pool and were charged with usury. Involving fifty-two defendants, the Julian case dragged on for five months, through eighty-three trial days; one witness was on the stand for eleven days. At the end, eleven defendants were acquitted and the others were dismissed. Another ambitious attempt at a show trial failed.[52]

Like so many others of its kind, the Julian case demonstrated the expense and difficulties of an attempt to crack down on fraudulent promotion. Federal officials claimed major victories against fraud in oil, real estate, and securities, but their campaigns and show trials really did little more than mollify public opinion. The effect of headline-grabbing prosecutions was limited because, for the most part, both federal and state regulators lacked adequate remedies for widespread violations of fraud statutes.

In 1922, for example, the most effective agents against fraud were the postal inspectors. Not only could postal authorities stop the flow of mail, and hence money, to promoters, but as the Fort Worth cases demonstrated, when experienced investigators came down hard on fraud artists, they were capable of producing strong evidence for prosecutors. The problem was that gathering exhibits and interviewing victims was time-consuming and costly, beyond the means of the Post Office Department. In order to mount its Fort Worth campaigns, the department had to divert investigators from other regions where fraud was at least as much of a problem. In January 1922, for example, inspectors worked on 129 cases in Fort Worth, but there were nearly twice that number awaiting action in Chicago and more than four times as many pending in New York City. The chief inspector of the department told the House Committee on Appropriations that he needed at least fifty more inspectors to cope with the surge of fraud. He did not get them. Under these circumstances, federal officials could do little more than prosecute what the *Oil and Gas Journal* called "the most flagrant cases of violations." As this reliable trade publication pointed out, "This number is but a very small percentage of the total number of such organizations which have been formed to fleece the public."[53]

Even if the department had hired fifty additional inspectors, fraudulent promoters could have evaded prosecution by modifying their operations, as the successful, if unillustrious, career of D. J. Simmons demonstrated. Simmons, a twenty-three-year-old big spender with a third-grade education, bought royalty interests on scattered junk acreage in Texas and Louisiana, promising a fifteen-to-one payout to 4,500 potential investors. His literature, prepared by pens in Fort Worth, also implied that he owned all of the royalty interests on designated leases, whereas he actually purchased from one-eighth to one-half of the interest. Though his holdings did not grow—his purchases of a big house in Fort Worth and a fast car left him strapped financially—Simmons's promises soared. When postal inspectors discovered his United Royalty Pool in 1925, he had raised about $9,000 by mail. By October 1925, when inspectors closed in, he was forecasting returns of 5,000 percent in forty-five days. After a fraud order was issued in Fort Worth, Simmons moved to San Antonio and continued his sales campaign, using envelopes marked "confidential," without his name and return address. By the time authorities discovered his new location, he had moved again.[54]

Promoters like Simmons could keep going because from the time a sufficient number of complaints had accumulated to warrant investigation, hearings, and a possible fraud order, the Post Office Department needed at least a year to act. Prosecution by U.S. attorneys took as much as a year longer, and some promoters, such as Paul Vitek, were never apprehended. The legal system, when it actually operated against fraudulent promoters, was slow and uncertain. But even when criminals were detected, arrested, and tried, most of their sentences were so light as to be no more serious than any other risk of doing business. The salesmen for B. M. Hatfield, who was sentenced to one year and a day for the promotion of the Mexia Syndicate, were fined only $500. H. E. "Hurry-Up Harry" Wilcox pleaded guilty to mail fraud and was fined $350. Salesmen and copywriters for Revere paid no more. When fines were higher, like those levied against Walter Marks, they went uncollected.[55]

If the Post Office Department's slowness hampered its pursuit of fraudulent promoters, the glacial pace of the Federal Trade Commission made it virtually impotent. Relatively young among federal agencies, the FTC was created to enforce fair trade regulations, and its main concentration was acting against restraint of trade. When it pursued dishonest oil promoters, it did so on the assumption that fraud gave them a competitive edge over honest oilmen and was thus an unfair and illegal competitive practice. The FTC, however, had even fewer agents than the Post Office Department. It could act on fewer complaints, and it took more time to

Easy Money

gather information. By the time the understaffed FTC was finally ready to act, its targets had often wrapped up their illegal promotions. Either they had made the money they expected and gone on to something else, or, as was true for Big Diamond, their venture ended in receivership. In either event, they had concluded the business the FTC sought to enjoin long before the agency secured a cease and desist order. So common was this situation that the commission's annual report for 1919 admitted it. But nothing was done to improve procedures, and the FTC remained, as the *New York Times* described it, "a fragile sword."[56]

Even when the FTC tried to move vigorously against repeat offenders, it could do little, as the adventures of Seymour Cox demonstrate. The commission's investigations began early in 1919, and at the end of September, it took its first step and issued a complaint. Cox responded in November. Thereafter, the FTC took no action until the end of January 1921, when it began an additional year of hearings, charges, answers, and postponements. It did not issue a final order stipulating deceptive and unfair practices until January 22, 1922. Cox ignored it. Nothing more happened until the FTC applied to the Fifth Circuit Court of Appeals for enforcement of its cease and desist order. The court granted a preliminary injunction against Cox six weeks later. From the time of its original action to enforcement, nearly four years elapsed. Cox made good use of the time to promote at least three additional ventures and to collect hefty writer's fees from Frederick A. Cook and others. He was already under indictment in two federal courts when the FTC completed its processes.[57]

In the final analysis, the FTC's most effective course lay in cooperation with the Post Office and Justice departments. The commission frequently forwarded exhibits and other information from its files to these agencies. In several instances its inspectors offered valuable aid because they were able to obtain fairly candid revelations from promoters who knew that nothing more serious than a cease and desist order could result from FTC attention. Some investigators even led oilmen to think that confession to the FTC secured immunity from further federal action; that assumption brought the promoters of General Lee Development to speak freely and provide what proved to be valuable information for federal attorneys. But overall, the involvement of the FTC was strictly stopgap, intended to fill a void left in federal law, which contained no major restrictions on the sale of securities.

Promotion on Trial

In the absence of a federal agency monitoring securities sales, regulation of them rested with the states. State statutes and enforcement procedures were highly varied. Beginning with Kansas in 1911, a steady progression of states passed legislation regulating the sale of securities. New York's "Martin Act" was seen as the toughest because it provided for criminal proceedings against fraud. Most statutes were limited to requiring registration of securities and salesmen before securities were sold to the general public; California and Texas laws were of this type.

In Texas the blue sky law, passed in 1913, had more loopholes than substance. It permitted the unregistered sale of "private stock," the device so often used by oil promoters, and failed to define the legal responsibility of brokers for claims and promises. Under the pressure of the Fort Worth trials, the legislature amended the law in 1923, specifically barring false dividends, merger schemes, and skimming. On paper the new law was a significant improvement, but it produced few changes in the ways fraudulent promoters did business.[58]

Under the new law, enforcement still rested with the secretary of state, whose office issued state charters to companies demonstrating they had assets to a specified value. In most instances, however, the valuation promoters placed on their assets was accepted by the secretary of state without question. In those few cases in which data were questioned, promoters could pay fees to employees of the secretary of state who inspected the assets listed, revised their opinions, and kept the fees. Only rarely was a promoter pressed to do more.[59]

This situation was in part the result of severe understaffing. During the 1930s the Texas blue sky office still had only twelve part-time employees, none of whom was an attorney. No significant cases were processed until the late 1930s, and even then the secretary of state and the attorney general were too shorthanded to mount more than symbolic prosecutions. By the 1950s the office was hopelessly behind. In one year it received more than 9,000 separate applications for securities activities, and it had the equivalent of four full-time employees to process and investigate them. One scholar described it as "the most hopelessly overworked of all blue sky offices."[60]

Though some states, among them Kansas and Wisconsin, were reputed by promoters to be hard territory to avoid trouble, there is little evidence to suggest that promoters were seriously restricted by regulation in most

Easy Money

states. Lack of uniformity and dilatory enforcement made the laws easy to evade, and promoters knew it.[61] The variety of securities peddled by promoters complicated enforcement as well. The Texas blue sky law of 1923, for example, did not touch sales of trust certificates or units, syndicate interests, leases, or royalties. Even where stock sales were regulated, if promoters sold "personal" stock as opposed to "treasury" stock, they could escape legal action. Increasing state regulation thus posed some complications for promoters, but they were never insuperable barriers to bilking the gullible. There were always loopholes to be found in the law, and sending some promoters to prison merely gave others incentive to look for them.

SEVEN

Adaptive Strategies

THE GOVERNMENT'S crackdown on Fort Worth promotion in 1923 did not end oil promotion by mail, but it did bring many operators to adjust their strategies. A few responded to the harsh spotlight on oil by switching to other types of promotion. Real estate and that old promotional war-horse, mining stock, were popular alternatives. Such a change of business often involved no more than the substitution of different nouns and adjectives in sales literature. Other promoters left the temporarily inclement Texas environment for other havens, commonly California and Florida. Many abandoned the device of the trust estate in business organization. It came as a grim surprise when the Fort Worth trials demonstrated that trustees could be held personally responsible for the illegal acts committed by trust employees; hired salesmen's wild promises, for example, were the trustees' liability. Promoters turned instead to organizing investment clubs, pools, and syndicates, and they often tried to sell something real, if of dubious value. Having seen what happened to that ace high flyer of promotional prose, Seymour Cox, they were more careful about their language, avoiding outright promises and hedging predictions of easy money. Above all, the canniest promoters tried to be less conspicuous.

The fund-raising activities of Roy Westbrook in the mid-1920s illustrate both adaptation to the possibility of stricter law enforcement and coping with perennial problems of capital formation among small independent oilmen.[1] A Fort Worth printer, Westbrook had ready opportunity to observe promoters at work, and by 1925 he decided he knew enough about the oil game to try his luck with his own company. Appropriately enough, he began by printing an ample supply of stationery with an elegant letterhead for his Westbrook Oil Company. He next looked up a Pennsylvania lease broker, J. W. Grant, who had picked up vast oil leases in the west Texas Permian Basin several years earlier; Grant had gotten most of his leases at the bargain price of ten cents an acre, so he was able to offer Westbrook over 21,000 acres in Winkler County for $8,000, a price even Westbrook could afford. Westbrook had no trouble raising the cash in Fort Worth, but he had to complete a test well before the end of the year to avoid paying $2,100 in annual rental fees. Cash short, Westbrook had to act fast.

The necessity for swift action, however, created a logistical problem. Westbrook intended to raise the money for his test well through a mail-order sales campaign of the variety he had seen countless other Fort Worth promoters use. The drilling deadline on his lease rental payment meant that he would have to spud in before he could get his sales campaign in high gear and bring in operating capital. Luckily, he was able to strike a bargain with a newly rich driller, who agreed to complete a well in return for 2,000 acres of Westbrook's block of leases. The driller, in turn, sub-contracted the work for a lease of 400 acres, and the well was under way by midyear of 1925.[2]

To raise operating capital, Westbrook chose to sell leases. He carved up a portion of his remaining leases into five-acre tracts and sold them through the mail, to distant investors, for $50 each. His sales campaign resembled those of Cook and Cox and others, for the lure was still quick riches. In a four-page letter, Westbrook took potential investors on a verbal tour westward from Fort Worth to Winkler County, always emphasizing the dazzling possibilities of wealth. Of Ranger, he reminded his readers, "Leases here also were bought for just a few dollars per acre at the start of operations. Later these same leases sold in excess of $10,000 per acre." Though Westbrook did not say so, his reader was to assume that buying a lease from Westbrook Oil would offer a similar chance for giant profits.[3]

Westbrook's hired pens were creative, but they never soared to the heights reached by Lucky Cox; the recent trials had a dampening effect on hyperbolic expression. Westbrook offered "A CHANCE FOR ENORMOUS PROFITS" and not the certainty of them. His literature incorporated the "hurry-up" theme, but hedged on deadlines. After the test well was spudded in, Westbrook mailed highly imaginative versions of his progress, but he usually added modifying phrases, such as "should this well be the producer we expect it to be. . . ." Hyperbole survived, but Westbrook used it with comparative restraint.[4]

Unfortunately, restraint did not prompt quick sales, and although Westbrook hired the Southern Brokerage Sales Company of Dallas to help him peddle his acreage, leases sold slowly. Westbrook was forced to sweeten his offer, but he did it by offering bonuses—shares in his company or participation in a lease pool—none of which could be mistaken for a simulated dividend drawn from paid-in capital. In short, he encouraged investors to buy, but he did not resort to deliberate deception to do it. Though he raised funds through the mail like many other promoters, he really was carrying on wildcat exploration. He could hope to make a profit on lease sales, but he would make his own fortune only if he discovered oil. Whether he actually expected to do so was another matter.

As luck would have it, Roy Westbrook found oil, opening the prolific Hendrick field. The discovery was a classic instance of a newcomer trying his luck at long odds no veteran would touch, and winning big. His excitement—and ambivalence—were conveyed in another four-page letter to investors:

I could not believe it could be true. I thought some one must be playing a practical joke on me so I began immediately to check back. I got confirmation on the two wires. Phoned Gerret Donnelly who was in charge of the well and found out that he had received the same messages. The jubilee started right then. My wife and little boy and girl enjoyed a real celebration while getting breakfast. I sat down to the table to eat but I was half way to the office in the car when I realized that I had not eaten a bite. I was too excited, too full of joy to want food. Because I knew I had made good my word with you and the rest of the people who had trusted me with their money.

I was glad of course for myself and for my loved ones. But I was glad too for you and every other loyal man and woman whose wonderful support had made this great success possible.

Mr. Thompson and I left for the field on the first train, the famous Sunshine Special, one of the fastest trains in the South, but it was far too slow that day. Arrived at Monahans at 2:04 Sunday morning and went to bed but could not sleep. I could not believe yet that we had really struck oil. But next morning when we drove out to the well and my eager eyes spied that towering black derrick I knew that our dreams had come true.

Drenched clear to the top, the derrick stood up in unmistakable evidence that oil had been struck and flowed over the top, marking

Easy Money

the discovery of what I firmly believe today will be one of the greatest oil fields in all Texas.[5]

Though his investors might well have wondered at his apparent surprise at success, it was genuine success nonetheless. By the beginning of 1986, the Hendrick field had produced more than 250 million barrels of oil. Westbrook organized his venture, promoted investors, drilled his well, and most remarkably, found oil. He did it all within the wide latitude of the law.[6]

Like Roy Westbrook, Paul Vitek raised money by mail-order sales for exploration he actually carried out. He was not lucky enough to discover a giant oil field as Westbrook did, but he found and produced oil, albeit not in the quantities he described to his investors. Though he employed the familiar and questionable promotional techniques associated with Fort Worth oil promotion, federal authorities never convicted Vitek of violating the law, for all they tried to do so. Unlike most promoters, moreover, Vitek was a careful manager of his promotional and other business operations. Thus he avoided the commonest errors of promotional artists; overall, the wily Vitek made few mistakes.

Vitek was one of the more unusual oil promoters of his day, for he was not a native-born American. Born in the Austro-Hungarian province of Bohemia, near Prague, Vitek emigrated to the United States in 1908. He worked in a factory, delivered milk in the Chicago area, and at age sixteen went to Oklahoma, drawn by an oil boom. There, according to his own account, he worked "around a derrick and drilling, as a helper." When the boom was over he returned to Chicago, where he married and found work with the Royal Insurance Company. In 1918 Vitek set up his own Chicago brokerage firm, selling stocks and bonds. Vitek never described the particulars of this operation, but it is unlikely that his brokerage firm specialized in blue-chip securities. In 1920 he found it expedient to leave Chicago for Fort Worth, where, in his own words, he entered "this oil promotion business."[7]

Once in Fort Worth, Vitek became closely associated with Dr. Frederick A. Cook, Leo Reardon, and their circle. Vitek took an office in the Farmers and Mechanics Bank Building, the seat of Cook's operations, and launched his Vitek Oil and Refining Company, a trust estate. Though Vitek later asserted that he relied on his own resources to launch this venture, he had more than a little help from his friends. Cook's tip sheets, the *Oil Tribune* and the *Arkansas Oil Gazette*, touted Vitek Oil, and Cook, Leo Reardon, and G. H. McGrath used their brokerage operations to peddle it to investors. Reardon and F. W. Wimberley, both of whom worked as pens for Cook, helped Vitek concoct his early literature; when S. E. J. Cox hired on to write for Cook's Petroleum Producers' Association, he also wrote for Vitek. Once written, Vitek's literature was reproduced and mailed from Cook's office. Vitek thus began his career in oil promotion as a protégé of Frederick A. Cook.[8]

Though happy enough to have Cook's help in promoting his venture, Vitek was wily enough to watch for his own opportunities. They came his way when the Vitek Oil and Refining Company got into the Smackover, Arkansas, oil boom. Late in 1922 Vitek drilled a well that came in for almost 15,000 barrels of oil a day. Like other wells in the district, its production quickly dwindled to several hundred barrels per day, but that was more than most Fort Worth promoters could boast of, and Vitek was quick to exploit it with his mentor Cook. Touting the well's production at 25,000 barrels a day and using a doctored photograph of his well gushing oil, Vitek bamboozled Cook into having the Petroleum Producers' Association pay $38,000 for part of Vitek's property. Cook thought PPA was getting $1/16$ of the working interest in the well; Vitek in fact sold him $1/16$ of the royalty interest, or only 1/128 of the production. For that matter, Vitek never paid PPA the royalty due it. Cook's student had bested his mentor. Unfortunately, this Arkansas adventure landed both of them in hot water with federal authorities, and in December 1924 a federal grand jury indicted Vitek and Cook, as well as Leo Reardon and G. H. McGrath, for mail fraud.[9]

Vitek alone stayed clear of federal authorities. By the date of the indictment, he had disposed of Vitek Oil to C. N. Haskell, a trade-off in which Vitek picked up cash and his stockholders received stock in Haskell's Southern States and Western States oil companies, both of which went bankrupt shortly thereafter. When news of the indictment reached him, Vitek fled to New York, where federal authorities failed to locate him. In 1925 he was arrested in Chicago but managed to avoid extradition. These adventures taught Vitek, who had a natural talent for covering his tracks, the value of a low public profile. He had learned, however, that promotion could bring in big money: Vitek Oil and Refining had raised an estimated $1.7 million.[10]

By December 1926 Vitek gauged that his difficulties with federal au-

Easy Money

thorities were far enough behind him to permit his return to Fort Worth. Even so, he took precautions. He did not put his name on the office he rented in the Neil P. Anderson Building, so that, as a disgruntled postal inspector remarked, "People coming along could never discover it was Mr. Vitek's office, unless they knew the room number." His letters to investors usually listed a post office box number rather than a building name as a return address. Just to make sure he avoided unwelcome attention, Vitek did not even have a telephone installed, a matter which he explained to incredulous postal officials as an attempt to keep his overhead for operations low.[11]

Despite his preference for the shadows, Vitek's return to Fort Worth did not go unnoticed by federal officials. Scarcely had he settled in when postal authorities tried to have him extradited to the Western District of Arkansas to stand trial. Fortunately for Vitek, Fort Worth law enforcement officials were not interested in pursuing him. The U.S. attorney's office refused to issue a fugitive warrant for Vitek, and he remained in business in Fort Worth. The Post Office Department, however, did get the Texas secretary of state to enjoin Vitek from selling securities in the state. If they could not stop him from doing business altogether, it was clear that postal officials meant to make his doing business difficult.[12]

Despite legal obstacles, Vitek launched the Vitek Oil Company, a Texas corporation, and, injunction or not, he sold $117,000 in common shares. Vitek Oil's principal assets were acquired with the minimum of cash, through agreements to drill test wells in return for interests in leases. Thus, at the company's organization, Vitek put in a forty-acre lease in Stephens County, Texas; subsequently, he picked up a seven-sixteenths working interest in a forty-acre lease in Carson County and an eighty-acre tract in Howard County. The Howard County tract offers a good example of the promotional trading of the time. Vitek acquired this property from Fort Worth promoter James Mascho, for $5,000 and the promise to drill a test well. Mascho had picked up the lease from another group of promoters, who had made a drilling commitment to Roxana Petroleum (Shell), which kept a half interest in the eighty-acre tract. Vitek picked up all of his leases without putting down much cash, but that did not stop him from making generous valuations of their worth: $110,000 for the Stephens County tract, for example, and $249,000 for the acreage in Howard County. Vitek honored his obligations to drill on these properties; per-

Adaptive Strategies

haps memories of the recent trials, as much as desire for production, led him to complete the tests he agreed to carry out.[13]

The results of Vitek Oil's drilling campaign in 1927 proved unspectacular. The Stephens County test yielded a small showing of gas, and the well was plugged and abandoned. The Carson County test came in, though with precisely how much oil is uncertain. In any event, the well was never connected to a gathering line and was ultimately sold for its derrick, collecting tank, and casing. Vitek had better luck in Howard County, where he brought in a 200-barrel well in July 1927. This production became Vitek Oil's most valuable asset. In the first six months of its existence, however, the company ran up expenses of between $140,000 and $150,000, a sum which Vitek explained entirely with respect to the wells he had drilled, but which also actually included the high costs of mail-order promotion.[14]

Though he knew he had to be wary of attracting the further attention of federal agents, Vitek took up additional profit-making opportunities. He followed the establishment of Vitek Oil with the organization of a brokerage operation, the Price Stock Exchange. The naming of this enterprise, as well as placing his secretary, Erna Stoll, at its ostensible head, again demonstrated Vitek's desire to obscure his business dealings from inquisitive law enforcement officials: Price seems to have been a name he chose at random. The Price Stock Exchange conducted its business from Vitek's office, where Miss Stoll and another stenographer tended its operations without the benefit of a telephone connection but with the "advisory" help of Vitek. The Price letterheads included the motto, "WE GUARANTEE." What they guaranteed was left unspecified. Its newsletter bore the heading, "Dealing in Listed and Unlisted Highly Speculative Oil and Mining Securities," language clearly calculated to protect Vitek from future legal problems. Vitek was not about to take unnecessary chances.[15]

With the Price Stock Exchange ready to skim commissions from investors' dollars, by the summer of 1927 Paul Vitek was ready for another promotional scheme, this one different from anything he had promoted before. An acquaintance, Guy Holcomb, found what looked like a sensational money-maker, a vacancy strip in the area of the fabulous Yates oil field in Pecos County, Texas. As the result of a surveyor's error in 1917, a narrow strip of land between sections 60 and 61 of Block 2, some ninety-three acres in extent, lay open to claim and purchase. Land surrounding

Easy Money

the strip was leased by the Transcontinental and Mid-Kansas oil companies, the two largest producers in the Yates field. Fortunes had been made
on vacancies. Fort Worth independent oilman Ed Landreth found one in
Crane County's McElroy field in 1927, and brought in well after well on
his acreage which, prior to his claiming the strip, had been controlled by
Gulf Oil. With Landreth's success in mind, Holcomb filed for the Pecos
County strip in 1927, but he knew he would need partners with ample
funds to press his claim in the face of inevitable legal opposition. With his
own vision of Ed Landreth's Crane County coup as inspiration, Vitek
decided to buy a half interest in Holcomb's strip. Undoubtedly it would
take a lot more cash than either he or Holcomb had on hand to win the
strip, but as he surveyed the lists of his investors, Vitek had an idea of
where that cash might be raised.[16]

Vitek's vehicle for this promotion was to be Vitek's Bonanza, Inc., a
Texas corporation capitalized at $50,000. Vitek's Bonanza offered inves-
tors the chance to buy shares in the potential profits of the strip at $20
each. Even Vitek admitted the enterprise was a pure gamble. After all, he
and Holcomb had only a hope of gaining title to the strip; it was not yet
in their hands. Thus, as Vitek promoted it, the strip was "the greatest
gamble," a "win or lose proposition for big stakes," a gamble for a chance
"to reap millions—the untold wealth laying under this strip of 'Golden
Land'." And, carefully hedging his language to avoid phrases federal investigators could seize on, Vitek told his investors, "I feel certain in my
own mind that we will win and win big."[17]

His optimism was premature. In taking on a legal battle with two large
oil companies, as well as other property owners on the strip, Vitek was in a
much more vulnerable position than Ed Landreth in Crane County. Landreth entered the contest for his strip with a $3 million bankroll from a
previous sale of properties and production. Vitek, by contrast, embarked
upon his venture with a debt of almost $32,000 accumulated by Vitek Oil.
By October 1927, as Vitek sent out the first letters for his Bonanza promotion, contractors and suppliers for Vitek's Howard County well were serving Vitek Oil with labor and mechanics' liens. In December 1927 the State
of Texas placed Vitek Oil in receivership, with former federal attorney
Henry Zweifel, Vitek's choice, as receiver. In the meantime, the Texas
Corporation Commission refused Vitek's application for a charter for
Vitek's Bonanza. Vitek's Pecos County strip scheme generated opposition

Adaptive Strategies

he could not handle with limited resources, and his win-or-lose proposition was a dead loss.[18]

Vitek's investors were in no position to learn of these dramatic developments. Solicited for the Bonanza, they bought shares for cash, money which Vitek would have to return to them unless he could think of a legitimate way to avoid it. The situation called for the familiar device of a reload to a new venture, the illusory salvage of the investor's loss. Not any promotion would do: he needed a venture that was unlikely to attract immediate federal attention, a venture which would not demand putting up as much capital as a state charter would require. Vitek found the sale of small royalty interests just what was needed.

The trade in royalties and interests in royalty pools was by no means new in the 1920s. It had long been a way for prudent operators and investors to diversify their holdings, spread their risks, and participate in frontier or developing areas at relatively low costs. How large this fraction of production was varied from region to region. In most United States oil fields of the twenties it was customarily one-eighth, but in California it was often one-sixth. On purchase of a royalty, the investor received a deed of ownership. Thereafter, when petroleum was produced he received payment proportionate to his fractionate ownership of production, ordinarily from the petroleum purchaser. Like land, the royalty interest could be divided, transferred, or sold by the owner.

Though royalty ownership enabled the investor to avoid sharing costs, it still entailed risks. Purchase of a royalty in an untried, wildcat area was, of course, highly speculative. If no oil were discovered, the investor would get no return. In producing areas, the risks of royalty speculation lay in how much petroleum could be produced, how long it could be produced, and how much it would bring on the market. Since petroleum is a depletable resource, the royalty owner had to expect that, unless prices rose dramatically and continually, declining production would mean dwindling income. What could not be known, particularly given the want of knowledge of reservoir engineering in the twenties, was how long the owner could expect to receive income from production. In a spectacularly rich area like the Permian Basin Yates field, royalties and production held up for decades. In problematic areas like the Winkler County Hendrick field, or like the Eastland County, Texas, oil fields of the early twenties, production came in strongly and then petered out or developed production prob-

Easy Money

lems. The value of royalties, of course, varied with the prospects of production. Generally speaking, however, to make money a royalty owner had
to acquire the property early in the life of a field; to make a real fortune, as
many investors hoped to do, one had to acquire royalty interests over a
large area. Even flush production would not make the owner of ½,000 of
⅛ of production from a five-acre lease rich quick.[19]

What Paul Vitek and promoters like Leo Reardon and H. H. Hoffman
knew was that hopeful investors outside the oil industry often did not
understand what they were getting when they bought royalties. They
tended to think they were getting something much bigger than they really
were—which suited royalty promoters admirably. But promoters did give
investors real property for their money, and that made royalty sales attractive to men who wanted to avoid legal entanglements.

Having spent most of 1928 embroiled in the legal tangles resulting from
the failure of Vitek Oil and the debacle of Vitek's Bonanza, in December
Vitek launched his first royalty venture, Winkler Royalty Interests, in
which he created 600 shares at $50 each. The royalties Vitek put into this
venture were in every instance small fractions of the original landowner's
⅛: 1/32 of the ⅛ interest in production from Section 44, Block 26; 1/64 of
the ⅛ in one half of Section 43, Block 26; and 1/64 of the ⅛ on Section 25,
Block 11. Translated into production, this was not very impressive. In
Block B-11, for example, Vitek was only purchasing one of every 512 barrels
of oil produced in Section 25. When Vitek sold royalties to investors, he
sliced the portions yet more thinly. The investor who sent Vitek $50 got
1/600 of the production due Vitek, or 7/100 of a gallon from each 512
barrels (21,504 gallons) of petroleum produced in Section 25. There actually was some production in Section 25, but there was no guarantee it
would be extensive or long-lived.[20]

Obviously, investors who looked into Winkler Royalty Interests with a
critical eye would wonder how long it would take to return their $50
investments with a profit. Given west Texas crude prices in 1928 and the
production already existing on Vitek's royalty acreage, there was scant
possibility for the investors to get their money back in less than thirteen
years.

To keep investors from such discouraging calculations, Vitek used several stratagems. He concentrated his sales energy upon those who had
already invested in his earlier ventures, offering them the chance to turn in

Adaptive Strategies

worthless shares in Vitek's Bonanza for credit of fifty cents on the dollar toward purchasing Winkler Royalty Interests. The purchaser of Winkler Royalty received not merely a share or certificate but a deed, a genuine enough document. Thereafter, each month Vitek sent the investor a check for fifty cents for each royalty interest purchased. All this gave the appearance of getting something back for money spent. Some 400 persons bought Winkler Royalty Interests, a result which led Vitek to launch a second and similar promotion, Winkler County Royalty, early in 1929. Twice the size of its predecessor, the venture had 1,200 royalty interests for sale at $50 each. Vitek succeeded in selling roughly half the royalties in this venture.[21]

Had Vitek been content merely to sell off tiny pieces of royalty, he would have cajoled his investors into a disappointing investment from which there was slim chance of good return, except by reselling the royalty at higher prices to someone more gullible. Vitek, however, added a refinement which ruled out even that modest possibility. Before he mailed the royalty deeds, he secured power of attorney from his investors. In short, the investors gave up their right to use what they had purchased: they could not sell or trade their minuscule interests, and any money they received came to them from Paul Vitek, who distributed royalty payments after skimming 5 percent for overhead costs of property management. Vitek sold his investors on this part of his scheme by the lure of huge profits from the eventual sale of the royalty for much higher prices, a sale which Vitek had to be prepared to transact at a moment's notice when his expertise indicated the time was right. In all, Vitek exercised the broad discretionary powers over capital and assets characteristic of a trust estate, but he did not have to form one to do so.[22]

It was hard for a man in the business of luring the gullible to protect himself from charges that he had promised investors a fortune and failed to deliver it, but Vitek did what he could. Like Roy Westbrook, he was now careful to construct his literature without hard and fast promises, emphasizing the "chance" his royalties had to appreciate in value. Such an approach left federal authorities with the relatively complex task of establishing the present and future value of those royalties before they could successfully charge Vitek with fraud. The government was not up to the challenge.

It was particularly fortunate for Vitek that his royalties in Winkler

Easy Money

County happened to lie near one of the most problematic and controversial oil fields in the United States in 1929, a field about whose future even industry experts disagreed.[23] There was no question that the Winkler County Hendrick field was a field of major importance; huge gushers were commonplace within it. But after a year of frenzied development, the field developed perplexing problems of water incursion; wells that had been lucrative oil producers suddenly began to flow greater and greater amounts of water, and no one knew exactly what had caused this problem. Many observers feared that water would eventually choke off oil production in Hendrick, but no one was in a position to predict when that development might take place. Hendrick producers responded to this situation with a voluntary, if uneasy, agreement to cut back production, hoping that this might slow water incursion and maintain field profitability. No one knew how long the agreement would hold or if it would accomplish its economic objective.

The complexity of Hendrick field problems made the task of evaluating Vitek's royalties formidable, and Vitek was fully aware of this difficulty when he appeared before postal authorities in Washington on August 14, 1929. To a charge that his properties did not show the kind of production likely to lead to big profits, Vitek answered that the production cutback had temporarily discouraged activity, and that development and production would both pick up in a short time, as would profits. In response to Postal Inspector Johnson's estimates of property values and future production, Vitek offered his own consulting engineer's much more promising estimates. When Johnson offered dampening information on prices for sour Hendrick crude, Vitek countered by introducing a new complication: he maintained that his royalties lay in a "sweet oil" area of the Hendrick field, an area in which the oil commanded a price twice that of the rest of the field because it did not have a high sulfur content. Vitek's "sweet oil" ploy was indeed a creative tactic. Although there had been some indication that sweet oil might lie at greater depths than existing Hendrick field production, no one had found such oil in commercial quantities in Winkler County by 1929; there was no "sweet oil area," save in Vitek's mind. The move succeeded because the government was unprepared to discuss the sulfur content of Hendrick crude; Vitek was thus able to dispute even the information the Post Office Department had on current oil prices and hence royalty values. In all, the hearing gave Vitek a

Adaptive Strategies

chance to do what he was best able to do, to make his properties sound much more valuable than they really were.[24]

Vitek's royalty promotions, constructed with a view to staying out of the hands of law enforcement authorities, brought him between $70,000 and $80,000. This was a far cry from the booty he estimated he had taken in while in cahoots with Cook. Promoting royalty interests, however, proved much safer. In April 1930 Vitek was indicted by a federal grand jury in Fort Worth for his earlier promotion of Vitek Oil in Texas, but federal prosecutors did not pursue his royalty ventures after a jury found him innocent. His adaptive strategy worked.[25]

Among the promoters who proved less skillful than Vitek at staying out of trouble was his longtime Fort Worth associate, Leo F. Reardon. Reardon stood trial with Dr. Cook in 1923, and at the end of 1924 he, Cook, and Vitek were associated by indictment in the Vitek Oil and Refining case. While Vitek fled to New York and Cook was in Leavenworth, Reardon surrendered and paid a $3,500 fine, but he escaped prison. By the mid-twenties Reardon was a marked man, and he had good reason to try to stay on the right side of the law. This did not mean he was willing to give up selling oil to small investors: after all, that was what he knew best.[26]

Like Vitek, Reardon saw trade in royalties as a safer way to raise money than the promotion of wildcat exploration; he also scented an opportunity to cash in on the publicity given the discovery of the bonanza Yates field. In 1927, therefore, Reardon and Joe A. Hoover organized three separate royalty companies to promote trade on Yates Ranch properties, and Reardon set to work writing and mailing news to investors of his clever purchase of one-sixteenth of Ira Yates's royalty interest on 5,808 acres. The tract, on closer examination, included only 100 producing acres along with 5,708 nonproducing acres, but that was obscured by verbal color worthy of Seymour Cox: "The ultra-violet rays of rainbow's end—the veritable pot of gold which makes the Lamp of Aladdin resemble a rusty lantern—has been found in the world-famous Yates Ranch of Pecos County, Texas."[27]

Reardon publicized his venture, sold stock, and only belatedly applied for a state charter, claiming assets of $100 million. The high figure attracted the attention of the secretary of state, who learned that Reardon had never executed his option to purchase the producing royalties from

Yates and that his valuation of assets was thus indefensible. Reardon's application for a state charter was denied. This action placed the promoters in an dangerous position: they had already sold securities based on claims of a state charter and the ownership of property to which they lacked a legal title. Worse yet, state and federal authorities were now aware of their predicament. For good reason, they rushed to cover their tracks.[28]

It was not easy to do. They already owed Ira Yates $30,000 for the nonproducing acreage. They could not pay him until they were given a charter and permission to sell stock; they could not sell stock legally until they acquired the producing royalty from Yates. In short, Ira Yates had the two promoters over a barrel; if he would not come to terms with them, they were out of business and into hot water.

The canny rancher exploited the situation fully, by doubling his price for the producing acreage. Reardon and Hoover were in no position to bargain. In turn, they tried to recoup by selling shares illegally, passing along the cost to their investors and awarding themselves shares of the watered stock to sell for eating money. Reardon told investors that the stock, worth no more than $1 per share, was trading at $12.50 and that mammoth wells were producing on the company's properties. In some correspondence Reardon announced that the price per share had just risen to $50! None of it was true. The stock did not sell well, and Reardon and Hoover tried assessing stockholders by making unauthorized drafts on their bank accounts. As this move did not raise operating capital, Reardon and Hoover tried to revive sales with a phony dividend. When this ploy failed, Reardon's royalty empire fell apart. His plan to sell properties at inflated prices was unsuccessful because he had been too ambitious, mismanaged the venture, and thereby placed himself at the mercy of keener men. In the end he was convicted of mail fraud again and was sentenced to a year in Leavenworth. Reardon's adaptive strategy might have worked, but he botched its execution.[29]

Another veteran of both promotion and federal indictment, Henry H. Hoffman, also tried the royalty game on an ambitious scale. Hoffman, who also went by Hubert Hoffman and H. H. Hoffman, had a long and shady record in the Houston oil community. He arrived there in 1915 and worked as a printer and real estate salesman. When oil prices rose in 1916, he organized the Hoffman Oil and Refining Company and set up the Hoffman Trust. Thereafter, on paper, his business empire grew, with the

Adaptive Strategies

H. H. Hoffman Company and the Hoffman Production Company as new creations in 1918; both were based on promotion of investments in small unproductive leases in the vicinity of Houston. By year's end, he had hired an office manager and founded both the Ranger-Burkburnett Oil Company and the Union Trust Company, a brokerage operation. He managed promotions as far away as Kentucky from the seven-story Hoffman Building in downtown Houston. In the years that followed, Hoffman launched the Dallas Comanche Oil Company, the Ranger Comanche Oil Company, and the Union National Oil Company—all based on small royalty holdings in Eastland County. He was indefatigable at thinking up new promotions.[30]

One reason there were so many ventures was that Hoffman's various companies regularly went into receivership. Ranger-Burkburnett, for example, failed in 1921, with $350,000 in stock issued and no assets. Usually Hoffman simply went on to his next promotion, but following this business failure he moved to Fort Worth to elude FTC examiners; then he traveled extensively on the East Coast and in Europe both to keep beyond the reach of the government and to promote the Blue Bird Oil Company, which he and Butler Perryman located back in Houston. He was caught up and convicted in the federal sweep in 1923, however, and served a term in Leavenworth in 1924 and 1925. As soon as he got out he went back to promotion, attracting the renewed attention of the FTC, which issued a cease and desist order in 1927. Typically, when nothing else happened, Hoffman continued to sell shares and certificates, but in common with many other fraudulent promoters, he altered his strategy to try to avoid further prosecution.[31]

Like Reardon and Hoover, Hoffman concentrated on the sale of royalty interests and shares in royalty ventures, promoting the Terrell County Royalty Company, the Howard County Royalty Company, and the Mid-Tex Corporation in 1929. Since they were all run along similar lines, Mid-Tex serves as an example of Hoffman's refinement of royalty sales techniques.

Hoffman purchased royalty interests in 320 acres of nonproducing land near the Hendrick field. He then divided the interest into halves, kept one of them personally, and divided the other into 2,000 units. A week or two after the purchase, he secured sucker lists from other promoters and began to sell the royalty units for $10 each. He touted his wares with all the

Easy Money

familiar advertising devices. When a noncommercial discovery well came in on a nearby lease, he told his investors that it was "a sensational new oil strike"—which in his various letters came in on any one of six different dates. Hoffman sent investors gusher photos, actually taken at a well one hundred miles away; telegrams promised 700 percent profits and bonuses of additional royalties. He always urged the immediate acquisition of more interests, "to secure a steady income every month for many years to come. DO NOT HESITATE THE FRACTION OF A SECOND—THIS MAY BE THE TURNING POINT IN YOUR LIFE."[32]

As the Mid-Texas promotion advanced, Hoffman acquired additional property in Winkler County from Paul Vitek, and he created 2,000 more interests in 1/640 of ⅛ of the royalty interest on 320 acres of land; he sold 907 of them. He told investors that this kind of royalty purchase was more prudent than common shares in oil companies because there would be "no promoter to cut in on your profits." And, indeed, there was no cut, for there was neither oil nor profits. Neither tract was sufficiently attractive to induce the lease owners to risk capital on test wells.[33]

If the leases had been exceptionally productive, however, investors would never have recovered the capital they placed with Hoffman because, as was typical of such promotions, each holding was microscopic. An investor actually owned ½,000 of 1/640 of ⅛ of ⅛ of the oil produced from 320 acres. If the tract had yielded $750 million in oil production, an extremely unlikely outcome, the maximum return to the investor would have been ninety cents. But Hoffman, among others, successfully obscured the truth and hooked thousands of would-be oil moguls on his scheme.[34]

The government was harder to deceive. Familiar with Hoffman's past, postal inspectors picked up his trail, gathered his promotional literature, and checked land records. They discovered the usual pattern of glittering promises and sordid deceptions, especially with the Terrell County promotion: Hoffman had never actually acquired the properties he sold there![35] Thus, in 1930, H. H. Hoffman returned to federal court. He pleaded guilty to mail fraud and received a two-year prison term. Fortunately for him, Judge James C. Wilson continued to take an indulgent course with promoters: the sentence was suspended for five years, and Hoffman was placed on probation. Wilson discharged Hoffman from probation after three years.[36]

Adaptive Strategies

At roughly the same time Henry Hoffman got into trouble promising fortunes from microscopic royalties, one of the most versatile promoters of his age landed in legal hot water. It was an event beyond his control, the stock market crash of 1929, that was his nemesis; ironically, after years of dubious oil dealing, promoting a printing company led to his fall. That promoter was Chester R. Bunker.

A Brooklyn boy like Frederick A. Cook, Bunker was beyond question superbly gifted at promotion. If he never quite achieved the soaring pinnacles of promotional bunkum as crafted by Seymour Cox or the canny ability to survive hostile federal scrutiny demonstrated by Paul Vitek, Bunker surpassed all oildom's pirates of promotion in the variety and audacity of his ventures and the flexibility of his business strategy. For over a decade, his promotional activity was unceasing and intense. Through the mails, he strung investors along with glittering promises of easy money; in daily business, he helped other promoters do the same thing. When it came to thinking up new ways to snare investors, Chester Bunker was unrivaled in his circle. Unfortunately, when it came to managing capital, Bunker showed the same weaknesses as many of his colleagues. That proved to be the decisive flaw of his career.

Like H. H. Hoffman and Roy Westbrook, Bunker began working as a printer. His involvement with promoters probably dated from 1918 when he took part in the short-lived Kentucky oil boom; he also published his first tip sheet, the *Kentucky Oil Ledger*, then. For the ambitious young Bunker, Kentucky soon ceased to be exciting, so he gravitated to that mecca of promotion, Fort Worth, one year later; there he commenced a grand paper empire of related oil ventures. Bunker and Company, a brokerage operation, hawked various stocks, including Kentucky Bell Oil and Gas, Texas Black B.O.Y. Royalty, and several of his own. Bunker Advertising concocted sales literature for his companies as well as for Paul Vitek and other Fort Worth operators. His first Texas tip sheet, the *Texas Journal of Commerce*, was succeeded by *Texas Oil World* and *Western World*. Bunker Printing produced his literature and that of other promoters. Altogether his various interrelated companies covered all aspects of promotion: copy, printing, advertising, and sales. It is even possible that Bunker achieved economies of scale by performing these services for both his own ventures and those of others.[37]

Beyond doubt, other promoters held Chester Bunker in high regard. Frederick A. Cook recognized his energy and abilities when he turned his

Easy Money

own tip sheet, *The Independent Oil and Financial Reporter*, over to Bunker to operate. The scale of his operations made Bunker a large employer, and his known skill as a promoter made him an important man in Fort Worth, where more mention was made of his legitimate operations than of his dubious ventures. In 1929 the American Petroleum Institute named him to one of its prestigious committees in recognition of his standing in the industry.[38] To that point, Bunker seemed to personify success. He had also been remarkably lucky at staying out of trouble. He had a close brush with the law in 1922, when he was indicted for mail fraud, but the indictment was dismissed by Judge Wilson. During the remainder of the decade Bunker assembled a veritable army of investors in more than a dozen ventures.

In short order, he launched the World Company, the Texanna Oil and Refining Company, World Oil Company, World Syndicates, the Marathon Fold Drilling and Leasing Club, the Pecos County Drilling Club, the Howard-Glasscock Drilling Club, the weekly *Western World*, a new securities company, Bunker's Wildcats, World Exploration, a consolidated printing and box manufacturing company, *Texas Monthly Magazine*, and a textbook and trade book company. Bunker even found the time to manage other promotions, including Galloway's "Laxa-Ginger Snaps," a purgative cookie confected of coarse cinnamon. He was up to selling anything.[39]

In all of his numerous ventures, Bunker was the idea man, the creator. As a manager of operations, however, Bunker was irregular and erratic; he delegated day-to-day operations to subordinates, most of whom were experienced in their various lines, and they kept the businesses going. But lack of management ability at the top was a serious weakness in Bunker's empire. So was want of ready cash, for the common element in Bunker's ventures was undercapitalization. The printing company, for example, was launched with borrowed money, which Bunker used to buy production machinery, and while it brought in considerable income, it was never out of debt during Chester Bunker's ownership. World Oil, his grandest promotion, had only $300,000 in capital stock, and two-thirds of the shares were exchanged for interests in earlier ventures. These earlier stock flotations never sold out; when allowance is made for Bunker's tactic of issuing generous stock bonuses, it is possible that only one-third of the possible interests that were folded into World Oil brought in money. After deducting brokerage commissions and costs, the amount of capital available for operations was small; for World Oil, Bunker was not likely to have raised more than $50,000. Worse yet, he spent most of this money on a costly unproductive lease on the edge of the Hendrick field and on what proved to be a marginally commercial property near the Yates field. Chester Bunker could create businesses, but he was not skilled at running them.

Bunker's single success in oil exploration was accidental. The venture was a wildcat promotion on the L. P. Powell ranch, in Crockett County, Texas, not far from the Big Lake oil field. He acquired his lease for about ten cents per acre and tried to sell leases, but met scant success. In the hope of turning the property to some use, he devised a scheme to use it to push subscriptions to his biweekly tip sheet, *World Oil*. The offer was simple: for every three-year subscription, $10 total cost, a buyer would acquire an interest in the prospective production from part of the Powell lease. He created slightly more than 20,000 interests and actually issued about 12,500 of them; the remainder were the property of World Oil. Bunker thus boosted his subscription list and thereby his advertising rates, but at the cost of drilling a test well in rank wildcat territory. His own compensation was limited to a small lease adjacent to the test well, which he carved out of his original lease without informing interest holders and divided with his driller and his secretary. When World Oil Company's Powell Number 1 came in, Bunker had his first grand success.

Bunker moved quickly to raise capital from his discovery, selling his acreage to the Humble Oil and Refining Company for $1.4 million, even before a confirmation well was undertaken. The bulk of the purchase price was to be paid out of production runs, but Bunker's driller received $75,000, Bunker and his secretary each drew $37,500, and $200,000 was paid to Bunker Printing. Certificate holders could expect payment from future income. Further payments to Bunker from Humble stopped, however, when certificate holders and Humble's attorneys learned of Bunker's offsetting lease. Bunker's subscribers claimed that they were entitled to all of the income from the sale of the lease and that Bunker's appropriation of the site next to the test well was illegal. Bunker countered that his prerogatives as trustee for the subscribers permitted him to take the tract. When the issue was finally settled in 1934, World Oil paid more than $400,000 in compensation to certificate holders, penalty for Bunker's indiscretion. By then it was of little interest to Bunker, because World Oil was in the hands of court-appointed trustees and Bunker himself was in Leavenworth.[40]

Had Bunker been a more capable manager, he would have put some of

Easy Money

the proceeds of his Crockett County windfall to work paying off bills and shoring up operations; doing so might in the end have kept him out of jail. But for a man who always had many more schemes in mind than he could execute, such a conventional use of ready cash was unthinkable. Worse yet, his Crockett County success encouraged Bunker to believe he could make big money looking for oil. Thus he took World Oil's money from the sale to Humble to purchase expensive leases close to production in the Yates and Hendrick fields in 1927. He used the Pecos County leases to promote a drilling club, which paid for a test well on a 3,460-acre block of leases. When he spudded in this test in mid-January 1928, Bunker was optimistic that it would "turn out a huge producer." Through engine trouble, cave-ins, and tedious fishing jobs, Bunker continued to send encouraging reports to his investors. When the crew pulled down the crown block, he wrote another upbeat report: "This delay merely stimulated interest in the well." When the well reached 3,105 feet, near its planned depth, Bunker sustained mystery and hope: "The well is being closely watched by the oil fraternity as it is in the eastern rim of a deep salt basin and is logging very much like the big Winkler County producers." Several days later, however, he had to plug and abandon the well after the drilling tools firmly jammed in the hole. There was no repeat of the Crockett County bonanza.[41]

When oil promotions flagged, Bunker turned to hard minerals, promoting mines in Texas, Arizona, and Nevada through World Exploration. As always, promotional costs were high and sales were disappointing, despite the energetic travels and bombast of "President Bunker," as his tip sheet styled him. "Success succeeds" and "Speculate with safety," he advised his readers.[42]

For all Chester Bunker's creativity, he was plagued by one glaring deficiency: he failed to make money. The only big return he ever got was from the sale of Crockett County leases to Humble; most of his other creations never generated funds from their operations. The sole exception to his record of business failure was his Fort Worth printing company, which made boxes and did other work for the large Fort Worth meat-packing houses. It also did printing for the State of Texas and printed three magazines, Bunker's tip sheets, and advertising brochures for a wide variety of businesses. Over the years, the printing company should have been a money-maker, but it was never profitable. The truth of the situation was simple: Bunker consistently diverted revenues from the printing company

Adaptive Strategies

to keep his other ventures alive. In a tangle of bookkeeping transactions, he milked the printing company. He charged his own salary to it, as well as $24,000 in annual rent paid to World Oil; the printing company paid the taxes and insurance on his property, along with interest on the bank note Bunker's World Oil had signed to acquire the property. The printing company even paid the cost of Bunker's brokerage operations during periods of no sales![43]

Even the printing company could not stand such plundering indefinitely, and as it began to falter in 1926, Bunker decided he would promote it. He reorganized it and began to sell it with the same devices he used in oil. In all, Bunker sold $111,000 worth of printing company stock to 642 investors, most of whom invested $200 or less. He found his targets through the sucker lists of his brokerage operation, and he concentrated on California, where he found about 12 percent of his investors, though the state contained only 5.6 percent of the population of the United States. Sales were slow, however, and they did not meet Bunker's needs for cash; actual capitalization of the printing company was barely adequate to launch its operation. In the long run, that meant it was unable to provide adequate support for the other ventures. In the short run, it had recurring cash flow problems, because Bunker's other ventures were slow to pay their printing bills; by November, they were more than $30,000 behind, and they never caught up during Bunker's management. When business turned down after the stock market crash in late 1929, the printing operation, and hence all of Bunker's empire, collapsed. In short order, World Oil went into receivership, and Chester Bunker was indicted for mail fraud in connection with the promotion and operation of the printing company.[44]

Chester Bunker's trial was not as grand as those of Cook and Cox earlier in the decade, but the federal government once again reinforced the prosecution with two special prosecutors. It also took the precaution of sending in Halstead L. Ritter to sit for Judge Wilson. For his defense, Bunker hired the local legal expert in mail fraud cases, Henry Zweifel, then in private practice. In the end, however, Zweifel secured the dismissal of only one count of the six-point indictment, and the judge sentenced Bunker to three years in prison. His appeal rejected, Bunker entered Leavenworth in April 1932. By that time, the golden age of oil promotion was over.[45]

"Poor Kitty"
I bought a little stock in oil,
I guess the broker lied.
No matter how I scratched its head,
The wildcat up and died![1]

THE GREAT speculative boom of the teens and twenties also expired when the stock market crashed in 1929. Promoters of industrial securities and their investors shared a common fate as plunging prices prompted margin calls and paper profits vanished, leaving debt, frustration, and resentment behind. Thus began the Great Depression. In truth, the previous fluctuations in the stock market and massive losses in real estate investments had already undermined small investors as a group. The euphoria spun out by the surges in securities markets merely obscured long-term weakness in the economy.

Oil was in trouble long before. After its price decline in 1921, the petroleum industry revived and activity resumed. But as successful exploration resulted in a long sequence of great discoveries, especially in Texas, California, and Oklahoma, the pace of oil exploration and production advanced from hectic to desperate. A tidal wave of crude oil swamped markets, steadily weakening prices, which fluctuated in response to surges and dips in production. As prices drifted downward, oilmen responded by producing ever greater quantities of oil, trying to make up by quantity what they lacked in prices. That, of course, intensified downward pressures on prices. Despite talk of conservation and some experiments in production control, nothing stopped the flood of oil. The final blow came with the discovery of the gigantic East Texas field in 1930. Thus it was that oil prices did not return to the levels of 1919–20 until the 1970s, and even then the actual gains against inflation were slow in coming.

Long before the depression, many promoters fell into financial and legal difficulties, giving investors reason to be skeptical about the benefits of popular capitalism. What happened to the artists of promotion the federal authorities used as examples in their crackdowns on mail-order promotion?

169

Afterword

Some promoters adjusted to their brushes with the law by changing the scenes of their operations. California was an attractive destination for Oklahoma and Texas promoters who saw ventures go sour; Oscar Houston of Big Diamond, for example, found his way to Long Beach, and, after serving his time, Chester Bunker headed to California, where he applied for a realtor's license.

Other promoters felt a pressing need to continue operations farther afield. Charles Sherwin and Harry Schwarz, of General Lee Interests, fell into that category. Out on bail, they shifted their operations from Fort Worth to Mexico City, where they promoted the Mexerica Mining Company. Mexerica's mailing address, however, was a post office box in Fort Worth, and before long postal authorities noticed it received fourteen sacks of mail a day. They stopped delivery and pressed Mexican authorities to apprehend Sherwin and Schwarz. That brought the two promoters to take a hurried trip to France during the winter of 1924, while their associate, Robert A. Lee, served time in Leavenworth.[2]

Knowing his former employers were still at liberty did not put Robert A. Lee in a charitable frame of mind. He did not serve more than eight months of his sentence, but, once paroled, he was still hard up for money. He naturally thought of the two men who promoted the schemes on which, like so many of General Lee's investors, he had pinned his hopes for income for the rest of his life, and in October 1924 he filed a civil suit against them, claiming breach of contract and asking $25,000 damages. But before he could get any money from them, Lee had to find Sherwin and Schwarz, and that was no easier for the old man than for federal authorities.[3]

Sherwin and Schwarz returned from France in the spring of 1924 and used Guadalajara, Mexico, as a base from which to sell several more mining promotions. Tiring of Mexico and mine promotion, however, they tried something more exciting and moved to Florida, where they joined the real estate promotion game. Then luck turned against them: the federal circuit court threw out their appeal, and when they stalled for more time by appealing to the Supreme Court, that body affirmed the lower courts' rulings.[4]

The two promoters were thus obliged to enter Leavenworth in the summer of 1925. Still, things were not as bad as they might have been, for in November, President Calvin Coolidge remitted the heavy fines levied on the promoters. Nor did they serve their full ten-year sentences. Charles

Easy Money

Sherwin was paroled by 1933 and went back to doing what he knew best; in 1934 he and Walter Marks were indicted for running a mail-order bucket shop in Dallas. In 1939 Sherwin was under federal indictment again, this time in Los Angeles. Once out of Leavenworth, Harry Schwarz was more successful at staying out of sight.[5]

Paul Vitek's skill at adapting strategy to avoid legal penalties for promotional sleight-of-hand kept him out of jail and let him continue to raise money for various ventures. As his Howard County exploration demonstrated, he was better at promotion than paying bills, a characteristic he shared with many other operators. Unlike many other promoters, however, he actually looked for oil, and, had he kept drilling, a lucky strike might have made his glittering promises come true. But on July 12, 1931, a well he was completing in the new East Texas field caught fire while he was on the rig. Badly burned, Vitek died two days later.[6]

In some ways, the subsequent fates of Dr. Frederick A. Cook and Seymour Cox were no less painful. During the first round of his appeals, Cook served time in the Tarrant County jail, where his wife delivered hot home-cooked meals, until the Internal Revenue Service seized their Packard and sold it at auction for $1,000. Cook received guests, including author Everett Harre, who left an autographed copy of *One Day and Forever*.

Much of Cook's time was taken up with further legal entanglements. In December he came to trial along with John C. Verser and the other promoters of the Revere Oil Company. Cook's role had been limited to the provision of copywriting, printing, and mail room services, so he claimed ignorance of fraud. The presiding judge, James C. Wilson, believed him and dismissed the charges. Cook's attorney secured a parole for his client from Judge Wilson, only to have it disputed by Henry Zweifel and reversed by the circuit court. Finally, when his appeal to the Supreme Court in the PPA case failed, Cook arrived at the federal prison at Leavenworth, Kansas, and began to serve his sentence on April 6, 1925.[7]

In prison, Cook served as a doctor and edited the prison newspaper, *New Era*. He also became an industrious jailhouse lawyer, petitioning Presidents Coolidge and Hoover for pardons, without success. When he was finally released in the spring of 1930, he looked older than his sixty-five years. Prison took a toll on Cook, but it never made him penitent. He continued to insist on his complete innocence, and he convinced a small

Afterword

but devoted following that he was still a hero, if an ill-starred one. A wealthy admirer secured a pardon for him from Franklin Delano Roosevelt several months before Cook's death in August 1940.[8]

Seymour Cox arrived back at Leavenworth in February 1933, three years after Cook's release. He had hardly settled into the prison routine before he was brought back to Fort Worth to stand trial for his phony Mexican mining promotion. This time he pleaded guilty and received a two-year sentence, which ran concurrently with his Oklahoma City sentence.[9]

Like Cook, he edited the prison paper, and he taught in the prison school. For the most part, however, he reflected on the unfair breaks life had dealt him. Cox stayed behind bars until November 1939; he served an extra thirty days beyond his term because he claimed to be incapable of paying his $5,000 fine. While her husband was in prison, Nelda lived in the Fort Worth YWCA and opened "Your Book Nook," in the Sinclair Building. She offered tours "personally conducted by Mrs. S. E. J. Cox," and sold a variety of titles, including *Kings of Commerce* and *A History of Financial Speculation.*[10]

Upon his release, Seymour moved back to Fort Worth, where he was generally accepted as an interesting local character, one with a massive chip on his shoulder. He belabored anyone who would listen with complaints about his stern father and his recent misfortunes. He did more than idle and grumble in his old age, however. In 1950 he developed a promotion for the Penner Oil and Gas Company of Nowata, Oklahoma. History repeated itself. In November 1951, at age sixty-seven, Cox was fined $1,000 and sentenced to two consecutive five-year sentences in prison on fourteen counts of violating Securities and Exchange Commission and postal regulations.[11]

Cox's health declined to the point that he was transferred to the federal clinic in Springfield, Missouri. In prison, in the hospital, and after his release, he tinkered away at a novel, *Girls, Gushers, and Roughnecks.* He had, after all, always excelled at writing fiction, and the prose was pure Cox: "A wildcat derrick . . . pointed upward like a finger of destiny." "An immense and immeasurable treasure vault hidden deep in the bowels of the earth"; "We expect to hit the pay and promote ourselves to millionaire's row." "When this well busts in, we'll be rich as Rockefeller." "We'll be millionaires when this well breaks loose." "Pay off big." Cox's imagination still flowed in familiar channels.[12]

Cox never lived to see his novel in print. He died at age eighty-seven in December 1971, and "the Napoleon of promoters" was buried in Houston, the site of his grandest dreams and most flawed illusions.[13]

At first sight it seems unlikely that there could ever be another Seymour Cox. Numerous changes in laws and regulations since the 1920s, some of them the result of protests against promotional practices that permitted the plunder of jazz-age investors, have created a maze of rules to be negotiated by those raising money for oil ventures. The Securities Act of 1933, notably, tightened the definition of fraud by forbidding misleading statements, strengthening the hand of federal prosecutors. The act also created a civil remedy, which was expected to be more effective than the time-consuming criminal proceedings. Major parts of this legislation, Section 17a most obviously, were created with the oil frauds of the 1920s in mind, because congressmen were convinced that the blue sky laws of states had been inadequate to deal with the likes of Seymour Cox.[14]

These measures served largely to restore investor confidence in the securities market. As one scholar has argued, the SEC in effect became the guarantor of trust in securities. There is little evidence, however, to suggest that the agency has been a significant deterrent to small-time confidence men. In part this result has followed from the commission's strategy of "promotion of disclosure more than the punishment of fraud." As its landmark action against Columbus Marion ("Dad") Joiner, the discoverer of the East Texas oil field, demonstrated during the early 1940s, by the time the commission acted against a fraudulent promoter, the scam had been concluded and the assets were dissipated.[15]

Some of the SEC's critics argue that it is still incapable of more than highly selective enforcement. Thus, like postal authorities of the era of Seymour Cox and Frederick A. Cook, the SEC has taken relatively little action against Ponzi schemes and small-scale operations. One observer described the activity of infrequently traded "pink sheet" companies as "a regulatory black hole." The SEC continues to inch its way to court, however, even when larger sums are involved. The $300 million Goldcor scheme for extracting gold from lava sands in Costa Rica was exposed by an investigative reporter in July 1988. The SEC acted five months later.[16]

Scam operations are still remarkably easy to organize. For a start, lists of investors can be obtained from over 300 list brokers for as little as twenty cents per target. With list in hand, a promoter can launch a penny stock sale or a boiler room operation, both techniques now especially effective when they are combined with radio and television marketing support. The penny stocks in minerals and other ventures still sell well among naive investors, who lose billions of dollars annually in what the North American Securities Administrators Association aptly characterized as "the shadowy netherworld of U.S. equity markets."[17]

If the basic techniques of floating dubious promotions remain familiar, the allure of a fortune from black gold has proven equally enduring. Neither the operation of the SEC nor the existence of federal statutes has kept time-honored oil scams from reappearing regularly and multiplying when boom-time prosperity whets investors' appetites for speculation. A decade before the SEC came into being, for example, many jazz-age promoters, in and outside oil, used the device of linking religious righteousness to profits. Then and more recently, that device permitted them to exploit evangelical Christians by assuring them that God will make the saved prosperous. Oil promoters have victimized the gullible faithful by claiming that God is their geologist and that the historical books of the Old Testament will lead them to oil bonanzas in the Middle East. This approach, used in the twenties, worked as well in the oil boom of the seventies. One oil promoter in Idaho raised $4 million from believers whom he convinced that "God is leading us to move ahead in this very area when no one else is interested." He went bankrupt, and state authorities sued him for securities violations. But when the faithful link spiritual and financial advice neither the SEC nor federal regulations are likely to keep them from losses.[18]

Pyramid schemes continue to be popular with fraud artists. Recently Stephen L. Smith raised $125 million from 700 investors, including his grandmother, to float the SH Oil Company. He paid initial dividends as high as 80 percent, though assets and income were meager. In the end, the federal government actually closed him down, and he received a fifteen-year prison term from a federal court in Florida.[19]

Because the excitement of an oil boom can reach all social classes, people from quite literally all walks of life can be caught up in speculation; the rich and famous are no more immune to the allure of windfall profits now than they were in the jazz age. Thus, at the beginning of the most recent oil boom, the Home-Stake Production Company swindled investors of $130 million; only $3 million went toward drilling for oil. Among the

Easy Money

investors caught in this scam were celebrities such as Barbra Streisand, Jack Benny, Barbara Walters, Liza Minnelli, and Senators Jacob Javits and Ernest Hollings; like Carlo Ponzi and Big Diamond, Home-Stake paid "dividends" from funds raised in security sales. In the end, Robert S. Trippet, the Home-Stake promoter, spent only one day in jail; his investors were still trying to recover their stakes in midyear 1989.[20]

Most oil promoters, past and present, have been content to pursue investors outside Hollywood, and they frequently fall back on traditional strategies. In 1981 Howard B. Sirota, a thirty-two-year-old Wall Street lawyer, was accused of some fast promotion in which he acted, like Seymour Cox, as "the general partner, the promoter, the underwriter, the explorer, the finder, the contractor." As one observer commented, "If you imagine a circular conference table, he jumps from seat to seat, negotiating with himself, paying himself exorbitant fees for his services. So when he's done maybe the only way he'd find oil would be to drill in a gas station and hit a tank."[21] Similarly, in 1982 Merle Lee Matlock, president of Petrowest, Inc., and Explorer Energy, Inc., was indicted by a federal grand jury in Dallas for bilking investors of $693,000, money supposedly destined for oil and gas exploration in west Texas. Matlock was accused of using this money for personal purposes and of selling interests in drilling leases he did not own. When the SEC filed suit, Matlock filed for bankruptcy.[22]

To those familiar with the business shenanigans of the twenties, Matlock's alleged adventures with other people's money have little novelty, nor does the frequent appearance of bankruptcy as a feature of these recent oil scams. Like Cox, many promoters in recent times have tried to use their talents to reach easy money and have seen riches slip through their fingers. Litigation surrounding their recent operations makes an analysis of how they lost money difficult for the scholar at present. If, however, we grant that their operations resemble those of jazz-age promoters, we may gain some insight to their recent fates from what was true of their predecessors' operations. That may, in turn, indicate why the profits of boom times so often prove to be illusory, even before boom turns to bust.

The newcomers to oil in jazz-age America learned that promoting their ventures to raise capital was not as certain of success as they expected. The same boom that attracted both the newcomer and his investors to the

Afterword

industry drew numerous other newcomers with the same objectives. To meet intense competition for investment capital, promoters tended to describe the financial return from their ventures in the most favorable light while doing their best to obscure risks. Depending on the language they used, it was easy to stray from optimism into fraud.

Newcomers and marginal operations were especially likely to slide in this direction because they generally lacked sufficient capital to carry through on ventures, and they did not have positions within established business circles from which to raise money. The leases they could afford to buy, moreover, tended to be cast-off or rank wildcat properties, with little appeal to established oilmen and sophisticated investors. Thus the investments offered by the newcomers tended to be so risky that they were driven to costly appeals to naive investors who had no understanding of the risks involved. That, too, made dishonesty tempting. In the end, given the realities of competition for capital in a high-risk industry, the line separating legitimate and dishonest practice was often a blurred one.

The less capital they had on starting out, the more likely it was for newcomers with honest objectives to wander into fundamentally dishonest practices. Eager to get started, promoters took negligible assets and tried to build companies around them; they exaggerated the value of assets and overcapitalized their ventures. Such promoters could hope that by floating a large issue of stock or units or shares they would end up with enough capital to sustain operations. They rarely succeeded.

The shortage of capital in the creation of many of their ventures commonly dogged the new oilmen through their careers. Most of them were always running behind, raising money after they had incurred operating expenses. Much of the time, moreover, they lacked accurate information on their financial status because they rarely kept careful track of either debts or costs. As a consequence, few of them recognized the exceptionally high costs of raising small amounts of money. Those who used the mail or salesmen to find investors usually ended up spending what came in to raise capital rather than to acquire and develop properties. For that reason, companies started on a shoestring commonly ended barefoot in the snow. This outcome was often as much a surprise to promoters as to investors.

Whether honest or dishonest, newcomers or veterans, the participants in the oil booms faced challenging business conditions. High prices and

Easy Money

rising demand for petroleum fed the boom-time mentality that it was never easier to make money in oil. It seemed as if there could be no possibility of loss. But when so many people got into the oil business because they believed that boom prosperity would last forever, it actually became progressively harder to make real profits. In upstream oil, participants did not compete for retail markets but for capital, prospects, supplies, land, and labor. Competition of many participants drove costs up at a rate faster than could be offset by rising prices of petroleum. That meant that it was harder to end up with profits once bills were paid: costs ate up profits. When the odd venture turned a profit, initial overcapitalization had "watered" the stock so heavily that even real dividends rarely provided good returns to investors. In the end, the glamour of oil investments outweighed their financial value.

To those intoxicated by the excitement of boom times, costs and rates of return on invested capital did not seem to be problems because their attention was fixed upon the future rather than the present. Caught up in accelerating speculation, boomers thought as speculators, losing sight of objective standards of financial performance. It was particularly easy for the hard-up promoters to be captivated by the future orientation of the boom mentality, for their present situations were usually painfully lacking cash. If new oilmen grossly underestimated the cost of doing business from want of having done it before, they could console themselves that future returns would let them settle all their bills. Even old hands were often careless in controlling costs because they, too, concentrated on future returns. Investors, as well, were blinded by the dazzling future; they lost sight both of how long it would take to get a good return on a small investment and of the possibility there would be no return at all. Speculative mania came to hide financial reality.

In the twenties, as in more recent booms, the short-term effect of the activity of unlucky, inept, or fraudulent promoters on the petroleum industry has been significant. Veteran oilmen have long recognized that the large influx of newcomers that has come with each boom has raised the costs of doing business, because they boost demand for goods, services, and capital much more quickly than supply markets expand. In the short run, the more inclined promoters are to ignore costs, the more they tend to increase costs for everyone else in the industry. If money is no object in paying for a lease, the price of all leases will rise. Thus, overall, the profit

Afterword

margins of veteran and newcomer, honest operator and fraud artist, shrink with boom activity.

As a boom progresses, then, more money goes into the finding of oil, but proportionately less oil is found and produced. Overall, the financial efficiency of the industry declines. Bungling newcomers like the promoters of Lubbock Oil and Big Diamond simply lack the know-how that can find oil without the assistance of a lucky fluke; fraud artists like Seymour Cox and Dr. Frederick A. Cook do not spend much effort trying to bring in production. Either way, the money such promoters take in yields few barrels of oil.

Now that the petroleum industry has moved through another intense boom and a decline even more severe than that of the thirties, it is clear that the example of these unsuccessful promoters of long ago still has much to teach us. In terms of the behavior of petroleum prices and expectations of energy demand, there are many parallels between what happened in the late teens and twenties and what happened in the seventies and eighties. In both periods petroleum seemed in short supply. In both periods inexperienced businessmen rushed to get into oil, and a horde of eager investors supplied them with capital. In both periods many people lost money, and for many of the same reasons.

At this point it is worth emphasizing that honest businessmen, like their fraudulent brethren, get caught up in boom-time speculation, face boom-time accelerated costs, and make boom-time misjudgments. Their investors, like the mullets pursued by crooked operators, also lose money. Short of regulation precluding high-risk investment altogether, it is difficult to see how such boom-to-bust casualties could be avoided. They are one of the unavoidable results of high-risk endeavor. But many of our examples of promotion, past and present, have been dishonest. If we assume that the distinction between honest and fraudulent promises can be readily drawn—not always an easy matter—could something more than what the SEC and federal regulation offer work to protect investors from boom-time fraud?

Part of the problem in cracking down on fraudulent promotion lies in the difficulty investors have always faced in learning enough about new and untried investments. Particularly if the investors are unfamiliar with the business in which they consider putting their money, or, as with petroleum, if knowledgeable investment evaluation involves technical and specialized expertise, it is difficult for most of them to scent fraud. Journalists have found it pointless to try to verify the credibility of promoters with state or federal regulatory officials. State officials rarely keep track of them until mountainous complaints produce political pressures for action. Federal agencies, such as the Commodity Futures Trading Commission, are unreliable and slow.[23]

Modern tax laws, moreover, have indirectly provided additional incentive to dishonest promoters because they have created a class of investors willing to use large sums in high-risk ventures, largely with a view to adjusting tax burdens. Such investors have been more attuned to the advantages of sheltering income than to the practical realities of return on investment. Commodity brokers, oil lease peddlers, and even rabbit breeders feasted on this new school of mullets. At the same time, legislators created numerous exceptions, such as "safe haven" provisions, which exempt small promoters from onerous and costly paperwork and from the disclosure requirements that apply in other instances. Such havens have been open to both legitimate promoters and pirates of the trade.[24]

Even if the disclosure process worked more smoothly, however, or if tax laws and loopholes were changed, the behavior of investors eager to get rich quickly during the twenties oil boom makes it clear that swindles would not be eliminated. As important as the availability of information is the investors' ability to understand the industry they are investing in and their willingness to exercise a measure of prudence in pursuing gain. Most investments cannot make a person rich in a hurry, but when investors have that goal uppermost in mind, they lose sight of economic reality. Herein lies the weakness of regulatory attempts to protect investors, past and present. Short of making investors' choices for them, regulators cannot save them from the runaway spills of ignorance spurred on by greed. Doing so would involve severe restriction on individual choice and an open economy, comparable to an attempt to save Americans from cardiac disease by removing butter and eggs from supermarket shelves. Without a regulatory prohibition of investment, how could one protect an investor like Martin Jachens who repeatedly gave money to Seymour Cox? Or investors like P. G. Wooster and N. J. Cary who had lost money in oil promotions before they lost it with General Lee? If repeated losses at "playing the oil game" did not educate them, what could have done so? In short, perhaps the main problem lies not with the working of regulation

Afterword

but with investor mentality, especially during boom times. As Charles P. Kindleberger has argued, there may be little that law and regulation can do to protect investors bent on speculation.[25]

The ultimate damage done to the economy by inept, unlucky, and crooked promoters was profound. When estimates of losses in oil, other securities, and real estate before 1929 are totaled, they add up to billions of dollars over little more than a decade. Much of this money was lost, moreover, by economically marginal investors and by farmers and small-town speculators, leaving them less able to cope with sharp declines in agribusiness and local economies. Black Thursday, October 24, 1929, captured headlines all over the world, but the tens of thousands of individual Black Thursdays passed without public notice.

But during the twenties, as in recent years, inept and shady promoters also did significant long-term damage to the American petroleum industry. Each new scandal has made it more difficult for honest oilmen to raise venture capital. The public reputation of the industry, repeatedly tarnished from the days of the Pithole boom in Pennsylvania onward, was tarred anew with every fresh round of disclosure of fraud and sharp trading. Over the years, dishonest promoters have damaged industry credibility and left the oil industry vulnerable to critics who would constrict its ability to raise capital and would bring it under more stringent governmental regulation. The entire American petroleum industry has, in short, paid a high price for the pursuit of easy money.

GLOSSARY

The reader who wishes to know more about oil field technology and terminology should consult J. E. Brantly, *History of Oil Well Drilling* (Houston: Gulf Publishing Company, 1971), and Robert O. Anderson, *Fundamentals of the Petroleum Industry* (Norman: University of Oklahoma Press, 1984).

The following terms appear in *Easy Money*:

Bailer. A cylindrical tool lowered into the well bore during cable tool drilling to remove rock cuttings and debris.

Casing. Steel pipe used in a well to support the walls of the hole and seal off the borehole from fluids.

Casing shoe. A heavy metal ring used on strings of casing in a cable tool-drilled well to strengthen the end of the pipe and permit driving the casing through a tight hole.

Crown block. A steel frame containing mounted pulleys, placed in the top of a derrick to hoist equipment.

Drilling straight up. Bearing the entire expense of drilling a well.

Elevators. Clamps to hold pipe, casing, or tubing as it is lowered into or lifted from the well bore.

Fishing job. Retrieving tools or other materials lost down a well and bringing them back to the surface; usually a time-consuming and costly procedure.

Mineral rights. Ownership of minerals under a tract of land, which includes the right to explore for and extract minerals.

Pay formation. Rock layer or strata producing petroleum.

Producing horizon. Rock layer or strata producing petroleum.

Poor boy. An operator who works on the leanest possible budget, often doing his own drilling, using secondhand equipment, on the cheapest acreage available.

Royalty. The proportion of the oil and gas produced from a lease that belongs to the mineral owner.

Section. One square mile of land.

Spud in. To begin drilling a well.

Glossary

Structure. Subsurface folds or fractures of rock that form petroleum reservoirs.

Underreamer. A bit-like device used to enlarge a well bore to the size of casing.

Wildcat acreage. Leases outside of the boundaries of known producing areas.

NOTES

ABBREVIATIONS IN NOTES

We have abbreviated the following sources after their initial use in each chapter:
FW   *Financial World*
FWP   *Fort Worth Press*
FWR   *Fort Worth Record*
FWST   *Fort Worth Star-Telegram*
HC   *Houston Chronicle*
MR   *Mineral Resources of the United States*
NYT   *New York Times*
OGJ   *Oil and Gas Journal*
PTO   Pioneers of Texas Oil Collection, Barker Texas History Center, University
        of Texas at Austin
SEP   *Saturday Evening Post*
WSJ   *Wall Street Journal*
WW   *World's Work*

PREFACE

1. "Oil on the Brain," H. De Marsan, Publisher, 43 Chatham Street, New York, n.d. [ca. 1865].

2. Charles P. Kindleberger, *Manias, Panics, and Crashes: A History of Financial Crises* (New York: Basic Books, 1978), pp. 9, 29, 81.

3. Roger M. Olien and Diana Davids Olien, *Wildcatters: Texas Independent Oilmen* (Austin: Texas Monthly Press, 1984).

CHAPTER ONE

1. *New York Times*, May 10, 11, 20, 1922.

2. *NYT*, May 13, 1921, October 3, 1922; Louis Guenther, "Pirates of Promotion: Methods of the Industrial Promoters," *World's Work* 37 (January 1919): 315, 319; John K. Barnes, "Harvest Time for the Get-Rich-Quick Promoter," *WW* 34 (October 1917): 157.

3. David H. Dunn, *Ponzi!* (New York: McGraw-Hill, 1975), pp. 46, 56, 118, 248–50. Out on bail after serving 3½ years of a federal sentence, Ponzi fled to Florida where he organized a fraudulent land syndicate; he was deported in 1934.

Notes to Pages 3–9

4. *The Statistical History of the United States from Colonial Times to the Present* (Stamford, Conn.: Fairfield Publishers, 1965), p. 150; Samuel G. Blythe, "Gambling with Grief," *Saturday Evening Post*, July 5, 1924, p. 3.

5. George Soule, *Prosperity Decade: From War to Depression, 1918–1929* (New York: Rinehart, 1947), pp. 80, 86; Maurice Leven, Harold G. Moulton, and Clark Warburton, *America's Capacity to Consume* (Washington, D.C.: Brookings Institution, 1934), pp. 102–5.

6. Soule, *Prosperity Decade*, pp. 57, 75, 82; Wesley C. Mitchell, *Income in the United States: Its Amounts and Distribution, 1909–1919*, 2 vols. (New York: National Bureau of Economic Research, 1922), 2:43–46; *The Business and Financial Record of World War Years* (New York: Herbert D. Seibert & Company, 1939), p. 248.

7. *Business and Financial Record*, pp. 78, 169, 305; William E. Leuchtenburg, *The Perils of Prosperity, 1914–32* (Chicago: University of Chicago Press, 1969), pp. 74, 77–78, 100.

8. Soule, *Prosperity Decade*, p. 76.

9. *Business and Financial Record*, p. 248.

10. Ibid., pp. 247–48, 296.

11. Ibid., pp. 273, 278, 295, 300.

12. Dorothy S. Brady, "Family Savings, 1888–1950," in *A Study of Savings in the United States*, ed. Raymond W. Goldsmith, Dorothy S. Brady, and Horst Mendenhausen, 3 vols. (Princeton: Princeton University Press, 1956), 3:154; Soule, *Prosperity Decade*, p. 86; George Creel, *How We Advertised America* (New York: Harper & Brothers, 1920), pp. 86–87; Mark Sullivan, *Our Times, 1900–1925*, 6 vols. (New York: Charles Scribner's Sons, 1936), 5:428–33; Robert T. Patterson, *The Great Boom and Panic, 1921–1929* (Chicago: Henry Regnery Company, 1965), p. 9; Roy C. Osgood, "Trends of Blue Sky Laws," *Investment Banking*, December 1932, p. 151.

13. Quoted in David E. Shi, *The Simple Life: Plain Living and High Thinking in American Culture* (New York: Oxford University Press, 1985), p. 216.

14. Quoted in ibid., p. 218.

15. Roland Marchand, *Advertising the American Dream: Making Way for Modernity, 1920–1940* (Berkeley: University of California Press, 1985), pp. 194–200.

16. Quoted in Leuchtenburg, *Perils of Prosperity*, p. 188.

17. Ibid., p. 189.

18. Robert S. Lynd and Helen Merrill Lynd, *Middletown: A Study in American Culture* (New York: Harcourt, Brace and Company, 1956), pp. 80–81.

19. Samuel Crowther, "Everybody Ought to Be Rich: An Interview with John J. Raskob," *Ladies Home Journal*, August 1929, p. 9.

20. O. R. Geyer, "Oil Makes Millionaires," *Scientific American*, Supplement no. 2162 (June 9, 1917): 360; Albert W. Atwood, "Rainbow's End," *SEP*, December 28, 1918, pp. 21–22; Gertrude Mathews Shelby, "Florida Frenzy," *Harper's Monthly Magazine*, January 1926, p. 178.

21. Crowther, "Everybody Ought to Be Rich," pp. 9, 36.

22. Ibid., p. 9.

23. *NYT*, June 22, 1919, August 20, 1921, July 24, 1922; Louis Guenther, "Pirates of Promotion: The Modern Bucket Shop," *WW* 37 (November 1918): 30; Louis Guenther, "Pirates of Promotion: The Wreckage," *WW* 37 (March 1919): 511.

24. *NYT*, June 22, 1919, August 20, 1921.

25. *NYT*, February 12, 15, 1922; Exhibit 26: receipt for $4,000 in securities sent to General Lee Development Interests by Alice Kane; Exhibit 160: list of securities given to General Lee Development Interests by Olga Herzog, United States v. Robert A. Lee et al., CR2267, U.S. District Court, Northern District of Texas, Fort Worth, Record Group 21, Southwest Branch (Fort Worth), National Archives; V. H. McNutt and Conrad Lambert, *First Principles of the Oil Business* (Kansas City, Mo.: McKinley Publishing Company, 1924), p. 69.

26. *NYT*, June 20, 17, 1921; Patterson, *Great Boom and Panic*, p. 21.

27. Frank Parker Stockbridge, "The Florida Rush of 1925," *Current History Magazine*, November 1925, pp. 181–82; John S. Jordan, "What's Left in Florida," *WW* 52 (September 1926): 571–72; "The Florida Boom Examined," *Literary Digest*, May 9, 1925, p. 72.

28. J. Leroy Miller, "In the Land of the Realtor," *Outlook*, January 13, 1926, p. 69; Frank B. Sessa, "Real Estate Expansion and Boom in Miami Beach and Its Environs During the 1920s" (Ph.D. diss., University of Pittsburgh, 1950), pp. 66, 97, 174–76; T. H. Weigall, *Boom in Paradise* (New York: Alfred H. King, 1932), p. 131; James M. Ricci, "Boasters, Boosters, and Boom: Popular Images of Florida in the 1920s," *Tampa Bay History* 6, no. 2 (1984): 31–57.

29. Shelby, "Florida Frenzy," p. 178; Miller, "In the Land of the Realtor," p. 69; *NYT*, March 22, 1925, sec. 2, p. 2.

30. Felix Isman, "Florida's Land Boom," *SEP*, August 22, 1925, pp. 14, 141–42.

31. Sessa, "Real Estate Expansion and Boom in Miami Beach," pp. 110, 178; Weigall, *Boom in Paradise*, p. 99; Shelby, "Florida Frenzy," p. 177; Homer B. Vanderblue, "The Florida Land Boom," *The Journal of Land and Public Utility Economics* 3 (May 1927): 124; *NYT*, March 22, 1925, September 6, 1925.

32. Kenneth L. Roberts, "Florida Fireworks," *SEP*, January 23, 1926, p. 13; Frederick Lewis Allen, *Only Yesterday: An Informal History of the Twenties*, Perennial Library ed. (New York: Harper and Row, 1964), p. 229; Reginald T. Townsend, "The Gold Rush to Florida," *WW* 50 (July 1925): 184; Stockbridge, "The Florida Rush of 1925," p. 183; *NYT*, November 16, 1925; Vanderblue, "The Florida Land Boom," p. 122.

33. Weigall, *Boom in Paradise*, pp. 133–34; Shelby, "Florida Frenzy," p. 177; Jordan, "What's Left in Florida," p. 571.

34. Sessa, "Real Estate Expansion and Boom in Miami Beach," p. 105; Weigall, *Boom in Paradise*, p. 108; Townsend, "The Gold Rush to Florida," p. 185; Miller,

"In the Land of the Realtor," p. 68; Shelby, "Florida Frenzy," p. 180.

35. Roberts, "Florida Fireworks," p. 85; Weigall, *Boom in Paradise*, pp. 109–10; Sessa, "Real Estate Expansion and Boom in Miami Beach," pp. 179–80; Paolo E. Coletta, *William Jennings Bryan: Political Puritan, 1915–1925* (Lincoln: University of Nebraska Press, 1969), pp. 150–51.

36. "While Real Estate Booms in Florida," *Literary Digest*, March 14, 1925, p. 60; for an example, see Louis Gold's advertisement for Fellsmere Estates in the *NYT*, November 15, 1925.

37. Weigall, *Boom in Paradise*, pp. 224, 231; Jordan, "What's Left in Florida," p. 575; Shelby, "Florida Frenzy," p. 181; Sessa, "Real Estate Expansion and Boom in Miami Beach," pp. 200–203.

38. Weigall, *Boom in Paradise*, p. 231.

39. Jordan, "What's Left in Florida," p. 574.

40. Gertrude Mathews Shelby, "The Crisis of Florida Fever," *Outlook*, May 5, 1926, p. 25; Charlton W. Tebeau, *A History of Florida* (Coral Gables: University of Miami Press, 1971), pp. 385–86.

41. Jordan, "What's Left in Florida," p. 571; Tebeau, *A History of Florida*, p. 386; *NYT*, September 8, October 10, November 2, December 7, 1925.

42. Tebeau, *A History of Florida*, p. 387; Vanderblue, "The Florida Land Boom," pp. 127, 131; for an account of how one developer lost money, see Glenn A. Niemeyer, "Oldsmar for Health, Wealth, and Happiness," *Florida Historical Quarterly* 46, no. 1 (1967): 18–28.

43. Vanderblue, "The Florida Land Boom," pp. 113, 116–17, 124; Stockbridge, "The Florida Rush of 1925," pp. 178–79; *NYT*, May 4, 1924.

44. Vanderblue, "The Florida Land Boom," p. 120; T. S. Van Dyke, *Millionaires of a Day: An Inside History of the Great Southern California Boom* (New York: Fords, Howard & Hulbert, 1890), pp. 57–58, 144; Albert W. Atwood, "When the Oil Flood Is On," *SEP*, July 7, 1923, p. 86.

45. William Rintoul, *Spudding In: Recollections of Pioneer Days in the California Oil Fields* (Fresno: California Historical Society, 1978), pp. 60–61, 83; Fred W. Viehe, "Black Gold Suburbs: The Influence of the Extractive Industry on the Suburbanization of Los Angeles, 1890–1930," *Journal of Urban History*, November 1981, pp. 3–26.

46. Atwood, "Oil Flood," p. 86; *NYT*, August 19, 1923.

47. Atwood, "Oil Flood," p. 86.

48. Albert W. Atwood, "Mad from Oil," *SEP*, July 14, 1923, p. 11; Atwood, "Oil Flood," pp. 86, 96; Walter A. Tompkins, *Little Giant of Signal Hill: An Adventure in American Enterprise* (Englewood Cliffs, N.J.: Prentice-Hall, 1964), p. 2; *NYT*, August 19, 1923.

49. *NYT*, August 19, 1923; Atwood, "Mad from Oil," p. 92.

50. Rintoul, *Spudding In*, pp. 46–47; Atwood, "Mad from Oil," pp. 10–11; *NYT*, August 18, 1923.
51. *NYT*, August 18, 1923; Atwood, "Mad from Oil," p. 11.
52. *NYT*, August 18, 1923; Atwood, "Mad from Oil," p. 92.
53. *NYT*, August 18, 1923; Atwood, "Mad from Oil," pp. 92, 94, 101.
54. *NYT*, August 18, 1923; Atwood, "Mad from Oil," p. 97.
55. *NYT*, August 18, 1923; Atwood, "Mad from Oil," pp. 94, 101; Viehe, "Black Gold Suburbs," p. 13.
56. *Oil Weekly*, August 1, 1922, p. 96.
57. Atwood, "Oil Flood," p. 93; Viehe, "Black Gold Suburbs," p. 23.

CHAPTER TWO

1. Harold F. Williamson, Ralph L. Andreano, Arnold R. Baum, and Gilbert C. Klose, *The American Petroleum Industry: The Age of Energy, 1899–1959* (Evanston, Ill.: Northwestern University Press, 1963), pp. 169–71, 190, 222–26; Department of the Interior, United States Geological Survey, *Mineral Resources of the United States, 1921*, Pt. 2, *Nonmetals* (Washington, D.C.: Government Printing Office, 1924), p. 290.
2. Williamson et al., *The American Petroleum Industry*, pp. 261–68, 292.
3. *MR*, 1917, Pt. 2, pp. 688, 1024; *MR*, 1918, Pt. 2, pp. 1090–91; *MR*, 1921, Pt. 2, pp. 254, 296; *MR*, 1922, Pt. 2, p. 416; *Derrick's Annual Review of Oil Fields for 1921* (Oil City, Pa.: Derrick Publishing Company, n.d. [1922]), pp. 35–36.
4. Williamson et al., *The American Petroleum Industry*, p. 60; *New York Times*, June 1, 1918, May 25, 1919; George Patullo, "Chasing the Rainbow," *Saturday Evening Post*, May 29, 1920, p. 12; Louis Guenther, "Pirates of Promotion: The Wreckage," *World's Work* 37 (March 1919): 512.
5. *NYT*, March 9, 1924; "Extraordinary Conditions in Oil," *Financial World*, September 1, 1917, p. 17, September 15, 1917, p. 28; J. W. Smallwood, "The American Oil Industry," *FW*, February 24, 1919, p. 1; "No Overproduction of Oil," *FW*, March 3, 1919, p. 1; Louis Guenther, "Pirates of Promotion: The Oil Stock Flotation Game," *WW* 37 (December 1918): 149–51.
6. Ray Morris, "Oil and the Investor," *WW* 39 (February 1920): 331; F. G. Swanson, interviewed by R. M. Hayes, February 20, 1955, Tyler, Texas, Pioneers of Texas Oil Collection, Barker Texas History Center, University of Texas at Austin; Burk Paschall, interviewed by M. C. Boatright, July 30, 1952, Breckenridge, Texas, PTO; John K. Barnes, "Harvest Time for the Get-Rich-Quick Promoter," *WW* 34 (October 1917): 155–56.
7. *FW*, September 15, 1917, p. 28; *NYT*, May 1, May 25, June 1, July 13, 1919;

Louis Guenther, "Pirates of Promotion: The Modern Bucket Shop," *WW* 37 (November 1918): 29.

8. O. R. Geyer, "Oil Makes Millionaires," *Scientific American*, Supplement no. 2162 (June 9, 1917): 360.

9. Henrietta M. Larson and Kenneth Wiggins Porter, *History of Humble Oil and Refining Company* (New York: Harper & Brothers, 1959), p. 16; American Petroleum Institute, *American Petroleum: Supply and Demand. A Report to the Board of Directors of the American Petroleum Institute by a Committee of Eleven Members of the Board* (New York: McGraw-Hill Book Company, 1925), p. 73; Walter A. Ver Wiebe, *Oil Fields in the United States* (New York: McGraw-Hill Book Company, 1930), p. 427; Charles D. Vertrees and George Abell, interviewed by S. D. Myres, February 21, 1971, Midland, Texas, Abell-Hanger Collection, Permian Basin Petroleum Museum, Library, and Hall of Fame, Midland, Texas.

10. Joseph A. Kornfeld, "A Half Century of Exploration in the Southwest," *Oil and Gas Journal*, May 31, 1951, p. 198; Samuel W. Tait, Jr., *The Wildcatters* (Princeton: Princeton University Press, 1946), p. 140.

11. David White, "Outstanding Features of Petroleum Development in America," in American Association of Petroleum Geologists, *Bulletin* 19, no. 4 (April 1935): 499–500; Exhibit 4: undated promotional letter, United States v. Robert A. Lee et al., CR2267, U.S. District Court, Northern District of Texas, Fort Worth, Record Group 21, Southwest Branch (Fort Worth), National Archives.

12. James A. Clark and Michel T. Halbouty, *The Last Boom* (New York: Random House, 1972), pp. 7–8, 17–19; *Western World*, September 22, 29, October 19, 1928, July 27, 1929.

13. Clark and Halbouty, *The Last Boom*, p. 8; Roger M. Olien and Diana Davids Olien, *Wildcatters: Texas Independent Oilmen* (Austin: Texas Monthly Press, 1984), pp. 56–57.

14. Exhibit 16 (Oklahoma): A. D. Lloyd, "Report of Mineralogical, Geological, and Topographical Survey for the Signal Hill Oil and Refining Company of Blanchard, Oklahoma," September 1916, pp. 5–7, Federal Trade Commission v. Big Diamond Oil & Refining Company, P. M. Faver, J. F. Dofflemyer, B. F. King, and O. E. Houston, Docket #795, Records of the Federal Trade Commission, Record Group 122, National Archives, Washington, D.C.

15. Testimony of Oscar Houston and B. F. King, Official Report of Proceedings, pp. 138–44, 166, FTC v. Big Diamond.

16. H. P. Nichols, interviewed by Mody C. Boatright, October 11, 1952, Tyler, Texas, PTO.

17. Exhibit 21: "The Honor of the Lees," U.S. v. Lee et al.; *Fort Worth Press*, May 30, 1923.

18. Joseph S. Morris, interviewed by Roger M. Olien and J. Conrad Dunagan,

Notes to Pages 34–41

February 24, 1987, San Antonio, Texas, PTO; O. W. Killam, interviewed by William A. Owens, September 5, 1956, Laredo, Texas, PTO.

19. Tait, *The Wildcatters*, pp. 76–77.

20. For examples of this approach to finance, see Olien and Olien, *Wildcatters*, pp. 20, 25–26.

21. H. A. Wheeler, "Wild Oil Boom in the North Texas Oil Fields," *Engineering and Mining Journal*, March 27, 1920, pp. 741–46; Dorsey Hager, "Geology of Oil Fields of North Central Texas," in AIME *Transactions* (New York: AIME, 1920), p. 520; *The Derrick's Handbook of Petroleum*, vol. 2 (Oil City, Pa.: Derrick Publishing Company, 1900), p. 181; Williamson et al., *The American Petroleum Industry*, pp. 34–35; Earl Oliver, "Appraisal of Oil Properties," in AIME *Transactions* (New York: AIME, 1921), p. 354.

22. *MR*, 1912, Pt. 2, pp. 335–38, 399; Larson and Porter, *History of Humble*, p. 127.

23. Wheeler, "Wild Oil Boom in North Texas Oil Fields," p. 741; Hager, "Geology of Oil Fields of North Central Texas," p. 520; Larson and Porter, *History of Humble*, pp. 126–28.

24. Wheeler, "Wild Oil Boom in North Texas Oil Fields," p. 741.

25. "The Company," Lubbock Oil Corporation, Correspondence File K-M; Oil and Gas Lease, February 19, 1918, Legal Documents, Lubbock-Bridgeport Oil Company and Lubbock Oil Corporation Papers, The Southwest Collection, Texas Tech University, Lubbock, Texas.

26. Leases, Legal File; Roscoe Wilson to J. E. Chase, March 6, 1919, Correspondence, 1919–22, File A-C, Lubbock Papers.

27. Contract, February 10, 1919, Legal Documents; Chase to J. L. Stephens, February 28, 1920; Will H. Evans to Chase, July 25, 1919, Correspondence File T; "The Company," January 1920, Correspondence File K-M, Lubbock Papers.

28. Chase to T. B. Saunders and N. F. Boone, February 19, 1920, Correspondence File R-S, Lubbock Papers.

29. Lowrey to Elder, January 3, 1919, Correspondence, 1919–22, File D-H; J. E. Chase to Thomas and Black, July 3, 1919, Correspondence, 1919–22, File T, Lubbock Papers.

30. Note Payable to W. O. and C. O. Rominger, March 10, 1919, Correspondence File A-C; Contract, February 10, 1919, Legal File, Lubbock Papers.

31. Chase to Roscoe Wilson, April 10, 1919, Correspondence File U-Y; Wilson to Chase, April 29, 1919, Correspondence File A-C, Lubbock Papers.

32. J. L. Steel, Wagner Supply Company to Lubbock-Bridgeport, May 17, 1919, Correspondence File U-Y, Lubbock Papers.

33. Forwarding Request, Lubbock-Bridgeport to Postmaster, Lubbock, May 2, 1919; Chase to S. P. Robbins, July 11, 1919; Robbins to Chase, July 12, 1919, Correspondence File U-Y; "Summary, Financial Statement," Lubbock-Bridgeport Oil

Development Company, July 17, 1919, Financial Documents, Lubbock Papers.

34. J. E. Chase to Frank P. Chase, May 9, 1919; Wilson to Chase, May 29, 1919; Chase to L. H. Cook and Company, May 31, 1919, Correspondence File A-C; Chase to Wilson, May 31, 1919, Correspondence File U-Y, Lubbock Papers.

35. Wilson to the Lubbock-Bridgeport Oil Company, June 19, 1919, Correspondence File U-Y, Lubbock Papers.

36. Chase to Thomas Black, July 3, 1919, Correspondence File A-C; Chase to Wilson, July 7, 1919, Correspondence File U-Y, Lubbock Papers.

37. Crump to Chase, August 10, 1919; Ura Embry to Chase, September 3, 1919; Crump to Chase, September 10, 1919, Correspondence File A-C, Lubbock Papers.

38. Chase to W. C. Jennings, October 16, 1919, Correspondence File J; Chase to O. C. Graves Oil Company, October 15, 1919, Correspondence File D-H; J. E. Chase to Frank P. Chase, October 15, 1919, Correspondence File A-C; Chase to Dr. E. E. Trabert, October 7, 1919, Correspondence File T, Lubbock Papers.

39. Chase to F. A. Howard, October 29, 1919, Correspondence File D-H, Lubbock Papers.

40. Enclosure and letter, Chase to Harry Hines and Company, September 8, 1919, Correspondence File D-H; Chase to W. C. Jennings and R. H. Lowrey, October 23, 1919, Correspondence File J, Lubbock Papers.

41. Financial Statement, February 1, 1920, Financial Documents; Chase to W. C. Jennings and R. H. Lowrey, Correspondence File J, Lubbock Papers.

42. Drilling practices and equipment are explained clearly in J. E. Brantly, *History of Oil Well Drilling* (Houston: Gulf Publishing Company, 1971), pp. 221–74, and in Robert O. Anderson, *Fundamentals of the Petroleum Industry* (Norman: University of Oklahoma Press, 1984), pp. 130–43.

43. Chase to Wilson, July 7, 11, 1919, Correspondence File U-Y; Chase to J. Hayden Moore, August 22, 1919, Correspondence File K-M; Chase to Jennings, August 28, 1919, Correspondence File J; Chase to Crump, September 13, 1919; Chase to F. P. Chase, September 15, 1919, Correspondence File A-C, Lubbock Papers.

44. J. A. Gubbie to Bridgeport Oil and Development Company, August 15, 1919, Correspondence File T; Expense Accounts, 1919–21, Financial Documents, Lubbock Papers.

45. Lubbock Oil Corporation to A. W. Black, January 5, 1920, Correspondence File U-Y; Chase to Dr. H. W. Evans, December 5, 1919, Correspondence File D-H; Chase to F. P. Chase, December 28, 1919, Correspondence File A-C, Lubbock Papers.

46. W. B. Hardy to Lubbock-Bridgeport, November 24, 1919, Correspondence File T; Telegram, Jennings to Chase, February 5, 1920, Correspondence File A-C, Lubbock Papers.

Notes to Pages 46–50

47. Wilson to Chase, December 23, 1919, Correspondence File A-C; Chase to W. F. Lewis, December 23, 1919, Correspondence File D-H; Memorandum for Drawing Mortgages, Legal File, Lubbock Papers.

48. Wilson to J. E. Chase, December 21, 1919, Correspondence File A-C; Chase to W. F. Lewis, December 23, 1919, Correspondence File D-H; Chase to Morris, September 18, 1919, Correspondence File K-M; R. H. Lowrey to J. E. Chase, October 28, 1919, Correspondence File A-C, Lubbock Papers.

49. Undated reorganization in longhand, Legal Documents; Transfer Documents by Lowrey, Legal Documents, Lubbock Papers.

50. Statement, January 30, 1920, Legal Documents, Lubbock Papers; Hager, "Geology of Oil Fields of North Central Texas," p. 520.

51. Trade Circulars from Trade Circular Advertising, January 22, 1920, and Western Advertising, February 3, 1920, Correspondence File A-C, Lubbock Papers.

52. Minutes, Board of Directors, Lubbock Oil Corporation, Bridgeport, Texas, January 22, 1910; J. E. Chase Expense Statement, Philadelphia Trip, January 31, 1920, Financial Documents; J. E. Chase to F. P. Chase, January 15, 24, 1920, Correspondence File A-C; Chase to William Etheridge, January 6, 1920, Correspondence File D-H; Contract, February 20, 1920, Legal Documents; Bank Statements, 1919–21, Financial Documents, Lubbock Papers.

53. [Lowrey?] to Bradstreet's, February 18, 1920; J. E. Chase to Frank P. Chase, February 19, 1910, Correspondence File A-C, Lubbock Papers.

54. Contract with F. E. Collins Investment Company, April 12, 1920, Legal Documents; Chase to Van Dyke, April 30, 1920; Van Dyke to Chase, May 6, 1920; F. McFarland to J. E. Chase, April 23, 1920, Correspondence File U-Y, Lubbock Papers.

55. Chase to Roscoe Wilson, April 19, 1920, Correspondence File U-Y; Boone to Chase, April 28, May 3, 20, 1920, Correspondence File A-C, Lubbock Papers.

56. Chase to Boone, May 18, 1920, Correspondence File A-C, Lubbock Papers.

57. Salary Receipts, June 20, 1920, Financial Documents; W. D. Crump to Chase, June 23, 1920, Correspondence File A-C; J. E. Chase to F. P. Chase, July 7, 1920, Correspondence File A-C, Lubbock Papers.

58. J. E. Chase to F. P. Chase, July 7, 1920; Roscoe Wilson to Chase, September 17, 1920; J. E. Chase to J. B. Collier, September 27, 1920, Correspondence File A-C, Lubbock Papers.

59. Drilling Contract with W. F. Dennis and E. J. Horner, October 5, 1920, Legal Documents; unidentified correspondent to Chase, December 21, 1920, Correspondence File C; Jennings to Uncle Jim, January 11, 1921; Jennings to Mother, January 17, 1921, Correspondence File J, Lubbock Papers.

60. Bank Statements, January–May 1920, Financial Documents; W. C. Jennings to C. C. Pearson, February 5, 1921, Correspondence File P; Chase to Crump, June

14, 1921, Correspondence File A-C, Lubbock Papers.

61. Jennings to Mr. Scott Reed, Internal Revenue Service, July 28, 1921, Correspondence File U-Y; Jennings to Chase, August 2, 1921, Correspondence File A-C, Lubbock Papers.

62. Chase to Crump, September 20, 1921, Correspondence File A-C; Jennings to W. E. Schott, September 4, 1921, Correspondence File R-S; Lowrey to Stockholders [undated], Correspondence File K-M; Chase to O. N. Jaye and Company, August 19, 1921, Correspondence File D-H; Chase to F. Witherspoon, July 24, 1921, Correspondence File U-Y, Lubbock Papers.

63. *The Derrick's Annual Review of Oil Fields for 1921* (Oil City, Pa.: Derrick Publishing Company, n.d. [1922]), pp. 35–37; *MR*, 1924, Pt. 2, pp. 253–54, 292, 296–97.

CHAPTER THREE

1. For early examples, see the prospectuses and stock certificates in the Ohio Historical Society and the Hagley Library, Wilmington, Delaware; see also Paul H. Giddens, *The Birth of the Oil Industry* (New York: Arno Press, 1972), p. 36.

2. See Roger M. Olien and Diana Davids Olien, *Wildcatters: Texas Independent Oilmen* (Austin: Texas Monthly Press, 1984), chaps. 1–3.

3. James McIntyre, "Very Few Operators Produce 68 Per Cent of Oil in Oklahoma," *Oil and Gas Journal*, February 28, 1924, p. 136.

4. Exhibit 62 (Faver): Dofflemyer to Faver, August 19, 1919, Federal Trade Commission v. Big Diamond Oil & Refining Company, P. M. Faver, J. F. Dofflemyer, B. F. King, O. E. Houston, Docket #795, Records of the Federal Trade Commission, Record Group 122, National Archives, Washington, D.C.; Giddens, *Birth of the Oil Industry*, pp. 32–36.

5. Louis Loss and Edward M. Corvett, *Blue Sky Law* (Boston: Little, Brown, 1958), p. 12.

6. Stock certificates for Silver-Burk Oil Company, Brookline Oil Company, Gladys Belle Oil Company, Terry Oil Company, Wheatly Oil Company, and Vitek Oil & Refining Company, in the authors' possession.

7. Exhibit 71: *Independent Oil and Financial Reporter*, May 2, 1922, United States v. Robert A. Lee et al., CR2267, U.S. District Court, Northern District of Texas, Fort Worth, Record Group 21, Southwest Branch (Fort Worth), National Archives; *Western World*, April 17, May 22, July 24, 1926, March 3, July 7, 1928; W. D. Hord, *Lost Dollars, or The Pirates of Promotion* (Cincinnati: Investors Publishing Company, 1924), pp. 43–44.

8. *Fort Worth Star-Telegram*, October 30, 1949; Hord, *Lost Dollars*, p. 38; Watson

Notes to Pages 56–60

Washburn and Edmund S. DeLong, *High and Low Financiers: Some Notorious Swindlers and Their Abuses of Our Modern Stock Selling System* (Indianapolis: Bobbs-Merrill, 1932), p. 65; Bryce Finley Ryan, "A Sociological Study of the Mail-Order Promoter and His Methods" (M.A. thesis, University of Texas, 1933), pp. 25–29.

9. Washburn and DeLong, *High and Low Financiers*, p. 65; *New York Times*, September 2, 1925.

10. Indictment, United States v. Robert C. Russell et al., CR1809, U.S. District Court, Southern District of Texas, Houston, Record Group 21, Southwest Branch (Fort Worth), National Archives; *Fort Worth Press*, June 1, 1923; Exhibits 22, 25, 27, 39, 45, 53, U.S. v. Lee et al. For an example of Chester Bunker's trade, see "List of Stockholders," United States v. Chester R. Bunker et al., CR4491, U.S. District Court, Northern District of Texas, Fort Worth, Record Group 21, Southwest Branch (Fort Worth), National Archives. See also Transcript of Hearings before the Solicitor in the Matter of Charges Against Shallcross 500% Syndicate and Smackover 500% Syndicate, June 18, 1923, pp. 12–17, Post Office Department, Record Group 28, National Archives, Washington, D.C.; *Fort Worth News-Tribune*, December 2, 1927; William Leavitt Stoddard, *Financial Racketeering and How to Stop It* (New York: Harper & Brothers, 1931), p. 8; *NYT*, February 19, 1922.

11. Exhibit 193, U.S. v. Lee et al.; Indictment, United States v. Walter L. Marks et al., CR3968, U.S. District Court, Northern District of Illinois, Chicago, Record Group 21, Southwest Branch (Fort Worth), National Archives; Transcript of Proceedings, United States v. Oscar L. Pardue et al., CR1811, U.S. District Court, Southern District of Texas, Houston, Record Group 21, Southwest Branch (Fort Worth), National Archives.

12. Joseph E. King, *A Mine to Make a Mine: Financing the Colorado Mining Industry, 1859–1902* (College Station: Texas A & M University Press, 1977), pp. 14–24, 38, 42, 44, 46–48, 51; Lewis Atherton, "The Mining Promoter in the Trans-Mississippi West," *Western Historical Quarterly* (January 1970): 35–50; Donald Chaput, "Fraud at Fresno?" *Pacific Historian* (Winter 1985): 48, 52, 55; Diana Davids Olien, "Selling Shares in Black Gold: Oil Promoters in the Jazz Age," *Journal of the West* (October 1989): 26–32.

13. George H. Smalley, "The Spenazuma Mining Swindle," *Arizona Historical Review* (July 1929): 86–97; Atherton, "The Mining Promoter in the Trans-Mississippi West," pp. 48–49; Louis Guenther, "Pirates of Promotion: The Wreckage," *World's Work* 37 (March 1919): 513–18.

14. Testimony of George B. Clark, Official Report of Proceedings, pp. 3–5, 9, 11; Testimony of P. M. Faver, Official Report of Proceedings, p. 204; Complaint, p. 3; Findings, p. 4; Exhibit 1 (Oklahoma): George B. Clark, interviewed by John M. Burkett, September 23, 1920, Wichita Falls, Texas; Exhibit 64 (Faver): J. F. Doffle-

myer to P. M. Faver, August 28, 1919; Exhibit 65 (Faver): Dofflemyer to Faver, September 2, 1919; Exhibit 15 (Oklahoma): A. M. Donoghue to J. M. Burkett, n.d., FTC v. Big Diamond.

15. Exhibit 65 (Faver): Dofflemyer to Faver, September 2, 1919; Testimony of Oscar Houston, Official Report of Proceedings, Oklahoma City, Oklahoma, May 18, 1922, pp. 125, 127, 139, 164–67; Testimony of Faver, p. 204; Complaint, pp. 1, 2, FTC v. Big Diamond.

16. Testimony of B. F. King, Official Report of Proceedings, p. 164; Testimony of Houston, pp. 125–26, 139–40; Testimony of Faver, p. 204.

17. Testimony of Houston, pp. 86, 100–101, 116–17; Complaint, p. 2; Findings, p. 3; Separate Answer of Respondent B. F. King to Complaint, August 6, 1921, p. 2, FTC v. Big Diamond.

18. Testimony of Faver, pp. 214–15; Testimony of Clark, pp. 13–16, 23–24; Exhibit 15 (Oklahoma): A. M. Donoghue to J. M. Burkett, n.d., FTC v. Big Diamond.

19. Complaint, p. 3; Findings, p. 4; Testimony of Houston, p. 104; Testimony of Faver, pp. 215, 217–19, 225; General Demurer submitted by Big Diamond Oil and Refining Company, J. F. Dofflemyer, and P. M. Faver, August 12, 1921; Exhibit 64 (Faver): Dofflemyer to Faver, August 28, 1919; Exhibit 65 (Faver): Dofflemyer to Faver, September 2, 1919; Exhibit 56 (Faver): Faver to U. M. Sanderson, August 9, 1918; Exhibit 58 (Faver): Faver to Dofflemyer, October 17, 1918, FTC v. Big Diamond.

20. Exhibit 62 (Faver): Dofflemyer to Faver, August 19, 1919; Testimony of Faver, p. 206; Testimony of Houston, p. 96; Separate Answer of Respondent Oscar E. Houston, March 7, 1922; Exhibit 10 (Oklahoma): brochure for Big Diamond Oil and Refining Company, FTC v. Big Diamond.

21. Exhibit 10 (Oklahoma): Big Diamond brochure, FTC v. Big Diamond.

22. Testimony of Faver, p. 229; Exhibit 23 (Oklahoma): Faver to Houston, September 9, 1918; Exhibit 24 (Oklahoma): Faver to Houston, September 13, 1918, FTC v. Big Diamond.

23. Testimony of Houston, p. 89; Exhibits 12–21 (Oklahoma), FTC v. Big Diamond.

24. Exhibit 13 (Faver): J. T. Cobb to Faver, April 24, 1918; Exhibit 5 (Faver): Faver to J. C. Russell, May 8, 1918; Exhibit 12 (Faver): Faver to J. T. Cobb, April 26, 1918; Exhibit 8 (Faver): Faver to John Berdahl, May 18, 1918; Exhibit 8 (Oklahoma): Answers by J. F. Dofflemyer and P. M. Faver to Federal Trade Commission Schedule A, April 26, 1919, FTC v. Big Diamond.

25. Exhibit 10 (Faver): W. R. McCann to Faver, May 9, 1918; Exhibit 77 (Faver): Dofflemyer to Faver, May 8, 1919, FTC v. Big Diamond.

26. Exhibit 65 (Faver): Dofflemyer to Faver, September 2, 1919, FTC v. Big Diamond.

Notes to Pages 65–69

27. Testimony of Faver, p. 237; Testimony of Houston, p. 128; Exhibit 39 (Oklahoma): Capital Issues Committee to Big Diamond Oil and Refining Company, September 24, 1918; Exhibit 30 (Oklahoma): Faver to Houston, October 30, 1918; Findings, p. 5, FTC v. Big Diamond; Chester Whitney Wright, *Economic History of the United States*, 2d ed. (New York: McGraw-Hill, 1949), p. 762.

28. Exhibit 56 (Faver): Faver to Joe Mitchell, August 9, 1918; Testimony of King, p. 181; Testimony of Houston, pp. 86, 116; Testimony of Faver, p. 236, FTC v. Big Diamond.

29. Exhibit 61 (Oklahoma): King to Faver, n.d. [August 1918]; Exhibit 56 (Oklahoma): King to Faver, September 7, 1918, FTC v. Big Diamond.

30. Exhibit 34 (Oklahoma): Telegram, Oscar Houston to Faver, September 3, 1918; Exhibit 26 (Oklahoma): Telegram, Faver to Houston, September 4, 1918; Exhibit 27 (Oklahoma): Telegram, Faver to Houston, September 8, 1918, FTC v. Big Diamond.

31. Exhibit 24 (Oklahoma): Faver to Houston, September 12, 1918, FTC v. Big Diamond.

32. Exhibit 56 (Faver): Faver to U. M. Sanderson, August 9, 1918, FTC v. Big Diamond.

33. Exhibit 50 (Oklahoma): Telegram, King to Faver, October 18, 1918, FTC v. Big Diamond.

34. Exhibit 107 (Faver): Dofflemyer to Faver, December 21, 1918; Exhibit 51 (Oklahoma): King to Faver, n.d. [October 1918]; Exhibit 30 (Oklahoma): Faver to Houston, October 30, 1918, FTC v. Big Diamond.

35. Exhibit 124 (Faver): Faver to Dofflemyer, October 26, 1918; Exhibit 126 (Faver): Faver to Dofflemyer and J. A. King, October 30, 1918, FTC v. Big Diamond.

36. Exhibit 62 (Faver): Dofflemyer to Faver, August 19, 1919, FTC v. Big Diamond.

37. Exhibit 99 (Faver): Dofflemyer to Faver, January 5, 1919; Exhibit 101 (Faver): Faver to Dofflemyer, January 7, 1919; Exhibit 74 (Faver): Faver to Dofflemyer, April 3, 1919; Exhibit 73 (Faver): Dofflemyer to Stahl and Andres, April 17, 1919, FTC v. Big Diamond.

38. Exhibit 82 (Faver): Faver to Dofflemyer, March 21, 1919; Exhibit 140 (Faver): Faver to Nellie Shepherd, February 4, 1919; Exhibit 157 (Faver): Faver to J. F. Pecula, February 10, 1919; Exhibit 141 (Faver): general letter to Big Diamond stockholders, February 24, 1919; Exhibit 81 (Faver): Faver to Dofflemyer, March 19, 1919, FTC v. Big Diamond.

39. Though Faver later told the FTC that the drilling rig's sale in 1918 yielded money for Big Diamond's "dividend," private correspondence between Faver and Dofflemyer makes clear the rig was sold in 1919. See Exhibit 91 (Faver): Faver to

Notes to Pages 69–75

Dofflemyer, March 11, 1919; Exhibit 82 (Faver): Faver to Dofflemyer, March 21, 1919; Exhibit 86 (Faver): Faver to Dofflemyer, March 28, 1919; Exhibit 44 (Oklahoma): Faver to King, March 22, 1919; Exhibit 83 (Faver): Faver to Dofflemyer, March 24, 1919, FTC v. Big Diamond.

40. Exhibit 70 (Faver): Dofflemyer to Faver, April 25, 1919; Exhibit 44 (Oklahoma): Faver to King, March 22, 1919; Exhibit 65 (Oklahoma): King to Faver, March 15, 1919, FTC v. Big Diamond.

41. Exhibit 70 (Faver): Dofflemyer to Faver, April 25, 1919; Exhibit 44 (Oklahoma): Faver to King, March 22, 1919; Exhibit 83 (Faver): Faver to Dofflemyer, March 24, 1919; Exhibit 87 (Faver): Faver to Dofflemyer, April 1, 1919, FTC v. Big Diamond.

42. Exhibit 62 (Faver): Dofflemyer to Faver, August 19, 1919, FTC v. Big Diamond.

43. Exhibit 8 (Oklahoma): Answers to Questionnaire, April 26, 1919; Exhibit 43 (Oklahoma): King to Faver, May 15, 1919; Exhibit 42 (Oklahoma): Faver to King, May 20, 1919; Exhibit 63 (Faver): Faver to Dofflemyer, August 25, 1919; Exhibit 59 (Faver): Dofflemyer to Faver, October 17, 1919; Exhibit 57 (Faver): Dofflemyer to Faver, October 10, 1919, FTC v. Big Diamond. The New York agent who absconded with funds was named Herrick; he may have been Fred Gresham, who used that name in running a bogus brokerage house in New York. See Louis Guenther, "Pirates of Promotion: The Oil Stock Flotation Game," *WW* 37 (December 1918): 153.

44. Exhibit 60 (Faver): Faver to Dofflemyer, November 12, 1919, FTC v. Big Diamond.

45. Testimony of Faver, p. 219; Separate Answer of Respondent J. W. McKinney to FTC Complaint, Findings, p. 6; Order to Cease and Desist, March 16, 1923, FTC v. Big Diamond.

CHAPTER FOUR

1. *Fort Worth Press*, November 21, 1927; Oliver Knight, *Fort Worth: Outpost on the Trinity* (Norman: University of Oklahoma Press, 1953), p. vii.

2. *FWP*, November 1, 25, 1922, December 29, 1923.

3. *Fort Worth Star-Telegram*, October 30, 1949; Knight, *Fort Worth*, pp. 196–97.

4. *Fort Worth Record*, May 2, 1918, January 30, 1919; Albert W. Atwood, "Rainbow's End," *Saturday Evening Post*, December 28, 1918, p. 22.

5. "History of Fort Worth," *American Journal of Health*, April 1930, pp. 418–20; *New York Times*, February 1, 1920.

6. *FWST*, July 21, 1929; *FWR*, May 21, 1919; "Architectural Description of Fort Worth," Texas Writers Project, Fort Worth Public Library Unit, vol. 42 (1941): 16, 732.

Notes to Pages 76–83

7. *FWP*, November 4, 1922, June 2, 1923; Application for Appointment of Receiver, November 4, 1922, Equity Docket #1185, U.S. District Court, Northern District of Texas, Fort Worth; Exhibit 149: Robert A. Lee to Ira Sickafeese, May 17, 1922, United States v. Robert A. Lee et al., CR2267, U.S. District Court, Northern District of Texas, Fort Worth, Record Group 21, Southwest Branch (Fort Worth), National Archives.

8. *FWP*, May 30, June 4, 1923; *FWST*, February 24, 1924; Indictment, U.S. v. Lee et al.

9. On the increasing popularity in advertising of the fictitious "friendly advisor," see Roland Marchand, *Advertising the American Dream: Making Way for Modernity, 1920–1940* (Berkeley: University of California Press, 1985), pp. 14, 305–8, 353–55.

10. Bill of Exceptions; Exhibit 2: Declaration of Trust, January 3, 1922; Exhibit 1: Declaration of Trust, February 4, 1922; Exhibit 3: Declaration of Trust, April 12, 1922, U.S. v. Lee et al.; *NYT*, April 29, 1923.

11. Exhibit 3: Declaration of Trust for General Lee Development Interests, April 12, 1922, U.S. v. Lee et al.

12. Albert W. Atwood, "Mad from Oil," *Saturday Evening Post*, July 14, 1923, p. 98; Lee Jones, Jr., interviewed by Roger M. Olien, March 18, 1981, Colorado City, Texas.

13. Exhibit 2: Declaration of Trust, January 3, 1922; Exhibit 4: initial circular letter, undated, U.S. v. Lee et al.

14. *FWP*, June 1, 1923; Exhibit 4: initial promotional letter, initial mailing kit, U.S. v. Lee et al.

15. Exhibit 4: initial promotional letter, U.S. v. Lee et al.

16. Ibid.

17. *NYT*, July 14, 1924; Indictment; Exhibit 1: Declaration of Trust, February 4, 1922; Exhibit 5: undated circular letter sent to Robert Howard, U.S. v. Lee et al.

18. *Houston Chronicle*, March 29, 1922; Exhibit 3: Declaration of Trust, April 12, 1922, U.S. v. Lee et al.

19. *FWP*, June 2, 1923; Exhibit 198: H. H. Schwarz to W. L. Marks, October 13, 1922; Exhibit 193: Telegram, Schwarz to Leslie Vincent Company, December 12, 1922, U.S. v. Lee et al. On the high cost of selling small issues, see Robert C. Higgins, *Analysis for Financial Management* (Homewood, Ill.: Dow-Jones Irwin, 1983), pp. 119–21.

20. Exhibit 6: undated letter and brochure, U.S. v. Lee et al.

21. Indictment; Exhibit 19: Lee to Alice M. Kane, January 21, 1922; Exhibit 21: Robert A. Lee, "The Honor of the Lees, 1649–1922," U.S. v. Lee et al.

22. Indictment; Exhibit 4: initial promotional letter; Exhibit 75: Robert A. Lee to A. L. Askanas, July 3, 1922, U.S. v. Lee et al.

23. Exhibit 35: Lee to N. J. Cary, March 3, 1922; Exhibit 100: Lee to Cary, April 22, 1922, U.S. v. Lee et al.

Notes to Pages 83–90

24. Indictment; Exhibit 168: Lee to P. G. Wooster, June 5, 1922; Exhibit 156: Lee to Kate Telford, April 24, 1922, U.S. v. Lee et al.

25. Indictment; Exhibits 156–58: Lee to Telford, April 24, July 19, August 7, 1922, U.S. v. Lee et al.

26. Exhibit 165: P. G. Wooster to Lee, May 3, 1922; Exhibit 167: Wooster to Lee, June 1, 1922, U.S. v. Lee et al.

27. Exhibit 92: I. H. Kirkland to Lee, May 13, 1922; Exhibit 94: Kirkland to Lee, June 20, 1922; Exhibit 96: Kirkland to Lee, September 4, 1922, and Lee to Kirkland, September 11, 1922, U.S. v. Lee et al.

28. Exhibit 33: Lee to Cary, January 16, 1922, U.S. v. Lee et al.

29. Exhibits 34, 35, 37, 38, 40, 41: Lee to Cary, January 18, March 3, March 13, March 27, April 13, April 22, 1922, U.S. v. Lee et al.

30. Exhibit 42: Lee to Cary, May 6, 1922; Exhibit 43: Cary to Lee, May 19, 1922, U.S. v. Lee et al.

31. Exhibit 43: Cary to Lee, May 19, 1922; Exhibit 45: subscription form signed by Cary, May 24, 1922; Exhibit 46: N. J. Cary to Lee, May 25, 1922, U.S. v. Lee et al.

32. Exhibit 43: Cary to Lee, May 19, 1922, U.S. v. Lee et al.

33. Exhibit 48: Cary to Sang, June 14 1922; Exhibit 49: Cary to Lee, June 15, 1922, U.S. v. Lee et al.

34. Exhibit 194: Telegram, Sherwin to Marks, June 26, 1922; Exhibit 50: Telegram, Lee to Cary, June 17, 1922; Exhibit 55: Lee to Cary, June 29, 1922; Exhibit 56: Cary to Lee, July 3, 1922, U.S. v. Lee et al.

35. Exhibit 57: Telegram, Lee to Cary, July 6, 1922; Exhibit 58: Schwarz to Cary, July 12, 1922, U.S. v. Lee et al.

36. Exhibit 59: Cary to Schwarz, July 14, 1922, U.S. v. Lee et al.

37. Indictment; Exhibit 67: J. E. Davis to Lee, September 2, 1922; Exhibit 139: W. C. Fulks and M. T. Fulks to Lee, June 9, 1922, and Telegram, Lee to Fulks, June 10, 1922, U.S. v. Lee et al.

38. Indictment; Exhibit 15: Lee to C. F. Throm, May 6, 1922; Exhibit 63: Lee to Throm, April 24, 1922, U.S. v. Lee et al.

39. Indictment; Exhibit 132: J. H. Bryant to Lee, November 9, 1922; Exhibit 185: Lee to Mary M. Strowbridge, October 25, 1922; Exhibit 46: Cary to Lee, May 25, 1922, U.S. v. Lee et al.

40. Exhibit 198: Schwarz to Marks, October 13, 1922, U.S. v. Lee et al.

41. Ibid.

42. Bill of Exceptions; Statement of Facts, U.S. v. Lee et al.; *NYT*, April 7, 1923.

43. Equity Docket #1185, U.S. District Court, Northern District of Texas, Fort Worth; Exhibit 29: Lee to Alice M. Kane, November 10, 1922, U.S. v. Lee et al.; *FWP*, October 30, November 4, 1922.

44. Exhibit 29: Lee to Kane, November 10, 1922; Exhibit 178: Lee to Wooster, December 11, 1922, U.S. v. Lee et al.

45. Exhibit 30: Lee to Kane, December 28, 1922, U.S. v. Lee et al.

46. Exhibit 31: Lee to Kane, January 23, 1923, U.S. v. Lee et al.

47. Hugh Eames, *Winner Lose All: Dr. Cook and the Theft of the North Pole* (Boston: Little, Brown, 1973), pp. 8–9; William R. Hunt, *To Stand at the Pole: The Doctor Cook–Admiral Peary North Pole Controversy* (New York: Stein and Day, 1981), pp. 10–11.

48. Hunt, *To Stand at the Pole*, p. 11.

49. Ibid., pp. 13–17.

50. Eames, *Winner Lose All*, pp. 27–28; Hunt, *To Stand at the Pole*, p. 17.

51. Hunt, *To Stand at the Pole*, pp. 21–32, 106; Eames, *Winner Lose All*, p. 19.

52. Hunt, *To Stand at the Pole*, pp. 33–57; *NYT*, September 2, 5, 9, 1909, October 14, 1909.

53. Hunt, *To Stand at the Pole*, pp. 132–33; *NYT*, January 31, February 13, 15, 19, 28, March 13, 14, 25, 1910, May 20, 1911, January 24, 1912, January 1, 1914, September 24, 27, 1915.

54. Testimony of Cook, 23:161, United States v. Frederick A. Cook et al., CR2273, U.S. District Court, Northern District of Texas, Fort Worth, Record Group 21, Southwest Branch (Fort Worth), National Archives. (The record of this case comprises thirty-one volumes; documents will be cited by volume and page number.) See also Thyra Thompson, Wyoming Secretary of State, to Arthur G. Randall, November 7, 1985, authors' papers; Arthur James Collier, "Oil in the Warm Springs and Hamilton Domes, near Thermopolis, Wyoming," *Bulletin 711*, United States Geological Survey (January 16, 1920); Ralph H. Espach and H. Dale Nichols, "Petroleum and Natural Gas Fields in Wyoming," *Bulletin 418*, United States Department of the Interior, Bureau of Mines (1941), p. 40.

55. Testimony of Cook, 23:162, U.S. v. Cook et al.; *Eastland County Deed Records*, 181:443–44.

56. Circular letter, brochure, undated, 23:13, 15, U.S. v. Cook et al.

57. Circular letter, 23:17, U.S. v. Cook et al.; "Quotation and Market Letter ending May 29th, 1920," copy, authors' files.

58. Testimony of Cook, 23:162, 164, U.S. v. Cook et al.; *Eastland County Deed Records*, 181:443–44, 208:46, 224:476, 263:264.

59. Testimony of Cook, 23:162–64; Exhibit 872, 22:11, U.S. v. Cook et al.

60. Ralph W. Hidy and Muriel E. Hidy, *Pioneering in Big Business: History of Standard Oil Company (New Jersey), 1882–1911* (New York: Harper & Brothers, 1955), pp. 10, 17.

61. Affidavit of D. W. Young, February 2, 1923; Application for Enforcement, Official Report of Proceedings, pp. 296–97, Federal Trade Commission v. Sey-

Notes to Pages 98–104

mour E. J. Cox, Prudential Oil and Refining, Prudential Trust and Securities, General Oil Company, Mrs. N. E. Cox, and Napoleon Hill, Docket #402, Records of the Federal Trade Commission, Record Group 122, National Archives, Washington, D.C.; Testimony of Cook, 23:167, U.S. v. Cook et al.

62. Testimony of Cook, 23:167–68, U.S. v. Cook et al.

63. Ibid.

64. Testimony of Cook, 23:197; Testimony of Ray, 23:65, 70, U.S. v. Cook et al.

65. Cook to Mrs. William H. Poetting, September 14, 1922, 5:67–71, U.S. v. Cook et al.

66. Cook to Shareholders, undated, 4:5–6; Testimony of Ruth DeVitt, 4:101, U.S. v. Cook et al.

67. Testimony of Brown, 9:124; Testimony of R. D. Mooney, 9:233, 236–37, U.S. v. Cook et al.

68. Circular letter, 4:13; Cook to "My Associates," October 28, 1922, 4:56–58, U.S. v. Cook et al.

69. Cook to C. W. Whitmer, January 12, 1923, 3:142, 144; Cook to Whitmer, December 22, 1922, 3:126, U.S. v. Cook et al.

70. Circular letters, 3:122–24, 143, U.S. v. Cook et al.

71. Exhibits Supporting Sworn Statement of John Burkett; Application for Enforcement, Official Report of Proceedings, p. 123, FTC v. Cox et al.

72. Exhibit 878, 22:74–76; Testimony of Matheney, 22:44–82, 174, U.S. v. Cook et al.; FWP, November 7, 1923.

73. Testimony of Cook, 26:3; Cook to Whitmer, December 22, 1922, 3:126; Cook to C. L. Warren, April 16, 1923, 10:96–97; Cook to C. L. Warren, April 16, 1923, 10:97, U.S. v. Cook et al.

CHAPTER FIVE

1. Financial World, February 17, 1919; Brief, p. 38, Federal Trade Commission v. Seymour E. J. Cox, Prudential Oil and Refining, Prudential Trust and Securities, General Oil Company, Mrs. N. E. Cox, and Napoleon Hill, Docket #402, Records of the Federal Trade Commission, Record Group 122, National Archives, Washington, D.C.

2. "Receiver to Stockholders, November 15, 1922," reprinted in The Fakes and Near Fakes of Oildom, ed. Frederick L. Haskins [pseud.] (n.p., n.d.) [Dallas, 1923]; Exhibit 16-G, Transcript of Fraud Hearings, May 21, May 22, 1923, Federal Trade Commission v. Fred L. Harris, alias Frederick L. Haskins, Docket #79, Records of the Federal Trade Commission, Record Group 122, National Archives, Washington, D.C.; Indictment, United States v. Seymour E. J. Cox, CR1574, U.S. District

Court, Western District of Michigan, Southern Division, Record Group 21, Chicago Branch, National Archives.

3. Testimony of Nelda E. Cox, pp. 974–1010; Testimony of Albert H. Klees, pp. 327, 340, Official Proceedings, Houston, Texas, February 23–March 7, 1921; Charges, pp. 1–3, FTC v. Cox et al.; Testimony of Martin Jachens, 9:2–7; Testimony of T. E. Nolan, 10:181–82; Testimony of Matt Medill, 9:26; Testimony of L. W. Zirjacks, 11:3; Exhibit 409, 9:218, United States v. Frederick A. Cook et al., CR2273, U.S. District Court, Northern District of Texas, Fort Worth, Record Group 21, Southwest Branch (Fort Worth), National Archives; *Houston Chronicle*, June 14, August 18, 1922; *Harris County Deed Records*, 422:443, 480:467, 497:325, 501:368, 504:27–35; *Houston City Directory*, 1918:368, 1919:412, 1920:506, 1921:516.

4. *Houston City Directory*, 1920:232; Testimony of N. E. Cox, Gene Aven, Oscar Kullenburg, and J. E. Hooper, FTC v. Cox et al.

5. Deed Records of Howard and Glasscock counties; Statement of the Federal Receiver of the Red River District, Official Proceedings, pp. 442–46; Circular Letter, Official Proceedings, p. 319, FTC v. Cox et al.

6. *Martin County Deed Records*; Declaration of Trust, *Harris County Deed Records*, 504:27–35; Cox to Frank H. Pollack, February 16, 1921, Indictment, United States v. Seymour E. J. Cox et al., CR1300, U.S. District Court, Southern District of Texas, Houston, Record Group 21, Southwest Branch (Fort Worth), National Archives.

7. *Harris County Deed Records*, 442:34, 518:416; *Houston City Directory*, 1923:565; *HC*, June 11, 1922.

8. *Fort Worth Star Telegram*, November 21, 1939; Exhibits: Cox to Ed Prather, December 6, 1919, and Cox to Alfred Carson, June 27, 1920, Indictment, U.S. v. Cox et al., CR1300; *Harris County Deed Records*, 442:34; *HC*, August 8, 1922.

9. *New York Times*, October 16, 1923; *Fort Worth Press*, October 31, 1922; *HC*, June 14, August 18, 1922; *Big Spring Herald*, April 13, 1921; Watson Washburn and Edmund S. DeLong, *High and Low Financiers: Some Notorious Swindlers and Their Abuses of Our Modern Stock Selling System* (Indianapolis: Bobbs-Merrill, 1932), p. 194.

10. *Houston City Directory*, 1922:858; Roger M. Olien, *From Token to Triumph: Texas Republicans since 1920* (Dallas: Southern Methodist University Press, 1982), p. 31.

11. *San Antonio Express*, October 25, 27, 1932; Theodore M. Filson to Hon. Brien McMahon, n.d., United States v. S. E. J. Cox et al., CR8722, U.S. District Court, Western District of Oklahoma, Oklahoma City, Record Group 21, Southwest Branch (Fort Worth), National Archives.

12. Testimony of Herman Danielson, 9:289, U.S. v. Cook et al.; Report and Findings of Fact, FTC v. Cox et al.

13. Testimony of Mrs. N. E. Cox, Official Report of Proceedings, pp. 974, 987, 1003, 1005, 1010, FTC v. Cox et al.; *NYT*, February 21, 25, 26, May 20, 1930.

14. Testimony of Albert H. Klees, Official Report of Proceedings, pp. 330, 342, 344, 358–60; Application for Enforcement, pp. 17–18, FTC v. Cox et al.; Testimony of Nolan, 10:164–65, 167, 170–71, 178–79, U.S. v. Cook et al.

15. Testimony of Nolan, 10:164–65, U.S. v. Cook et al.; Testimony of Klees, Official Report of Proceedings, pp. 358–60, FTC v. Cox et al.

16. Testimony of Jachens, 9:2–7, U.S. v. Cook et al.; *FW*, March 17, April 21, 1919.

17. Exhibit: Cox to W. P. Johnson, September 2, 1920; Indictment, p. 44, U.S. v. Cox et al., CR1300.

18. *HC*, June 14, 1922; Complaint, p. 9; Statement of the Receiver, Official Report of Proceedings, p. 1010; Brief, pp. 20–21, FTC v. Cox et al.

19. Complaint, pp. 3, 5, 9, 10, 11–13; Cox's Response, p. 9; Charges, p. 3; Brief, pp. 9, 10, FTC v. Cox et al.

20. Testimony of James L. Woolson, Official Report of Proceedings, pp. 502–55, FTC v. Cox et al.; *HC*, January 25, 1924.

21. Cox to Carson, U.S. v. Cox et al., CR1300.

22. Ibid.

23. Cox to Carson, U.S. v. Cox et al., CR1300; *Big Spring Herald*, April 26, 1936, October 11, 1970; Findings, p. 25, FTC v. Cox et al.

24. *Big Spring Herald*, August 6, 1920.

25. Cox to Carson, U.S. v. Cox et al., CR1300; *Big Spring Herald*, April 26, 1936, October 11, 1970; Findings, p. 25, FTC v. Cox et al.

26. Testimony of W. P. Johnson, Official Report of Proceedings, pp. 376–78, FTC v. Cox et al.

27. Exhibit: Cox to S. M. Lane, July 27, 1921; Indictment, pp. 18–19, U.S. v. Cox et al., CR1300.

28. Cox to Frank H. Pollack, July 11, 1921; Indictment, p. 11, U.S. v. Cox et al., CR1300.

29. *HC*, January 23, 24, 1924; Indictment, pp. 4–5, United States v. Butler R. Perryman et al., CR1808, U.S. District Court, Southern District of Texas, Houston, Record Group 21, Southwest Branch (Fort Worth), National Archives.

30. Circular of November 7, 1922, Indictment, p. 7, U.S. v. Perryman et al.

31. Ibid.

32. Circular, November 8, 1922, Indictment, p. 37, U.S. v. Perryman et al.

33. Exhibit 130: "To My Prospective Partner," 5:121, U.S. v. Cook et al..

34. Exhibit 800-2: Circular Letter, January 9, 1923, 18:88, U.S. v. Cook et al.

35. Ibid., 18:86.

36. *The Oil Tribune*, January 2, 1923.

37. Exhibit: Circular, undated, 8:120–21, U.S. v. Cook et al.

38. Indictment, p. 30, U.S. v. Cox et al., CR8722.

39. Ibid.

40. Ibid., p. 31; *NYT*, January 20, 1930, January 29, 1931; James R. Scales and Danney Goble, *Oklahoma Politics: A History* (Norman: University of Oklahoma Press, 1982), pp. 125–26; Indictment, p. 5, U.S. v. Cox et al., CR8722; Washburn and DeLong, *High and Low Financiers*, p. 183.

41. Indictment, p. 5, U.S. v. Cox et al., CR8722; *NYT*, January 20, 1930, January 29, 1931; Washburn and DeLong, *High and Low Financiers*, p. 187.

42. Washburn and DeLong, *High and Low Financiers*, p. 183.

43. Indictment, pp. 5, 50, U.S. v. Cox et al., CR8722; *NYT*, February 18, May 20, 1930.

44. Indictment, pp. 7, 13, U.S. v. Cox et al., CR8722.

45. *HC*, June 4, 14, 1922; *Big Spring Herald*, January 14, 21, 1921; *Harris County Deed Records*, 472:326–36.

46. *HC*, June 4, 1922; Application for Enforcement, pp. 17–19, FTC v. Cox et al; *Harris County Deed Records*, 50:384.

47. Testimony of J. E. Hooper, pp. 511–16; Testimony of W. P. Johnson, pp. 369–74; Testimony of Oscar Kullenberg, pp. 253–54, 263–64, 279, 283; Testimony of Albert H. Klees, pp. 360, 363, Official Report of Proceedings, FTC v. Cox et al.

48. Joe Pickle, "The Wizard of Oil," *West Texas Today*, May 1940; Testimony of W. M. Kimbell, Official Report of Proceedings, p. 429, FTC v. Cox et al.; Testimony of Herman Danielson, 9:242, U.S. v. Cook et al.

49. *HC*, June 14, 1922; *FWP*, November 31, 1922.

CHAPTER SIX

1. *New York Times*, October 9, 1921, February 10, 1924; *Review of Reviews*, April 1921, p. 443.

2. *NYT*, June 1, 3, 6, 17, 1919.

3. *NYT*, June 25, 1920; criminal docket books, U.S. District Court, Southern District of Texas, Houston, and Northern District of Texas, Dallas, Record Group 21, Southwest Branch (Fort Worth), National Archives.

4. Robert K. Murray, *The Politics of Normalcy: Governmental Theory and Practice in the Harding-Coolidge Era* (New York: W. W. Norton, 1973), pp. 108–11.

5. *Financial World*, October 13, December 15, 1917, March 17, April 21, 1919.

6. Sworn Statement of John M. Burkett, January 17, 1923, Writ of Enforcement, Fifth Circuit Court of Appeals, p. 8, Federal Trade Commission v. Seymour E. J. Cox et al., Docket #402, Records of the Federal Trade Commission, Record

Notes to Pages 125–34

Group 122, National Archives, Washington, D.C.

7. *Big Spring Herald*, April 13, 1921.

8. Indictment, United States v. S. E. J. Cox et al., CR1300, U.S. District Court, Southern District of Texas, Houston, Record Group 21, Southwest Branch (Fort Worth), National Archives.

9. *NYT*, March 15, 1922; *Houston Chronicle*, March 14, 1922.

10. Warrant of Removal, Southern District of New York, March 14, 1922, U.S. v. Cox et al., CR1300; *HC*, March 14, 1922.

11. *HC*, May 29, 31, June 1, 2, 1922; *NYT*, May 31, 1922.

12. *HC*, May 31, 1922; *NYT*, June 4, 1922.

13. *HC*, June 9, 1922.

14. The Court's Charge, U.S. v. Cox et al., CR1300; *HC*, June 10, 1922.

15. *HC*, May 30, June 11, 1922.

16. *NYT*, April 7, 1923; *Fort Worth Press*, November 9, 1922, March 12, 1923.

17. Criminal Docket, vol. 5, U.S. District Court, Northern District of Texas, Fort Worth, Southwest Branch (Fort Worth), National Archives; *FWP*, April 20, 21, 1923; *NYT*, April 3, 1923.

18. *NYT*, April 7, 21, 1923; *Oil and Gas Journal*, July 19, 1923, p. 70.

19. *OGJ*, May 3, 1923, p. 112; *FWP*, May 15, 1923, March 13, 1924.

20. Indictment, Motion to Quash Indictment, Plea in Abatement, Plea of Immunity, Bill of Exceptions, Statement of Facts, United States v. Robert A. Lee et al., CR2267, U.S. District Court, Northern District of Texas, Fort Worth, Record Group 21, Southwest Branch (Fort Worth), National Archives; *NYT*, May 9, 1923; *Fort Worth Press*, May 15, 21, 1923.

21. *FWP*, May 28, 29, 1923.

22. *FWP*, May 28, 1923.

23. *FWP*, May 28, 29, 30, June 1, 2, 1923.

24. *FWP*, June 6, 1923; Judgment, Bill of Exceptions, Order Allowing a Writ of Error; R. A. Lee Commitment, U.S. v. Robert A. Lee et al.; Indictment, United States v. Oscar Pardue et al., CR1811, U.S. District Court, Southern District of Texas, Houston, Record Group 21, Southwest Branch (Fort Worth), National Archives; *NYT*, June 6, 1923, July 11, 1924.

25. Testimony of Henry Zweifel, 30:31–32, United States v. Frederick A. Cook et al., CR2273, U.S. District Court, Northern District of Texas, Fort Worth, Record Group 21, Southwest Branch (Fort Worth), National Archives.

26. *FWP*, October 31, 1923; *Fort Worth Star-Telegram*, October 15, 1923; "John Milton Killits," *The National Cyclopedia of American Biography* (New York: James T. White and Company, 1941), 29:147–48.

27. *FWP*, October 31, 1923.

28. Lewis L. Gould, *Progressives and Prohibitionists: Texas Democrats in the Wilson*

Era (Austin: University of Texas Press, 1973), pp. 16–19.

29. Ibid., p. 19.

30. Norman D. Brown, *Hood, Bonnet, and Little Brown Jug: Texas Politics, 1921–1928* (Austin: University of Texas Press, 1984), p. 6; Gould, *Progressives and Prohibitionists*, pp. 265–76.

31. Testimony of Henry Zweifel, U.S. v. Cook et al., 30:10, 12, 14–15, 20–26.

32. See U.S. v. Cook et al., 1:53.

33. Transcript, 4:22, 51, U.S. v. Cook et al.

34. Ibid., 7:113–17.

35. Ibid., 7:108, 110, 116.

36. *FWP*, October 27, 1923.

37. Ibid.

38. See the memorandum by Judge Killits, May 27, 1937, in the Vilmjar Steffanson Collection, Dartmouth College Library.

39. Transcript, 7:9, 5:174, 16:329, U.S. v. Cook et al.

40. Ibid., 30:42.

41. *FWST*, November 20, 1923.

42. Transcript, 31:55–57, U.S. v. Cook et al.

43. *FWST*, November 23, 1923.

44. Judgment, U.S. v. Cook et al.; *FWP*, November 22, 1923; *FWST*, November 22, 23, 1923; *NYT*, November 22, 23, 24, 1923.

45. *FWP*, November 22, 1923.

46. Indictment, Statement of Particulars, Sentences; William M. Franklin to Clerk of District Court, November 25, 1932, United States v. John C. Verser et al., CR2274, Northern District of Texas, Fort Worth, Southwest Branch (Fort Worth), National Archives; *Deeds*, Pecos County, Texas, 35:601, 93:352, 106:543, 109:191.

47. *HC*, January 21, 1924.

48. *HC*, January 29, 1924.

49. *HC*, January 29, 1924.

50. *NYT*, January 29, 1924.

51. Criminal Docket, vols. 5 and 6, U.S. District Court, Northern District of Texas, Fort Worth; *OGJ*, July 5, 12, 1923.

52. *NYT*, May 8, 20, 24, June 17, 26, 28, July 1, 9, 17, 27, 1927.

53. *OGJ*, May 4, 1922.

54. Memorandum, Horace J. Donnelly, Solicitor, to Postmaster General, November 12, 1925, Fraud Record No. 4572, Records of the Post Office Department, Record Group 28, National Archives, Washington, D.C.; *Western World*, August 13, 1927.

55. See Sentences, CR2268, CR2240, CR2267, and CR2486, Northern District of Texas, Fort Worth.

56. Gerard C. Henderson, *The Federal Trade Commission: A Study in Administrative Law and Procedure* (New Haven: Yale University Press, 1924), p. 234; *NYT*, April 29, 1923.

57. Case File, FTC v. Cox et al.

58. John M. Elliott, *The Annotated Blue Sky Laws of the United States* (Cincinnati: W. H. Anderson, 1919), p. 814; Robert R. Reed and Lester Washburn, *Blue Sky Laws: Analysis and Text* (New York: Clark Boardman Company, 1921), p. 127; House Bill 177, *General Laws: Texas*, 38th legislature, 2d called sess., 1923; *Austin-American*, June 1, 3, 4, 6, 7, 9, 1923.

59. Testimony of Judge Teagle, United States v. Robert C. Russell et al., CR1809, U.S. District Court, Southern District of Texas, Houston, Record Group 21, Southwest Branch (Fort Worth), National Archives; *OGJ*, June 7, 1923, p. 98.

60. Jacob Murray Edelman, *Securities Regulation in the 48 States* (Chicago: Council of State Governments, 1942), p. 48; Louis Loss and Edward M. Cowett, *Blue Sky Laws* (Boston: Little, Brown, 1958), p. 59.

61. *FW*, December 30, 1918; David D. Levin, *Petroleum Encyclopedia: Done in Oil* (New York: Ranger Press, 1942), pp. 917–18.

CHAPTER SEVEN

1. Westbrook's promotions from 1925 to 1930 are chronicled in his extensive correspondence with C. I. Dearing, an investor from Indianapolis. The letters are in the archives of the Panhandle-Plains Museum, Canyon, Texas.

2. For general information on the project and the Hendrick field see Samuel D. Myres, *The Permian Basin: Era of Discovery* (El Paso: Permian Press, 1973), pp. 484–94.

3. Promotional Letter, "At the Beginning of 1926," Dearing Papers.

4. Westbrook to Dearing, March 20, April 8, 1926, Dearing Papers.

5. Westbrook to Dearing, July 26, 1926, Dearing Papers.

6. Railroad Commission of Texas, *Annual Report to the Governor, Oil and Gas Division: 1985* (Austin, 1986), p. 371.

7. Transcript of Hearing, August 14–15, 1929, Vitek Oil Company, Docket No. 223, Post Office Department, Record Group 28, National Archives, Washington, D.C. (hereafter cited as Vitek Oil Company); Testimony of Paul Vitek, November 17, 1923, 30:76, United States v. Frederick A. Cook et al., CR2273, U.S. District Court, Northern District of Texas, Fort Worth, Record Group 21, Southwest Branch (Fort Worth), National Archives; *New York Times*, March 2, 1930.

8. *Fort Worth City Directory*, 1923. Transcript of Hearing, p. 28; Testimony of Paul Vitek, 30:75; Testimony of F. W. Wimberley, October 16, 1923, 4:107, 111–12, 114;

207

Notes to Pages 151–60

Testimony of Mrs. Virginia Brown, October 18, 1923, 4:17; Testimony of B. C. Wynn, October 18, 1923, 4:93; Government Exhibit 131A: *Oil Tribune* 1, no. 11 (February 10, 1923), in 6:104; Government Exhibit 697: *Arkansas Oil Gazette* 1, no. 11 (March 24, 1923), in 18:46, U.S. v. Cook et al.

9. Testimony of Cook, 23:185–92, U.S. v. Cook et al.; Indictment, United States v. Paul Vitek et al., CR2164, U.S. District Court, Western District of Arkansas, Texarkana, Record Group 21, Southwest Branch (Fort Worth), National Archives.

10. Indictment, Capias, Hearing, August 14–15, 1929, pp. 28, 37–48, Vitek Oil Company.

11. Hearing, pp. 46, 124–25, 186, Vitek Oil Company.

12. Ibid., pp. 30–31.

13. Ibid., pp. 53, 80–85; lease by Paul Vitek from Orbit Oil Company, March 24, 1927, *Howard County Deed Records*, 65:538.

14. Hearing, pp. 41–42, 52–53, 81–85, Vitek Oil Company; *Western World*, July 16, 1927.

15. Hearing, pp. 10, 15, 54–56, 88–89, Vitek Oil Company.

16. Ibid., pp. 52, 62–63, 67. On Ed Landreth's strip, see Roger M. Olien and Diana Davids Olien, *Wildcatters: Texas Independent Oilmen* (Austin: Texas Monthly Press, 1984), p. 30.

17. Hearing, pp. 4, 7–9, 65, 69, Vitek Oil Company.

18. Ibid., pp. 81, 82, 177. The case is State of Texas v. Vitek Oil Company et al., No. 77831, 48th Judicial District, District Court of Tarrant County, Texas, December 17, 1927. A copy of the proceedings is found in the *Howard County Deed Records*, 5:185.

19. Edwin I. Reeser, *Oil Royalties* (Tulsa: Dexter Publishing Company, 1929), p. 117; Carl S. Webber and Walter S. Sachs, *Investment in Producing Oil Properties* (Philadelphia: Walter S. Sachs and Company, 1958), pp. 2–3.

20. Hearing, pp. 35, 38, Vitek Oil Company.

21. Ibid., pp. 20–21, 26, 35–36, 37–38, 114, 115, 120, 141, 185.

22. Ibid., pp. 11, 137–38.

23. See Olien and Olien, *Wildcatters*, p. 48.

24. Hearing, pp. 34–35, 38, 39–40, 45, 97–98, 106–7, 118, 129–30, 141, 182–83, Vitek Oil Company.

25. Ibid., pp. 46, 173–74; Indictment, Capias, Verdict, United States v. Paul Vitek, CR4494, U.S. District Court, Northern District of Texas, Fort Worth, Record Group 21, Southwest Branch (Fort Worth), National Archives.

26. *Fort Worth Press*, December 13, 1922, May 13, 1925; Indictment and Judgment, U.S. v. Vitek et al., CR2164.

27. Advertisement, *Western World*, November 12, 1927.

28. Exhibit G-1: Yates Royalty Charter; Exhibit: Memo of Agreement between

Notes to Pages 160–66

J. A. Hoover and Leo F. Reardon, September 14, 1927, United States v. Joe A. Hoover and Leo F. Reardon, CR4502, U.S. District Court, Northern District of Texas, Fort Worth, Record Group 21, Southwest Branch (Fort Worth), National Archives.

29. Exhibit: Reardon to Mrs. Julia Funderburk, November 21, December 24, 1927; Circular, December 14, 1927; Reardon to Funderburk, May 25, 1928; Exhibit G-13: Circular, n.d., U.S. v. Hoover et al.; *Western World*, October 13, 1928.

30. *Houston City Directory*, 1915, 1917, 1918, 1919; *FW*, March 24, 1919; *Harris County Deed Records*, 438:414, 455:208, 504:546; *Harris County Mortgage Records*, 169:7.

31. *Houston City Directory*, 1921, 1922; Federal Trade Commission v. H. H. Hoffman et al., Docket #865, Records of the Federal Trade Commission, Record Group 122, National Archives, Washington, D.C..

32. Letter of February 19, 1929, Indictment, United States v. Henry H. Hoffman, alias Hubert Hoffman, CR4590, U.S. District Court, Northern District of Texas, Fort Worth, Record Group 21, Southwest Branch (Fort Worth), National Archives.

33. Letter of April 8, 1929, U.S. v. Hoffman.

34. *Winkler County Deed Records*, vols. 36, 37, 39; Indictment, U.S. v. Hoffman.

35. Indictment, U.S. v. Hoffman.

36. Judgment, Application and Order Discharging Probation, U.S. v. Hoffman.

37. Mrs. Chester R. Bunker to Mrs. Ernest Granville, n.d., "World-Powell" file, Permian Basin Petroleum Museum, Library, and Hall of Fame, Midland, Texas; *Western World*, September 11, 1926; *Fort Worth City Directory*, 1920, 1921, 1923; Indictment; Testimony of Chester R. Bunker, United States v. Chester R. Bunker et al., CR1932, U.S. District Court, Northern District of Texas, Fort Worth, Record Group 21, Southwest Branch (Fort Worth), National Archives.

38. Testimony of H. R. Robinson, 13:297, 300, U.S. v. Cook et al.; *Western World*, November 9, 1929.

39. *Western World*, March 26, August 26, 1927, December 11, 1929; *Oil Weekly*, June 25, 1926, p. 80; *The Petroleum Register*, 1924 (New York: The Oil Trade Journal, 1924), p. 312; *Fort Worth City Directories*, 1919–1930; "Minutes of the Incorporation of World Oil Company, Incorporated," Equity 601: J. H. Sales v. World Oil et al., U.S. District Court, Northern District of Texas, Fort Worth, Record Group 21, Southwest Branch (Fort Worth), National Archives.

40. Complainants' Amended Supplemental Petition, p. 3, Equity 601; *San Angelo Standard*, June 11, 1925; *National Petroleum News*, May 26, 1926; *FWST*, March 4, 1934.

41. *Pecos County Deed Records*, 44:266, 671, 49:465, 59:63–75, 62:58, 75:183, 76:27, 573, 83:374, 94:23. *Western World*, January 14, February 11, 18, April 7, July 14, 21, August 4, 1928.

42. *Western World,* October 2, 1926, March 3, December 8, 1928, February 23, 1929.

43. Testimony of C. H. Struck; Accounts Payable, November 30, 1927, October 31, 1928, United States v. Chester R. Bunker et al., CR4491, U.S. District Court, Northern District of Texas, Fort Worth, Record Group 21, Southwest Branch (Fort Worth), National Archives.

44. Testimony of Struck; Accounts Receivable, November 30, 1927; Response of Ed Bateman to the Postal Inspector, September 26, 1929; Testimony of B. K. Isaacs; W. L. Mosely to Dear Stockholder, n.d. [1927], U.S. v. Bunker et al., CR4491; *FWST,* March 4, 1934.

45. Minutes, 12:207, U.S. v. Bunker et al., CR4491; Order on Petition, United States v. Chester R. Bunker et al., CR6429, U.S. Circuit Court of Appeals, Fifth Circuit, Record Group 21, Southwest Branch (Fort Worth), National Archives.

AFTERWORD

1. E. Blake Whiting, "Poor Kitty," *Financial World,* April 18, 1921, p. 719.

2. *New York Times,* July 11, 1924; *Fort Worth Press,* March 13, 1924.

3. *Fort Worth Star-Telegram,* February 24, 1924; *FWP,* October 3, 1924.

4. *NYT,* July 11, 1924; *FWP,* March 13, 1924, April 27, 1925; Mandate of July 27, 1925, File 30,322, U.S. Supreme Court; Appeal from the District Court, File 7546, U.S. Circuit Court of Appeals, Fifth Circuit, Record Group 21, Southwest Branch (Fort Worth), National Archives.

5. Presidential Order, November 9, 1925; Indictment of June 5, 1934, United States v. Robert A. Lee et al., CR2267, U.S. District Court, Northern District of Texas, Fort Worth, Record Group 21, Southwest Branch (Fort Worth), National Archives.

6. *FWST,* July 13, 14, 1931.

7. United States v. John C. Verser et al., CR2274, U.S. District Court, Northern District of Texas, Fort Worth, Record Group 21, Southwest Branch (Fort Worth), National Archives; Oral Opinion Rendered by Judge James C. Wilson at Fort Worth on March 17, 1927, United States v. Frederick A. Cook et al., CR2273, U.S. District Court, Northern District of Texas, Fort Worth, Record Group 21, Southwest Branch (Fort Worth), National Archives; Opinion, U.S. Circuit Court of Appeals, Fifth Circuit, United States v. Frederick A. Cook et al., CR5056, filed with CR2273, Record Group 21, Southwest Branch (Fort Worth), National Archives; *FWST,* February 4, 1925.

8. *NYT,* March 18, 1927, March 8, 10, 1930.

9. *FWST,* November 21, 1939.

10. Nell [*sic*] Cox to David Tant, August 30, 1933; Mrs. S. E. J. Cox to Clerk,

Notes to Pages 171–79

March 25, 1936, United States v. S. E. J. Cox et al., CR5534, U.S. District Court, Western District of Oklahoma, Oklahoma City, Record Group 21, Southwest Branch (Fort Worth), National Archives.

11. Hon. Joe Ingraham, interviewed by Roger M. Olien, November 10, 1985, Houston, Texas; *Odessa American*, November 14, 1951.

12. E. Lawton Bragg to Joe Pickle, September 1952, courtesy of Joe Pickle, Big Spring, Texas; S. E. J. Cox, *Girls, Gushers, and Roughnecks* (San Antonio: Naylor Publishing Company, 1972), pp. 1, 2, 9, 15, 26.

13. *Austin-American*, April 4, 1927; *San Antonio Express*, December 21, 1971.

14. Louis Loss, *Securities Regulation*, 2d ed. (Boston: Little, Brown, 1961), 1:105, 3:1432.

15. Susan Shapiro, *Wayward Capitalists: Target of the Securities and Exchange Commission* (New Haven: Yale University Press, 1984), pp. 190–91; Thomas K. McCraw, "With Consent of the Governed: SEC's Formative Years," *Journal of Policy Analysis and Management* 1 (Spring 1982): 348; see the various proceedings and documents in Case 24: Securities and Exchange Commission v. C. M. Joiner Leasing Corporation and C. M. Joiner, *Records and Briefs*, United States Supreme Court, October Term, 1943, vol. 10.

16. Bruce Ingersoll, "School for Scam," *Wall Street Journal*, February 2, 1988.

17. Robert M. Bleiberg, "Ponzi Was A Piker," *Barron's*, September 18, 1989, p. 11.

18. Bruce Ingersoll, "Inundated Agency," *WSJ*, December 19, 1985; Earl C. Gottschalk, Jr., "Churchgoers Are the Prey As Scams Rise," *WSJ*, August 7, 1989.

19. *NYT*, June 4, 1989.

20. For an extensive study of Home-Stake, see David McClintick, *Stealing from the Rich: The Home-Stake Oil Swindle* (New York: M. B. Evans, 1977); "A Star-Spangled Swindle," *Newsweek*, July 8, 1971, pp. 55–57; Hyman P. Minsky, "Financial Resources in a Fragile Financial Environment," *Challenge*, July–August 1975, pp. 7–10; *WSJ*, Centennial ed. (1989), 83:122G.

21. *Washington Post*, September 5, 1981.

22. *Dallas Morning News*, December 15, 1982.

23. Bleiberg, "Ponzi Was A Piker," p. 86.

24. McClintick, *Stealing from the Rich*; Allan Sloan, "Drilling for Suckers," *Forbes*, June 4, 1984, pp. 36–38; Richard L. Stern and Lisa Gubernick, "The Smarter They Are the Harder They Fall," *Forbes*, May 20, 1985, p. 38; Walt Bogdanich, "Ponzi Scams Allegedly Increasing," *WSJ*, May 8, 1985; *WSJ*, September 11, 1984, April 12, 1985, December 22, 1986.

25. Charles P. Kindleberger, *Manias, Panics, and Crashes: A History of Financial Crises* (New York: Basic Books, 1978), p. 81.

INDEX

Index

Index

Index

Index

Index